Back from the Dead

CONTRIBUTIONS TO ZOMBIE STUDIES

White Zombie: Anatomy of a Horror Film. Gary D. Rhodes. 2001

The Zombie Movie Encyclopedia. Peter Dendle. 2001

American Zombie Gothic: The Rise and Fall (and Rise) of the Walking Dead in Popular Culture. Kyle William Bishop. 2010

Back from the Dead: Remakes of the Romero Zombie Films as Markers of Their Times. Kevin J. Wetmore, Jr. 2011

Generation Zombie: Essays on the Living Dead in Modern Culture. Edited by Stephanie Boluk and Wylie Lenz. 2011

Race, Oppression and the Zombie: Essays on Cross-Cultural Appropriations of the Caribbean Tradition. Edited by Christopher M. Moreman and Cory James Rushton. 2011

Zombies Are Us: Essays on the Humanity of the Walking Dead. Edited by Christopher M. Moreman and Cory James Rushton. 2011

The Zombie Movie Encyclopedia, Volume 2: 2000–2010. Peter Dendle. 2012

Great Zombies in History. Edited by Joe Sergi. 2013 (graphic novel)

Unraveling Resident Evil*: Essays on the Complex Universe of the Games and Films.* Edited by Nadine Farghaly. 2014

"We're All Infected": Essays on AMC's The Walking Dead *and the Fate of the Human.* Edited by Dawn Keetley. 2014

Zombies and Sexuality: Essays on Desire and the Walking Dead. Edited by Shaka McGlotten and Steve Jones. 2014

Back from the Dead

*Remakes of the
Romero Zombie Films
as Markers of Their Times*

KEVIN J. WETMORE, JR.

CONTRIBUTIONS TO ZOMBIE STUDIES

McFarland & Company, Inc., Publishers
Jefferson, North Carolina

ALSO BY KEVIN J. WETMORE, JR.
AND FROM MCFARLAND

Catholic Theatre and Drama: Critical Essays (2010)
*Portrayals of Americans on the World Stage:
Critical Essays* (2009)
*The Empire Triumphant: Race, Religion and
Rebellion in the* Star Wars *Films* (2005)
*Black Dionysus: Greek Tragedy and
African American Theatre* (2003)
*The Athenian Sun in an African Sky: Modern African
Adaptations of Classical Greek Tragedy* (2002)

LIBRARY OF CONGRESS CATALOGUING-IN-PUBLICATION DATA

Wetmore, Kevin J., 1969–
  Back from the dead : remakes of the Romero zombie films as markers of their times / Kevin J. Wetmore, Jr.
    p.   cm.— (Contributions to Zombie Studies)
  Includes filmography.
  Includes bibliographical references and index.

  ISBN 978-0-7864-4642-1
  (softcover : acid free paper) ∞

  1. Romero, George A.—Criticism and interpretation.
  2. Zombie films—History and criticism.   3. Film remakes—
  History and criticism.   I. Title.
  PN1998.3.R644W48   2011
  791.43'675—dc23   2011018764

BRITISH LIBRARY CATALOGUING DATA ARE AVAILABLE

© 2011 Kevin J. Wetmore, Jr. All rights reserved

*No part of this book may be reproduced or transmitted in any form
or by any means, electronic or mechanical, including photocopying
or recording, or by any information storage and retrieval system,
without permission in writing from the publisher.*

On the cover: Poster art and production stills from the 1968 film
Night of the Living Dead and the 1990 remake; the 1986 film
Day of the Dead and the 2006 remake of *Dawn of the Dead.*
Cover design by Mark Berry (www.hot-cherry.co.uk)

Printed in the United States of America

*McFarland & Company, Inc., Publishers
Box 611, Jefferson, North Carolina 28640
www.mcfarlandpub.com*

To my fellow Midnight Society charter members:
Sarah Broyles, Meg Bodi, and Lacy Hornick,
and the Halloween Excursion Club:
Anthony Miller, and Andy and Jennifer Allen.

Acknowledgments

Gratitude and credit are due to:
George Romero and the casts and crews of the films discussed herein. Your work has given so many of us so much pleasure.
Pittsburgh — the city, the people and the University of.
Loyola Marymount University and the support of its administration and faculty. My colleagues at LMU, especially Katharine Noon, Mark Seldis, Jim and Beth Holmes, Dan Weingarten and Grant Garinger, S.J., who have been subjected to my taste in cinema and cultural studies on more than one occasion and lived to tell the tale. The LMU library has also been very helpful in finding rare sources. Thanks as well to colleague, friend and teacher David Sanchez, who has shaped my thinking on apocalypses.
Various friends who have shared the pleasure of the films: Tom Quinn, Matt Berube, Marc Yaeger, and Christina Petrillo. A mad shout out to Cody Kopp, Devin Kasper and Josh "Worm" Miller as well.
My parents, Eleanor and Kevin Sr., who dealt rather well with a child fascinated by horror, death and corpses (reanimated or otherwise) from an early age.
The rest of my family: Lisa, John, Sean, Tom, Eileen, Toni, and Phantom and Gizmo, who continue to put up with an adult who remains fascinated by the same.
Lacy Hornick, for rewatching them all with me again for this book.
And thanks to everyone who has ever written an article about Romero and his films who has NOT titled it "Knight of the Living Dead"— it's been done, people. Find a new cliché for a title.

Table of Contents

Acknowledgments — vi
Introduction: The Dead Are Rising — 1

I. *Night*

1. "We may not enjoy living together, but dying together isn't going to solve anything":
   Night of the Living Dead (1968) — 29
2. "I'm fighting; I'm not panicking":
   Night of the Living Dead (1990) — 47
3. "This has got to be the strangest load you've ever hauled!":
   30th Anniversary Special Edition (1998) and
   Children of the Living Dead (2001) — 64
4. "Hey, are you, like, freaked out about zombie movies?":
   Night of the Living Dead 3-D (2006) — 78
5. "Now you better watch this and try to understand what's going on":
   Night of the Living Dead: Survivor's Cut (2005)
   Night of the Living Dead: Reanimated (2009)
   Night of the Living Dead: Origins (2011) — 94

INTERLUDE: LIVING DEAD, LIVE!
Night of the Living Dead on Stage and in Other Media — 103

II. *Dawn*

6. "We're blowing it ourselves":
   Dawn of the Dead (1978) — 121
7. "Number One: Trust":
   Dawn of the Dead (2004) — 136

INTERLUDE: "DID YOU KNOW THAT MOVIE WAS BASED ON A TRUE CASE?"
    Return of the Living Dead (1985)   154

III. *Day*

8. "From now on, everyone is under martial law!":
    Day of the Dead (1985)   171

9. "Somebody will come. They have to":
    Day of the Dead (2008)   187

IV. Back for the Dead

10. "Isn't that what we're doing? Pretending to be alive?":
    Land, Diary, Surviving and the World of the Dead   201

Conclusion   226
Filmography   231
Bibliography   235
Index   241

Introduction:
The Dead Are Rising

"Movies resurrect the beautiful dead..."
— Susan Sontag, "Film and Theatre"

Pittsburgh 1993 and Before: A Personal Descent into Zombie Culture

In August of 1993 I was moving into a new apartment in the city of Pittsburgh where I was about to begin graduate school. I purchased a newspaper to read while eating breakfast before unpacking and discovered that that weekend was the "Zombie Jamboree"—the twenty-fifth anniversary of *Night of the Living Dead* celebration in Pittsburgh. I had been unaware that this event was happening that weekend; but the world stopped as soon as I learned of its existence. Thus, I did not unpack the weekend of August 27–29, 1993, just before school started. Instead, I spent the weekend at Monroeville Mall. Rather than set up and get settled, it made more sense to go to where *Dawn of the Dead* had been filmed and celebrate one of my favorite films with thousands of other fans and the people who had made it.[1]

I met George Romero (whom I have subsequently met a few other times in passing), John Russo, Karl Hardman, Kyra Schon, Russ Streiner and Marilyn Eastman. I talked with Tom Savini about the 1990 remake of *Night* and also met numerous other figures from horror and sci-fi cinema. It was, all in all, an auspicious way to begin my life in Pittsburgh, a city that takes pride in its zombie heritage. It was also a treat to meet and interact with individuals I had seen numerous times. A lifelong horror fan, I came of age in the eighties, just as home video systems came into popular existence. The first time I saw *Night of the Living Dead* was when it was broadcast on MTV in the early eighties, and I have seen it hundreds of times since. The advent of VHS meant that my friends and I could see *Dawn of the Dead* and *Day of the Dead* multiple times. We went to the remake of *Night* in 1990, and then saw it again on video when it came out a year later.

It is this new (at the time) technology that allowed for multiple viewings of a film. It also allowed us, after seeing the remake of *Night* in 1990, to be able to drive to one of our homes and rewatch the original. In the two decades since, multiple technologies have come forward (DVD, Blu-Ray, etc.) which allow not only for multiple comparative viewings but what John Bryant calls "fluid texts." One can observe alternate endings, directors' cuts, extended versions and other variations, all without leaving the couch. Furthermore, fan-based (and sometimes artist-based) reworkings of the original films transform even the original narrative, such as in the *Thirtieth Anniversary Edition* or *Night of the Living Dead: Reanimated*. These phenomena mean that even the originals are already unstable texts, with no single, definitive version to call *the* text. I shall explore the specific challenges of reading remakes and unstable originals below.

My love of horror and especially zombies has continued into my professional career. As an academic and an actor, I have studied and written about zombie films, and also acted in several of them.[2] My parents used to ask me why I was interested in all these things. I have been asked the same question by friends and colleagues through the years. Apart from the obvious answers (because I like them, they bring me pleasure, etc.), I also must note that they do bring meaning to my life and are part of my own identity. I am a zombie fan, as I am a Steelers fan, and as I am a theater professor and an actor. Like with many fans, and presumably readers of this book, zombies are now part of what I am, and the current culture continues to feed that need.

The Horror of It All: Reading Romero Through Sociophobics

In his seminal text *Hollywood from Vietnam to Reagan*, Robin Wood posits that Romero's trilogy is "one of the most remarkable and audacious achievements of modern American cinema and the most uncompromising critique of contemporary America" (287). If this is true (and I see no reason to argue it is not), what are the critiques of America that are made in each film and what are we to do with the remakes of these films? Do they offer similar critiques? One of the complaints about the remake of *Dawn* was that it did not have the same social commentary and critique of consumer culture as the original. But does that mean it is devoid of social criticism? The answer this volume provides is a resounding "no." The originals and the remakes all mean something, and all offer their own representation of social concerns.

Films do not just mean, they generate meaning. While it is possible to "read too much into" a particular text, we should note that a film is always the product of far more than the filmmaker's intentions. For example, while 9/11 is never mentioned once in the remake of *Dawn of the Dead*, it is nevertheless a presence in that film and in the minds and experiences of all who see it. The original *Return of the Living Dead* is very much rooted in the nihilism of the American punk scene in 1985, which would be impossible if the film had been made twenty years later. Whereas the film that was made twenty years later, *Return of the Living Dead 5: Rave to the Grave*, is rooted in contemporary rave culture, which did not exist in 1985.

Horror is simultaneously a subversive and conservative genre. It questions and subverts institutions (family, school, church, police, etc.) while essentially reinforcing the status quo. The return to normalcy at the end of many horror films is often a reinscribing of white, male, patriarchal authority. Zombie horror is paradoxical as well, in that we are horrified by the zombie apocalypse, but for the survivors, all rules are void. And the viewer almost always sides with the survivors. Zombie horror can be a form of wish fulfillment. Many is the viewer whose response to these films is, "If I were in that situation I would..." followed by a list of activities which one would not dare and could not do in the real world. When the dead rise we are free to shoot, torture, destroy, burn, and collect and use any and every weapon imaginable to do horrible things to zombies (and sometimes to other living humans). We can take over a mall and make it a private kingdom. We can make targets of (admittedly dead) human beings. What would horrify us if we saw it on the evening news delights us in a zombie film.

Robert Abele sees this situation as a lack of empathy: "You don't care about killing them. They're dead in the first place, so there's no pathos connected to slaughtering them"—there is no sympathy or empathy in killing the already dead (D7). Yet Romero's films consistently demonstrate the emotional and moral complexity of killing the dead. The original *Dawn* shows the apartment residents attempting to preserve the dignity of the reanimated dead even as a racist S.W.A.T. team member begins shooting the living. Whereas Ben has no qualms about shooting the dead Harry and Helen in *Night*, there is true pathos in Roger and Peter's last exchange before a bullet in *Dawn*. In the remake of *Dawn*, Ken's killing of Frank lacks the pathos of Roger's death, but it is still an emotional moment. The level of horror or pathos in the killing of a zombie is directly related to the audience's emotional connection to the character. The shooting of the celebrity-look-a-likes in the *Dawn* remake is actually a cause for bathos. Ironically, though the audience knows Steve very well by the point he is zombified, there is a great deal of emotional satisfaction in Ana shooting him. The second death of a zombie is always a cause for emotion — occasionally sorrow, but more often than not an adrenaline-fueled satisfaction or amusement.

Scholars and fans use a variety of methodologies to read these films. The most common and popular is psychological analysis. The aforementioned Robin Wood has explored horror through Freud's idea of the "return of the repressed"— that which we thought we had suppressed erupts into our lives. Most frequently, scholars of horror use psychoanalysis to survey what, in essence, is the cinema of fear, examining how the things that cause fear in a horror film are rooted in our psychosexual development. James Twitchell's seminal *Dreadful Pleasures*, for example, offers a Freudian model for viewing horror and its appeal: "Horror has little to do with fright; it has more to do with laying down the rules of socialization and extrapolating a hidden code of sexual behavior" (66). It is certainly true that one can examine horror movies and find a good deal of "hidden codes of sexual behavior," from Jason and Michael punishing teens who have sex to Norman Bates' unresolved mother issues; and this includes zombie films.

Reynold Humphries offers a psychological analysis of the cemetery scene which opens *Night*, for example. He sees the Cemetery Zombie as a patriarchal authority figure "returning to punish children who do not submit to a repressive family structure" (113). He sees Johnny's stated desire for candy, rejection of church, and fond memory of his prank on his sister and his grandfather cursing him as evidence of Johnny's infantile state, rejecting parental authority (113).

The most popular methodology of examining Romero's films seems to be an economic, class-based, often Marxist methodology. George Romero, interviewed in the documentary *American Nightmare*, states, "The zombie, for me, was always the blue collar kind of monster. He was us." Others have seen the zombie as a proletariat figure — the masses exploited by a small group of elite. *Dawn* is analyzed by most as a critique of consumer capitalism. The Romero-inspired *Shaun of the Dead* demonstrates that if a zombie outbreak did occur, most of us would not be able to tell the difference between zombies and working class people stuck in "McJobs." By the end of the film, the zombies are back behind the cash registers and pulling the shopping carts, indistinguishable from how they were before the outbreak. Our lives are dead and drained of meaning; we are stuck performing unrewarding, unenlightening, minimum-wage labor, which is the equivalent of being a zombie.

Romero's films have also been examined in terms of ethnicity and gender, what we might term "identity studies" methodology. Ben's ethnicity, in a sea of white faces, and Barbara's passivity in the face of male aggression (both living and dead), lend themselves to ethnic or feminist analysis. The fact that Cholo from *Land* is Latino is not irrelevant to Kaufman's desire to keep him out of Fiddler's Green. We can read Romero in terms of the behavior by and towards his characters.

This volume uses all of these methodologies and more, as it is a study of the sociophobics of Romero's zombie films and their remakes. David L. Scruton reminds us, "Fear is a social act that occurs within a cultural matrix. 'To fear' and 'to be afraid' are social events which have social consequences" (10). Scruton proposes using not just psychology to understand fear, but other social sciences as well. He proposes to engage in "sociophobics": "the study of human fears as they occur and are experienced in the context of the sociocultural systems humans have created" (9). A sociophobic study of horror cinema explores how the wide variety of fears present in society when the film is created is made manifest in the movie. The horror film offers fear as a social phenomenon, produced by society. Filmmakers look at what scares us individually and collectively and then places those fears on the screen, sometimes overtly, sometimes covertly, sometimes unaware of the meaning behind the film — but the sociophobia is always present in the modern horror film.

Scruton outlines three "basic taxonomies of fear":

1. Physical fears: death, sickness, suffering, etc.
2. Social fears: taking a test, asking someone out, etc.
3. Fear for (on behalf of) others (8).

Romero's films (like all horror films) focus on the first and third. Fear of the dead, fear of our own death, and fear that our loved ones might die or, worse, might be transformed by death into something that can hurt or kill us. But these fears are always also rooted not just in psychological but also sociological elements. 9/11, for example, transformed horror. Behind *Return of the Living Dead* is a fear of toxic chemicals being dumped in residential areas; behind the remake of *Dawn* is a concern about the inability to maintain meaningful relationships on any level in contemporary America. Fear is never just fear for the self, it is fear of threats from the outside. Kendall R. Phillips reminds us that a horror film monster is more than the allegorical embodiment of our collective fear, and that focusing on any allegory present in the film ultimately reduces or removes the terror such films intend to create (5–6). It is my hope to locate the context of the reimagined horrors of the remakes, rather than reduce the films down to simple allegories or real-life concerns.

Judith Halberstam refers to monsters as "meaning machines" that demonstrate the fears, anxieties and concerns of the cultures that produced them (21). Or, as best-selling author-cum-horror philosopher Stephen King observes, "When the horror movies wear their various sociopolitical hats — the B-picture as tabloid editorial — they often serve as an extraordinarily accurate barometer of those things that trouble the night-thoughts of a whole society" (*Danse* 131). What Halberstam and King are advocating is that even the most exploitive, ridiculous horror film still manages to root its fears in sociophobics. For our purposes, the zombie film always wears a "sociopolitical hat" and, as I hope this study will show, does "serve as an extraordinarily accurate barometer" of some of the fears of the United States when the film was produced.

The zombie especially serves as a particularly protean "meaning machine." "In proper hands," writes Joshua Bearman, "the zombie story is less about zombies than the human survivors — a tool for social, psychological and economic commentary" (118). I would argue that even "in improper hands" the zombie film still reflects the fears of the human community that produced the film, and though lesser films make for lesser tools of commentary, the commentary is still always there as subtext. In Romero's hands, the zombie is terrifying in and of itself, but it also refers to some sociophobic outside the reanimated dead. Mario DeGiglio-Bellemare, in a review of *Land of the Dead*, states that "Romero's zombies represent social change" (DeGiglio-Bellemare). Those who fight the zombies, as often as not, are those who resist an irresistible change.

We must remember, however, that horror is culturally bound. As Jim Harper observes, zombie films made in Japan are significantly different than those made in the west. In Japan, zombies are not reanimated corpses but irradiated living victims transformed into monsters — long before *28 Days Later* made western zombies not-quite-dead, too. The reason for this, as Harper explains, is that films about reanimated corpses "don't work in cultures that practice cremation" (43). We must be cautious, therefore, when considering these films and look to the culture that created them. I, as author, and you, as reader, must also be careful not to universalize or reduce the films down to a single common experience.

Those authors who analyze more than a single film, and perhaps even Romero's entire corpus, have either offered a diachronic analysis (considering the changes over time) or a synchronic analysis (considering what the films mean in a single, current social milieu). It is my hope in this volume to offer both a diachronic and synchronic analysis of the films, considering what they mean in the original contexts but also how remakes of the films force us to consider how the meaning changes over time. Likewise, we must historicize each film — films have both historicity and transhistoricity. This volume focuses on what the film meant when it was created, while occasionally considering how it is read now. While no one watching *Return of the Living Dead* today reflects on Love Canal or the creation of the Superfund, they are present in that film. It continues to mean and to scare, however, without that knowledge. Similarly, it is possible to watch *Night of the Living Dead 3D* without thinking of the cemetery and mortuary scandals of the first decade of the twentieth century and still find moments of the film disturbing. But those scandals are part of what shaped the film and what the film reflects back upon the society that created it. Lastly, we must consider the transhistoricity of these films. *Night* continues to scare, though audiences are no longer concerned about the civil rights movement or the American presence in Vietnam.

Other film genres will also come into play in this study, and what Susan Sontag says of science fiction can equally be asserted of horror: "Science fiction films are not about science. They are about disaster, which is the oldest subject of art" ("Imagination" 213). Horror concerns disaster in Sontag's understanding of it. Disaster "releases one from normal obligations," dehumanizes those going through it, and is "accommodating and negating the perennial human anxiety about death" (215, 222, 223). Both Romero's films and the remakes and reimagingings of them are disaster films as well as horror. There is also considerable overlap with other subgenres within horror: the slasher film, the haunted house film, and the good, old-fashioned monster movie.

In the end, we must ask of the remakes of Romero what Isabel Cristina Pinedo asks of all horror films: "What does this say about us? How does it help us understand the social world in which we live? How does it help us develop strategies for bringing about progressive social change?" (3). The key word here being "progressive." I noted above that horror as a genre tends to be paradoxically conservative and progressive. Romero himself and some of the makers of the remakes follow a socially progressive ideology in defining the sociocultural problems in the United States. In other cases, however, a reactionary ideology dominates the narrative, transforming Romero's progressive original into an intransigent conservative film, cautioning against the dangers of progressivism. In the end, I am less interested in how Romero's films and the remakes of them attempt to change the world, and more in how they reflect the world, what they say about "us," and how they construct the real dangers of the world.

One might be able to look at how the United States has changed simply by charting the presidential administration at the time of the release of the Romero original and remakes:

Night (1968): Johnson (Democrat)
Dawn (1978): Carter (Democrat)
Day (1985): Reagan (Republican)
Night (1990): Bush I (Republican)
Night 30th Anniversary (1998): Clinton (Democrat)
Dawn (2004): Bush II (Republican)
Land (2005): Bush II (Republican)

Night 3D (2006): Bush II (Republican)
Diary (2007): Bush II (Republican)
Day (2008): Bush II (Republican)
Survival (2009): Obama (Democrat)

Out of eleven films, four have been made under Democratic administrations and seven have emerged under Republican ones. It is also worth noting that three of the four films made during Democratic administrations were released towards the end of those administrations, as the nation was undergoing a pendulum swing back to the political right. *Night* was released a month before Nixon was elected, *Dawn* came in the waning months of the Carter administration, and the 30th Anniversary Edition of *Night* was created after the impeachment of President Clinton by a Republican congress, moving towards the election of the second President Bush.

The second Bush presidency has been a fountain of zombie culture, and Romero's recent films, remakes and other zombie films (such as *Homecoming*, *ZMD: Zombies of Mass Destruction* and *Zombie Strippers*) all either directly or indirectly refer to the Bush administration and the crises that have occurred under it. *Land of the Dead* is a direct critique of the Bush administration, whereas the remake of *Dawn* is a somewhat reactionary response to 9/11, as is the remake of *Day*. The zombie is rising as the most popular monster of our culture of the moment, overthrowing the perennial favorite the vampire. Romero set the model for the political zombie film

It is universally agreed that Romero changed the genre, not just horror but specifically the zombie film. For the rest of this introduction I will analyze the zombie film before Romero, consider what Romero added, examine how remakes work, and then finally outline the rest of the volume.

"White" Zombie

Night represents a reversal of previous zombie films. In films such as *White Zombie* (1932) and *I Walked with a Zombie* (1943) the horror comes from, as the title of the former suggests, a white American going through the process of zombification that happens to black people from Haiti. In these films there is a European (read: white) zombie master who creates and controls black zombies in Haiti. The horror of the plot is that the zombie master then wishes to transform a Euro-American, usually female, into a zombie. As Jaime Russell observes, many of these films posit "the equation of the zombie with America's racial others" (34). The heroes are white Euro-Americans, the zombies are people of African descent.

Their ethnicity is prominently featured, and actually of key importance. In his excellent *Book of the Dead*, Jamie Russell states that the zombie first came to the screen during the Great Depression: "The zombie — a dead worker resurrected as a slave into the hellish afterlife of endless toil — was the perfect monster for the age" (23). In other words, the fear was of endless work with no reward. And yet, zombies were not in and of themselves a threat. They had no will; they could not act on their own. The actual horror came from the zombie master, and that white people could be controlled and exploited as blacks were. The zombies were controlled — there was a maker, someone behind the scenes, a "Zombie Master." This individual could control the zombies and bend them to his will. Zombies did not do evil on their own, they were ordered to do so. In this sense, Russell's Great Depression thesis lends itself to *White Zombie*, but another sociophobic comes into play eleven years later with *I Walked with a Zombie*, when America was at war with three fascist nations and had reason to fear a master who could bend entire peoples to his will. There is a little bit of Hitler in *I Walked with a Zombie*.

But the real horror came from white people being turned into slaves like black people were. Thus the zombie film from the very beginning was rooted in American ethnicity and fear over what might happen to white people. Although, in fairness, it was always a white Zombie Master who was exploiting the black zombies, and thus a white Zombie Master enslaving the white zombie, the source of horror was that what had been happening to people of African descent for centuries could happen to people of European descent.

Romero and company removed both the zombie master and the immediate sociophobic that whites might be victimized like blacks. But through the unintentional casting of Duane Jones as Ben, the racial Other is not only present but again reverses the model established by *White Zombie*. Ben is a forceful, intelligent leader who never draws attention to his ethnicity; but by repeatedly challenging middle-class, middle-aged, middle American Harry Cooper, and accepting Tom as a willing follower, he embodies the threat perceived by Middle America not only from the Civil Rights movement, but from its more militant wing (as embodied by the Black Panthers and Malcolm X). Ben is emblematic of neither of these, but his very ethnicity demonstrates Harry's (read: white America's) powerlessness.

Simply by casting Duane Jones and removing the zombie master, Romero radically transformed the zombie film. So much is this transformation associated with him that we refer to "Romero zombies," and even now, in the wake of *28 Days Later*, can refer to the "post–Romero zombie." In order to understand not only what Romero added to the genre but also what other filmmakers now reimagine or respond to in remakes, let us examine the things Romero and his artistic associates did to the zombie with *Night*.

What Romero Added

First of all, there are no zombies in *Night of the Living Dead*. The "z" word is never once used. The reanimated dead are called "ghouls," "things," and "them." The first term is employed once the characters (and the media) realize the reanimated dead are eating the flesh of their victims. In fact, the film's original title was *Night of the Flesh Eaters*. Likewise, later films used the "z" word sparingly. It only occurs once in *Dawn* and very rarely in the other films. The preferred term is "those things" or "them," although derogatory terms begin to crop up (for example "stenches" in *Land of the Dead*).

The zombies also function differently in Romero's films than in their predecessors. Although no longer slaves to a zombie master, working without recompense, but rather autonomous monsters, Romero's zombies, at least in *Night*, still use tools — the cemetery zombie uses a rock in order to try to break Barbara's car windows. Later, other zombies use rocks to smash out the truck headlights. Karen kills her mother with a trowel. The zombies also seem to feel pain and react to stimuli. Lastly, they eat things other than humans, as one zombie is seen eating a bug pulled off a tree, implying they crave all flesh, not just human.

The motif of the tool-using zombie will continue throughout Romero's milieu — Bub in *Day* maintains a memory of books, razors and guns. In *Land*, Big Daddy continues to use the tools of his trade and even responds to the air hose bell of a gas station. Butcher cuts a hole in the wall with a cleaver, and the zombies seemingly (re)discover tool use in a film in which the humans misuse tools constantly. *Survival* shows a zombie postal worker repeatedly delivering the same letter; a zombie chained up in a kitchen, going through the motions of cooking and cleaning; and an attempt by Muldoon to domesticate the dead in order to have them continue to function as they did in life.

This continued tool use in Romero's films may be a holdover from the original zombie films — the zombie as slave laborer. In this case, by *Survival of the Dead*, Romero has committed to the idea that the dead can be trained to perform manual labor.

As noted earlier, the first thing Romero changed was to create an autonomous zombie. Romero's zombies lack the Zombie Master. They are not under the control of anything but instinct. *White Zombie, I Walked with a Zombie*, and even the comparatively more recent *The Incredibly Strange Creatures Who Stopped Living and Became Mixed-Up Zombies* (1964) all feature a character that controls the zombies. Romero removed this character and concept. But that was just the beginning of the zombie transformation.

The second key invention, other than autonomy of the zombie, is the flesh eating. *Night* calls them not "zombies" but "ghouls," and the film was originally called *Night of the Flesh Eaters*. The Caribbean zombie is a soulless laborer. The Romero zombie is an animated, cannibalistic corpse. The consumption of the flesh of the living is key to the Romero zombie and will figure frequently in the use of the zombie as metaphor. It is because of Romero that zombies consume.

Interestingly, this cannibalism will be narrowed by Dan O'Bannon in *Return of the Living Dead* to just brains, as will be explored in the second interlude, so much so that in popular culture it is now a given that zombies eat brains, not just flesh (though in *Night* it is clear they will eat any and all flesh, not just human). So connected is the zombie with brain eating that Seth Grahame-Smith began his adaptation of Jane Austen's novel *Pride and Prejudice and Zombies* with the line, "It is a truth universally acknowledged that a zombie in possession of brains must be in want of more brains" (7). Shows which parody popular culture, such as *The Simpsons* or *Robot Chicken*, employ the popular belief that zombies eat only brains for humorous effect.[3] Romero added cannibalism, O'Bannon added brain-eating.

Third, Romero also took the zombie out of the realm of superstition and the supernatural and placed them in the realm of science. However, unlike other fifties and sixties films that moved zombies into the realm of science, for Romero the science itself is just as mysterious. In the precredit sequence of the *Dawn of the Dead* remake, a spokesperson answers all questions with, "We don't know." Zombies are not supernatural, but science cannot save us. John Langan has said of Romero's zombies:

> While you can trace aspects of their behavior to a host of monsters that have come before (like vampires, they rise from the dead; like ghouls and werewolves, they eat our flesh; like Frankenstein's monster, they're reanimated corpses; like most monsters, they have a particular weakness that will kill them immediately), they boil all that down to the basics: they're back from the dead, they want to eat us, they can be killed with a shot to the head [qtd. in Adams, 1].

And yet, in Romero's films, the explanations as to why these are the basics (the dead reanimate, want to eat us, and are vulnerable to brain trauma) are often missing. While the earlier films offered both supernatural and/or scientific explanations, Romero casts all possible reasons into doubt. In *Night* there is talk of radiation from a returning probe to Venus, but there is no conclusive science that can reverse the reanimation or even be proven concretely. *Dawn* offers no explanations—the best science can do is to tell you what to do with dead bodies to ensure they do not reanimate. No reason or explanation for the reanimation is given, other than Peter's grandfather's Macumba theology: "When there is no more room in hell, the dead will walk the earth." Doctor Logan explains that the R-complex of the brain (the reptile cortex) reanimates the body in *Day*, but this does not explain why it does so. As

David Pagano puts it at its most basic, "They simply exist" (78). No explanation is given because none is needed.[4]

Fourth, by changing the means of transmission from magical ceremony aimed at an individual corpse to something that can be spread by bite or wound (plus the fact that even those who are not directly injured by zombies reanimate when they die), Romero allowed for both exponential growth of the zombies and the opening of zombiedom to all. In the case of the former concept, as the series continues, the number of humans declines and the number of zombies grows. By *Day* and *Land*, zombies have replaced humans as the dominant life form on the planet. In the Caribbean zombie films, the reanimated individual was targeted by the Zombie Master; one did not inadvertently become a zombie. The fear that one might become a zombie is still present in Romero, but now reanimation is not targeted. It can and will happen to all, and it happens much faster when one perishes because of a zombie attack. Transmission of zombie status is rapid and guaranteed. In the earlier zombie films there are only a handful of actual zombies. In Romero's work there are hundreds, then thousands, then millions.

Fifth, as noted earlier, although there is always social context and the presence of a sociophobic subtext, Romero added the overt social commentary found in many of the films. Romero has repeatedly said he prefers to use horror as allegory.[5] Jaime Russell correctly identifies that what Romero did (unintentionally) with *Night* was to transform the zombie film and even the horror film as a subject of study:

> By collapsing the boundaries between the normal and the monstrous, the living and the dead, Romero signaled a new stage in the zombie's development. Zombie filmmakers no longer had to hide behind half-baked plots and silly special effects. Instead they could approach serious issues with a grim, apocalyptic nihilism that was shocking and exhilarating in equal measure.... Romero may have done more to popularize socio-political readings of film among horror fans than any other director living today [189].

In short, in addition to adding autonomy, cannibalism, scientifically justified but equally mysterious origins, and exponential, untargeted growth, Romero is also responsible for elevating the zombie film to the level of socio-political and socio-cultural commentary. Romero took zombies and horror seriously.

Romero's six zombie films (as well as many of the remakes) also have recurring themes and motifs which reflect the sociophobics of zombies:

1. Humans are more dangerous than the living dead.

In every single Romero film and remake, the humans always do something that leads to their defeat and or deaths at the hands of the living dead. In *Night*, more deaths are caused by humans than by zombies; Ben kills Harry directly, surviving the night, only to be shot himself by humans in the morning. The biker gang lets the zombies back into the mall in *Dawn*, and Stephen's decision to fight the bikers leads directly to his death and the need for Peter and Fran to flee. The soldiers are as dangerous as the living dead in *Day* and much more unpredictable.

2. Grim humor becomes yet another source for horror.

When Sheriff McClelland sees the burned trucks and the remains of Tom and Judy, he jokes, "Somebody had a cookout here." What horrified the audience just a short while before is a source of grim humor for the posse. This motif (making light of the dead) is a recurring theme in Romero's work. In some cases the grim humor manifests as irony, in other cases it is simply very black humor, often at the expense of the characters. What was painful is transformed into something humorous.

3. Suspicion of the role of the media.

In all six of his films, and again in many of the remakes, the media comes under particular scrutiny. All of Romero's characters live extremely mediated lives, and even though they have experienced zombie attacks, they neither understand nor know what is going on until a television or radio tells them. In *Night*, first the radio then the television offers information, none of which is particularly useful. In *Dawn* we are shown a television station manager who purposefully allows misleading and dangerous information (the location of emergency shelters, some of which have been overrun) to continue to be broadcast for fear that people might stop watching if the information was not being given. In other words, he would rather give wrong information that might result in many deaths than correct information that might result in fewer viewers during the apocalypse. *Diary* is a film-length critique of citizen media, in which nothing is real unless viewed online or through a camera lens.

4. Lack of trust in authority figures.

From Captain Rhodes in *Day* to Kaufman in *Land*, from the National Guard soldiers turned highway robbers in *Diary* to the family patriarchs in *Survival*, all authority is suspect, and both its motives and practices must be questioned. At best, authority is like the sheriff in *Night* who oversees the shooting of Ben: uninformed and inadvertently prone to accidents that kill. More often, however, authority figures in Romero's films are like Rhodes and Kaufman: psychotic and more than willing to exploit and kill others in order to achieve their own ends.

5. The corruptibility of the individual.

Despite the circumstances, someone will act stupid and selfish, resulting in death and destruction in every Romero film and remake. Harry in *Night*, Steven in *Dawn*, the soldiers in *Day*, and Cholo in *Land* are all examples of individuals who do something obviously counterproductive and stupid, which directly results in their deaths or the deaths of others. No matter how intelligent or safe someone is, any character is capable of being corrupted by the petty needs and desires of the ego. Even Ben responds with anger and violence against Harry. All of his efforts result in people dying, and in the end he locks himself in the cellar (which he swore would only happen as a last resort) after everyone else in the house has died, many as an indirect result of his actions. This corruption inevitably ends in death and the destruction of anything the survivors have worked to create.

    6. "We" versus "they" and how we are the same.

    The horror in these films comes not only from "them" but from the fear that we will transform into one of them. Romero adds two of our oldest fears together: the fear of being eaten and consumed by something, and the fear of transformation, of becoming something else and no longer one's self. Related to this is the idea that "we" will not only become "them," we already *are* them. In the 1990 remake, Barbara looks from the zombies to the rednecks tormenting them and says, "They're us. They're us and we're them."

    These films also call into question the ideas of identity, self and "I." Death is supposed to end all physical activity and allow one to "move on" or "go to a better place." These films show the horror of one's body continuing on after "I" am gone. My body becomes something soulless and evil, and might attack my spouse, children, parents, loved ones or friends. The difference between "us" and "them" is simply one of behavior, and even then it is directly related to whether or not one is alive or reanimated.

    We should also note two things about Romero-style zombies. The first is that part of the horror emerges from this transformation that occurs when one dies and becomes a zombie. Rosemary Jackson, in her seminal *Fantasy: The Literature of Subversion*, cannily observed the relationship between deconstructed bodies and deconstructed identities: "Fantasies of deconstructed, demolished or divided identities and of disintegrated bodies oppose traditional categories of unitary selves. They attempt to give graphic depictions of subjects *in process* suggesting possibilities of innumerable other selves, of different histories, different bodies" (177–8). Zombies maintain our outer identity (nurse, businessman, Hare Krishna) as defined by clothing, but inner identity has been erased and homogenized. All zombies, at heart, are an erasure of our own identity, replacing it with that of monster.

    The second is that even after our identity is erased and replaced with a monster, we still have much in common with our pre-zombified self. Linnie Blake, writing of the original *Dawn*, perceives zombies and humans as having much in common. They both try to survive, can replicate, "and both must destroy the enemy in order to do so" (93). The only difference between the two: "their choice of weaponry and tactics: the many hands and teeth of the very many zombies versus the military hardware of the small band of survivors" (93). The most horrific thing is that "they" are "we"—just more bloody and with more decayed clothing.

7. Claustrophobia.

Romero's original films all take place in very tight quarters that do not allow for free movement. *Night* is set in a farmhouse and eventually ends in a basement. *Dawn* expands the space by moving to a mall, but it is still enclosed and limiting. In *Day* we move underground to a military base. While bases tend to be sizable, this one is underground and is linked to a series of caverns. Sarah's room is a small cinderblock cell. Even in *Land*, where the characters exist inside a walled city, Romero's camerawork reflects the series of enclosed spaces the characters all find themselves in — rooms, underground chambers, inside Dead Reckoning, tollbooths — so that every space is small and hemmed in. The trailer in *Diary*, which ends in a small panic room and the barn, and the armored truck in *Survival* echo this encircled motif.

8. Escaping to an island or escaping to Canada.

The instinct in many of Romero's characters is to escape the zombie apocalypse by traveling south "to an island" or north to Canada. The cops in *Dawn* are escaping to an island. When asked "Which island?" one answers, "Any island." At the conclusion of *Day* the surviving characters flee to a tropical island, presumably in the Caribbean. *Survival* features Plum Island, which O'Flynn goes on the web to promote as a safe place, although, as always in Romero, the humans are more of a threat than the zombies.

In *Land*, Riley sees "heading north" to Canada as the only option of possible safety and freedom. Canada is also mentioned as a possible refuge in *Dawn*. DeGiglio-Bellemare observes that the Canada-as-freedom motif echoes negative periods in American history, recalling the neighbor to the north as a destination both for draftees during the Vietnam War and the final stop of the Underground Railroad during the pre–Civil War period of slavery.[6] Ironically, of course, Romero himself escaped to Canada, where he now lives and works, and where his new films are made outside the Hollywood system. In Romero's career and films, as occasionally in American history, Canada means more freedom than in the United States. This notion of escape is rooted in Romero's repeated critique of the United States. If things are not going well in America, one can escape by heading north or south, out of the country. Salvation (whether spiritual or literal) is not found in America — one must leave to be safe.

9. Children are dangerous.

As will be further explored in the first chapter, the youth of America are an endangered species at best and a dangerous species at worst. Children do not survive in Romero or his remakes. None of the films or the remakes feature anyone (living) younger than early teens. Karen dies in *Night* and then kills her parents. The kids in the closet prove dangerous and deadly in *Dawn*, as does Vivian in the remake of *Dawn*. There are no children present in *Day*, and they are tangential at best in *Land*. The sole child in *Diary* is already a zombie when we meet him, and he attacks the college-age students. Children are a burden at best and a danger at worst, and they do not live regardless.

10. Humans are dangerous, but danger is omnipresent from "them."

In *Night* it is noted that taken singly, the "things" are not dangerous (which we should not take at face value, as all the zombie killings shown in the film are of a single zombie killing a human: Johnny and the Cemetery Zombie; Helen and Karen; even Barbara is seized by Johnny, and the others make room as she is pulled out of the house), but that they are very dangerous in groups. Yet, the fact that a single bite is a death sentence means that an individual zombie is just as dangerous as a group of them, and the single zombie is almost always more dangerous. In *Dawn*, the zombie whose scalp is cut off by the helicopter is presented as a very real threat, in as much as it is not noticed, where a crowd would be. In the same film, the children zombies that threaten Peter, and the single zombie that bites Roger, are far more dangerous than the slow crowds in the mall. In *Land*, the first death shown is that of Mike, a rookie and one of Cholo's men, who reaches over a store counter to grab dropped cigars and gets bitten by a single, hiding zombie. The single zombies in the opening, the hospital and the warehouse in *Diary* cause multiple deaths, and cause more problems than the crowd of zombies around the barn.

The zombie apocalypse is mundane in a way — no aliens, no giant lizards, no fire from heaven or people raptured away leaving sinners to face evil incarnate — just your next door neighbor trying to bite you and make you more like him or her. On some level the horror of the zombie apocalypse comes from this mundane aspect. That is why in films set at the beginning of it, many characters have no idea initially that anything is wrong. This initial unawareness is followed by confusion over the situation, which often results in further death and chaos. What is profoundly disturbing about zombies is how mundane they are — just dead folk trying to kill you.

11. No optimism. You cannot win; the best is you do not die (yet).

Tony Williams argues, "Romero's films have always been characterized by a lack of false optimism, a willingness to look objectively at the hard facts of reality, and a recognition that any victories may be tentative (or even unlikely)" (1). This vision is not simply emblematic of the era, but rather one Romero's work has held since *Night* through eight subsequent presidential administrations, several wars, and radical technological and social changes to his current work (as of this writing, *Survival of the Dead*). The remakes of

Romero's work frequently (but not always) share this lack of false optimism and a focus on the fact that "any victories may be tentative." The remake of *Dawn* and *Return of the Living Dead* both end with the deaths of all characters and the implication that there will be no victory for humanity: the world will soon be entirely dead.

These eleven motifs occur in all of Romero's films, and are, more often than not, present in the remakes. They form a collective sociophobics of the horror of society and of other people. Just as Romero's films changed the original zombie formula, these motifs also form a new formula that allows for social commentary while simultaneously positing a hierarchy of danger and safety which reflect Scruton's taxonomies.

Defining Terms of the Living Dead

In the traditional sense, Romero's reanimated corpses are not zombies (in fact, in the original film they are referred to as "ghouls" because they eat the flesh of the dead). As the title suggests, they are "living dead"—human beings that have died, and their corpses begin to move and demonstrate rudimentary signs of intelligence. They follow noise to prey, they can manipulate simple objects (in the original film they use rocks as tools to put out the headlights of Ben's car and to smash the window of Barbara's), and they can tell the difference between a living human and other reanimated corpses.

As noted earlier, the only reference to a "zombie" in the original trilogy is in *Dawn of the Dead*. The "z" word becomes more common in *Land of the Dead*, although it is also mostly absent from *Diary of the Dead* and *Survival of the Dead*. The characters in the films refer to the living dead by a variety of terms: "them," "those things," "ghouls," "stenches," and simply "the dead." The key element here is that, as the television broadcast states in *Night*, the bodies of "persons who have recently died have been returning to life and committing acts of murder." In other words, "zombies" must have died (cessation of all vital functions and brain activity) and then have been reanimated. Secondary is the drive to attack the living and kill and eat them. Romero's films and other related films suggest three possible causes for the reanimation of dead humans: radiation from the "Venus probe," some kind of virus, or God.[7] In all cases, however, regardless of cause, the monster in question is a dead human body that then reanimates.

The "infected" of *28 Days Later* and *28 Weeks Later* are technically not zombies, as the human being never died. Instead, they are infected with the "rage virus," which makes they behave like fast zombies, but they are technically still alive. The zombies of the remade *Dawn* and *Day* follow this model of the faster, more aggressive zombie, although in the former case they are true zombies (not becoming aggressive monsters until after bodily death). In the case of the *Day* remake, the zombies are technically not dead either. They are much closer, in fact, to the "infected" of the *28* series, as they are infected with a virus that first causes flu-like symptoms, followed by a nose bleed, then a very rapid transition into a badly disfigured and aggressive monster with a drive to attack the non-infected. In short, the *Day* remake zombies are, in fact, not zombies.

My larger point in arguing what is and is not a zombie, particularly in this last case, is to show that no matter how influential Romero's work has been on the zombie subgenre, even remakes of Romero are profoundly shaped by the other zombie/"infected" narratives out there. There is a larger zombie culture that has transcended Romero's creation and is now creating what anthropologists call "feedback": those filmmakers that create in response to Romero are now seeing Romero respond to their work. The zombie film in the twenty-first century is almost always full of intertextual referents and references.

Reading Remakes, Re-Envisionings and Adaptations

The twenty-first century has seen an explosion of "re-imagination." Remakes have frequently dominated horror in the last ten years, from mid-century classics such as *The Haunting, 13 Ghosts, House of Wax* and *The House on Haunted Hill*, to recreations of eighties slasher flicks, including *Halloween, Friday the 13th, My Bloody Valentine, The House on Sorority Row* and *A Nightmare on Elm Street*. Sequels, as well, have occupied considerable space in horror cinema: *Saw II* through *VI, Descent 2, Final Destination 3* (in which death itself is the "killer"), and such hybrids as *Freddy vs. Jason* and *Alien vs. Predator*. Sequels are, for all practical purposes, remakes of their original. Horror is full of the return to the same narrative, just with variation.[8]

The reasons for remaking a film are many, but at the top of the list is economics. In her book *A Theory of Adaptation*, Linda Hutcheon observes that there is a good deal of money to be made from a property that is already known (86); but there are also other reasons: "cultural capital," or "personal and political motives" (91–2). The films *Night of the Living Dead 3D* and *Day of the Dead 2: Contagium* would not have attracted nearly as much attention if they had not relied upon well-known, popular titles.[9] Constantine Verevis argues that the title is the first marker of intertextuality with the original, and that sometimes the title is "among the few elements retained from the original" (130).

In addition to the economic motive, remakes and sequels also demonstrate the idea of "cultural capital" as well. While Hutcheon uses the term to refer to such things as stage adaptations of *Great Expectations* or using Shakespeare as a source for a film such as *10 Things I Hate About You*, it also refers to material already familiar to an audience that the audience appreciates and respects—which, in the case of zombie films, refers to Romero.

Every Romero zombie film after *Night* is in some ways a "remake." They are set in the same world, telling virtually the same story: how a small group of individuals cope with the rising of the aggressive, cannibalistic dead. The films themselves are intertextual and self-referential, and by *Diary* they are self-aware. They reference each other, both in terms of narrative and visuals. As early as *Dawn*, *Night* is "quoted" in the film as the heroes' helicopter flies over Western Pennsylvania and sees a posse much like that in its predecessor. Lines from *Night*'s television broadcast are literally quoted in *Dawn*'s television broadcast. Each subsequent chapter visually references the earlier films, as well as sharing a world and the above-mentioned motifs.

What this intertextuality and cross-referencing does is create a series of allusions that can be read by the viewer but are not necessarily read "in order." Linda Hutcheon also reminds us that the different versions of the "text" exist "laterally, not vertically" (169). As an older horror fan, I encounter students who have not seen the original films in order, as I did, but encountered them side-by-side or in a different configuration. Some people saw *Diary* but did not see *Land*. Some have never seen the original *Night* but love the remake of *Dawn*.

Writing a decade ago, Leo Braudy states, "It is also a time of hyperconsciousness of film history, fed by the availability of old films on cable channels and in video stores" (332). Furthermore, current industry practice is to re-release a new DVD of an original film when a remake is released to theaters. Thus, one can see the remake in the theater and then go home and watch the original immediately, or even watch the original right before seeing the remake. Or they can see a single film without knowing or seeing any of the others.

Hutcheon reminds us that audiences for remakes fall into two categories: "knowing and unknowing" (120). One must ask what shapes the audience's expectations in viewing a film. A "knowing" audience is not necessarily one that has seen the original *Dawn of the Dead*, but rather is an audience whose understanding of zombie horror has been shaped by *28 Days Later* or *Return of the Living Dead 3*. Either of these films would produce a radically different set of expectations in the viewer who is now encountering the remake of *Dawn* without having seen the original *Dawn*. Faster-moving zombies would be expected, and not result in the objections that some fans of the original (and Romero himself) raised in response to the remake. When I saw the 2004

Dawn of the Dead, I knew the original by heart. Several of those with me in the theater had not seen the 1978 film at all, and thus our experiences (and perceptions of the film) were remarkably different. As a result, reception theory when talking about cinema in general and a canon of zombies films in particular can be a bit tricky. When I speak of "the audience," it is a general, idealized audience of knowledgeable fans, and not those who are viewing the film in isolation. Admittedly, the latter would probably not be reading this book.

To these I would also add a third category of "fan expert." In this category are those who have not only seen the originals, but are *very* familiar with them. They have watched the films multiple times, both on the big and small screens. They have heard the DVD commentaries and watched all the special features. They have read the books (such as this one) and debated with friends about the relative merits and quality of both originals and remakes. This group is not merely a "knowing" audience, they are a "hyperknowing" one. Horror and zombie subgenre fans tend to be knowledgeable, dedicated and judgmental. They are informed critics, and more than willing to express opinions about every aspect of original and remake.

Thomas Leitch further complicates our understanding of remakes by observing the "paradoxical promise" of the same but different film (44). We go to a remake because we enjoyed the original and want that first viewing experience again. But the expectation is also that something different will be done with the narrative or characters, as we also wish to be surprised. Hence the negative critical reaction to Gus van Sant's remake of *Psycho*, which was not a "reimagining" but literally a shot-by-shot remake of Hitchcock's film in color and with different actors. Nothing new was added, nothing was taken away. Van Sant made the same exact film, which made many (myself included) wonder why we would not simply go watch the original? The exercise seemed academic at best, and the waste of a good deal of talent and resources at worst. Virtually all other remakes, however, embody Leitch's "paradoxical promise" of a different version of the same thing — what Verevis refers to as "innovation and repetition" (177). John Biguenet also reminds us of the variety of allusive forms in cinema: visual, literary, musical, etc., which can point to other films, culture, literature, etc. (132). So remakes not only "quote" the original but can quote a variety of other texts, not necessarily cinematic.

Scott A. Lucas and John Marmysz offer a new model for understanding remakes, which I incorporate into this study. They argue that those who have seen the original are not passive viewers of the remake but "active participants" in deriving meaning from comparison with the original (13). They further see viewing not as "a one-way process" but as a "dialogue" between "originals, copies, and their multiple authors and interpreters" (12). The point of this book is to examine the dialogue between the different films, and between the films (individually and collectively) and the audience. As noted above, the movies engage in an extensive shaping of sociophobics which rise from the cultural moment when the film is created. But the horror is not limited to the cultural fears of the moment. More general human fears and concerns also play out across the screen.

Consequently, I am less interested in the "fidelity" of the remakes to the original, or the relationship between remake and original, than I am in how the remake is as much a reflection of the period in which it was created as the original is a reflection of its period of origin. The differences between remake and original also demonstrate where the new sociophobics are arising.

With the release of *Survival of the Dead*, Romero's sixth zombie film, we might be tempted to divide Romero's work into two trilogies: *Night, Dawn*, and *Day*, the original trilogy from 1976 to 1985, and *Land, Diary*, and *Survival*, the post–2001 films. Yet, narratively, this structure does not work as well as dividing the films into a tetrology and a pair of linked films. Romero himself claims that *Night, Dawn, Day* and *Land* form an overarching narrative from the beginning of the rise of the dead to the complete collapse of even post-rise societies (Lacher D3). *Diary* returns us to the first moments of the dead returning, and *Survival*, using a minor character from *Diary*, then carries the story forward for the next few months and the creation of those post-rise societies. Thus, *Diary* and *Survival* are in some ways also "remakes," inasmuch as they return to the beginning of the story and retell the collapse of society and how and why small groups survive for as long as they do.

Resurrecting the Beautiful Dead

In this volume I explore the six (as of this writing) original zombie films made by George A. Romero and then examine the remakes that have been made of the first three. This book is not a survey of zombie cinema, a list of films and reviews, or even a tribute to Romero as a filmmaker.[10] It is a series of close readings of Romero's films and the remakes and reimaginings of them in order to understand how the remake uses the same story to reflect current fears. I will also consider stage adaptations of *Night of the Living Dead* and its adaptation into other media.

I am less interested in the clichéd and usual readings of these films (*Night* as analogy for Vietnam or the Civil Rights movement, *Dawn* as indictment of consumer society), although these readings are important and valuable and will obviously come into play in any socio-cultural understanding of Romero's work. Having said that, I will build upon existing criticism to offer my own readings of these films.[11] I am more interested in some of the other influences that are often less-mentioned (the shaping influence of *The American Way of Death* and the subsequent congressional hearings on the funeral industry after *Night*, for example), and how the shifting sociocultural matrix of the historical moment of the remake renders the context of the original irrelevant. There is no Vietnam War or civil rights movement in 1990, or 1998 or 2006, for example, but there is a new *Night of the Living Dead* in those years. So the shifts that occur within the narrative, characters, setting and action demonstrate the new social fears present in this new zombie film.

For the purposes of this study I will consider the original films in their original contexts. I shall then look at the changes in the remakes that indicate a shift in social anxiety. The volume is divided into four sections. The first section is *Night* and concerns the three different versions of *Night of the Living Dead* (1968, 1990 and 2006), as well as John Russo's additions for the 30th anniversary DVD and the "reanimated" version (in which scenes from the original were replaced with a variety of animated versions while maintaining the original soundtrack), plus the forthcoming *Night of the Living Dead: Origins*. An interlude follows, exploring the adaptation of *Night* in other media, most specifically on stage as a theatrical performance. The second section, *Dawn*, covers the original *Dawn of the Dead*, its variations (European version, special extended version, etc.), and then Zach Snyder's 2004 remake. This section is followed by an interlude on *Return of the Living Dead*, which is not a Romero film but which has profoundly shaped the popular understanding of the Romero zombie (it is from *Return* that the idea that zombies crave brains comes — in Romero's films, all human flesh is fair game, but brains now seem canonical; see Interlude 2). The third section, *Day*, covers the original 1985 version and the 2008 remake. The final section, "Back for the Dead," offers an extended analysis of *Land*, *Diary* and *Survival*, as well as the continuing influence of Romero in the context of popular zombie culture.

I take the films at face value and ask you, the reader, for the purposes of this study to reserve judgment on the films themselves while we examine them. Some remakes are not very good films. Some are, quite frankly, shameful exploitations of Romero's brand name and are poorly written, acted and directed. I do not write in order to pass judgment or impose my taste. Instead, I am interested in teasing out the meanings of the remakes, no matter how good or bad, and how they reflect the world in which they were created. *Night of the Living Dead* gave us a template for looking at the world. The subsequent films continue to give us ways of understanding our own society, culture, and reality. The fact that some do so poorly, or in a manner crassly and cravenly designed to make money off of a more talented person's vision, or even in a manner patently ridiculous does not mean they do not do so. In other words, while *Night of the Living Dead 3D* is a terrible film with almost no redeeming artistic value, that does not mean that it cannot tell us about what we fear and why we fear it (it only makes it unpleasant to watch).

One thing I do consider is how Romero's original narratives are taken and transformed into another genre or form. Both John A. Russo's unofficial sequel, *Children of the Living Dead*, and *Night of the Living Dead 3D* not only change the focal point of the fears, they change the tropes and elements common to the zombie film transforming themselves into slasher movies. *Diary of the Dead* is an original zombie film by Romero, but it is just as much first-person pseudo documentary in the mold of *The Blair Witch Project*, *Cannibal Holocaust* or *The Last Broadcast* as it is a "zombie film." While I am more interested in the sociocultural meaning of these films and how they narrate sociophobics, and less interested in their literary aspects, it is still important to remember that genre and form also shape and change both fears and meanings. One fears a serial killer and zombies for different reasons, though both can kill you.

We should also remember that no one (the author included) goes to a zombie film for the scathing social critique of late capitalism and the American political establishment. I have never left a theater saying, "Dude, that use of the zombie as a metaphor for *lumpenproletariat* was AWESOME! It terrified me so much." The rise in zombie culture has also seen a rise in zombie scholarship, both deeply academic and amateur/fan. Fan writing tends to be enthusiastic but unsophisticated, and just as often offers opinion as analysis; whereas academic writing can be dry, dull, and looks on its subject matter with contempt. While it can be difficult to critique that which you love, I believe it is a necessity both to recognize the limits of academic criticism and of fan criticism, and to critique the films honestly and accurately. I hope this volume combines a fan's passion and knowledge with an academic's understanding of larger context. Thus, there will be no discussion in this volume of how awesome the decapitations of a zombie by helicopter are or how a particular scene should be loved by all fans.

> *"Yeah, they're dead, they're all messed up."*
> — Sheriff McClelland, *Night of the Living Dead*

Notes

1. This event was documented in the film *Zombie Jamboree: The 25th Anniversary of* Night of the Living Dead. Sadly, the John Russo-written and directed documentary fills much of its 60 minutes with television commercials made by the Latent Image, previews for and footage from other (non-zombie) Russo films and his "Scream Queens" line, and poorly-framed and shot footage of the event itself, mostly interviews with people who had nothing to do with *Night*, *Dawn* or *Day*.

2. I played "Jerry" in the much-maligned *Day of the Dead 2: Contagium*, a sequel-in-name-only to Romero's film. I have also appeared in a few independent zombie films which have not found distribution. It is a good deal of fun to work on such films, both as a zombie and as their human victim. It is an odd thing to see yourself torn apart and eaten.

3. In the third "Treehouse of Horror" (*The Simpsons*, season 4 [9F04]), Bart accidentally reanimates the dead, but the zombies do not harm or attack Homer because they cannot locate his brain. Similarly, zombies frequently show up on *Robot Chicken*, always attacking people for their brains. In one particularly memorable sequence (from "Cracked China," episode 2.7), a man in a bomb shelter asks the individuals groaning the word "brains" on the other side of the door, "Are you radioactive zombies or survivors thanking the one attribute that's kept you alive?" After a brief pause a voice comes from the other side of the door: "Zombies — didn't feel right to lie to you," which not only employs the brain motif but also locates humor in the fact the zombies having an ethical need to be honest about what they are, even as they seek to eat said brains.

4. In fact, it seems that when a specific cause is located, such as in *Day of the Dead 2: Contagium*, *Night of the Living Dead 3D* and *Children of the Living Dead*, the effect is to lessen the horror and the crisis itself. What is particularly terrifying in the open-endedness and ambiguity of *Night* and *Dawn* is that something that has no definite answers cannot be easily solved or taken care of (not to mention the Lovecraftian idea that fear of the unknown is the oldest and deepest fear in humanity). Anything with an explanation can be cured.

5. See Lacher and "10 Questions," for example, of Romero's assertion of his preference for allegory and his disdain for recent horror, especially so-called "torture porn," which he sees as not having "any substance underlying it" (Lacher D3).

6. In a wry observation on *Dawn*, Gregory A. Waller refers to the characters proposing to fly to Canada during a time of national crisis as "latter-day draft dodgers" (*The Living*, 308).

7. Both Peter in *Dawn* and the Reverend Hicks in the 30th anniversary re-edited *Night* suggest the dead might be reanimating because of a divine plan. Peter's famous line about "when there is no more room in hell, the dead will walk the earth" is presented as a Macumba apocalyptic vision. The Reverend Hicks uses fundamentalist Christian apocalyptic terminology to describe the rising of the dead as a sign of the beginning of the end.

8. There are, admittedly, excellent remakes: *The Thing* and *Invasion of the Body Snatchers* leap to this author's mind. And there are some excellent sequels: *Aliens* is the obvious choice; and I have always been of the opinion that *Saw II* is the equal of, if not surpassing, the original.

9. I have always felt that the negative reviews of *DOTD2:C* were significantly influenced by the decision of the producers to call it *Day of the Dead 2* when it was not related in any way to *Day of the Dead*— not via narrative, characters, artists who worked on the original (there was simply no connection). Had Taurus Entertainment simply released a zombie film called "Contagium," much of the Romero-fan ire would have been removed and the film might have received slightly more positive reviews. Might have.

10. Those looking for surveys will find an embarrassment of riches available to them of varying depths, quality and coverage. Among the better and more interesting ones are Jamie Russell's *Book of the Dead* (2005), arguably the most comprehensive look at the genre to date, Glenn Kay's *Zombie Movies: The Ultimate Guide* and Arnold T. Blumberg and Andrew Hershberger's *Zombiemania*, both of which offer lists summaries of specific films, Shawn McIntosh and Marc Laverette's *Zombie Culture* and Kyle William Bishop's *American Zombie Gothic*, which, although a little dry, offer an academic analysis of zombies in the American gothic literary tradition, relying upon formal and psychological criticism. One early survey is Peter Dendle's *The Zombie Movie Encyclopedia*, which has no entries from the explosion of the past decade but offers considerable analysis of early zombie films. From the same period and among the "lesser lights" of zombie literature is Andy Black's *The Dead Walk*, a volume from before the current tide of zombology but a rather uninformed and uninspired survey of "zombie films" which also includes *A Clockwork Orange* (?), mummy movies and the occasional vampire film. Of far more value are more recent fusion analyses combining both academic and popular approaches, such as Jonathan Maberry's *Zombie CSU* and Kim Paffenroth's Stoker Award–winning *Gospel of the*

Living Dead. There are also several volumes on the individual and collective works of George Romero, the best of which is Ben Hervey's BFI volume on *Night of the Living Dead.* Paul R. Gagne's *The Zombies That Ate Pittsburgh* represents one of the first surveys of Romero's work, and, more recently, Tony Williams's *The Cinema of George Romero: Knight of the Living Dead* also offers a survey of his work to date.

11. Interestingly, the only work that focuses solely on remakes of Romero, other than magazine articles, is Shane Borrowman's "Remaking Romero" in *Fear, Cultural Anxiety and Transformation: Horror, Science Fiction and Fantasy Films Remade.* Even then, Borrowman focuses primarily on the recent (for him) *Dawn* remake. No single work has focused on analyzing Romero's work and the remakes and sequels, official or unofficial, thereof, and what they mean in the next contexts. This book is an attempt to rectify this gap.

I
Night

1
"We may not enjoy living together, but dying together isn't going to solve anything": *Night of the Living Dead* (1968)

In the introduction to his collection of essays *American Horrors*, Gregory A. Waller identified 1968 as the beginning of "the modern era of the American horror film" (2). That is the year that both *Rosemary's Baby* and *Night of the Living Dead* were released. Until this point, for much of the past thirty years horror had been a genre aimed at children and teenagers. *Night* and *Rosemary's Baby* were very much adult horror films whose subtext was even more disturbing than their surface text. *Night* is the film that got the whole ball rolling. It changed filmmaking. It changed horror. It has, in some ways, become a Rorschach test — multiple and conflicting interpretations of the film have emerged, depending on the point of view of the viewer. The "living dead" may be perceived as metaphors for numerous things — whether the masses or the Vietnamese or the dangers of conformity.

Night premiered in Pittsburgh on 2 October 1968. Its genius is its simplicity. It is part siege film, in which a small group of emblematic characters must defend the place in which they are trapped from a large, dangerous and incomprehensible force out to enter that space and wreak havoc, such as *Rio Bravo* or *Assault on Precinct 13*. It is part post-apocalyptic film, in which a small group of emblematic characters survive an event that ends the world as we know it and attempts to continue to survive, such as *The Shape of Things to Come* or *Day of the Triffids*. It is part horror film, in which a small group of emblematic characters are killed off one by one by a supernatural or natural but evil menace, such as *Friday the 13th* or *The Blob*. It is cinema verité, unadorned naturalism — it is believable in its narrative and in the depiction of its characters. And yet, for all that, it has been read in numerous different ways as political or social metaphor.

As Gregory Waller reads it:

> It depicts the failure of the nuclear family, the private home, the teenager couple, and the resourceful, individual hero; and it reveals the flaws inherent in the media, local and federal government, agencies and the entire mechanism of civil defense ["Introduction" 9].

In other words, *Night* displays not only the failure of family, home, government and media, it is also a critique of the construction of American life in mid-century cinema: "the hero," the "teenage couple" and the mechanism of civil defense are all tropes from the horror/sci-fi/teen cinema of the fifties and sixties. Together they manage to save the day. *Night* completely devastates these tropes.

There is no army that comes to the rescue (which may also be symbolic of the reality that America's military is present in Vietnam, not at home), no national guard (ditto). Only a posse of local law enforcement and redneck hunters. The teenagers die in an explosion, and the hero himself is shot and killed by the very posse that would ordinarily rescue him. The notion of "home" is also under direct assault in *Night*. Although clearly a farmhouse in Middle America, the place of *Night* is not a "home." None of the people in the house own the house or live there. All seven sought shelter there when things turned bad. It is not their home. They are thrown together by chance and then slowly die, sometimes inadvertently.

The deaths themselves are of key importance. More people die at the hands of humans than living dead in *Night*. The film, in one sense, is a paradigmatic movie about small-group infighting doing more damage than the monsters, and the siege of the mundane. In addition to the specific sociophobics and specific historical references of the film, there are also comments on human nature and group dynamics. When in a panic, the film seems to say, we are more likely to die by the hands of those on our side than the enemy without. It is ironic, but the oxymoronic "friendly fire" does kill more humans than ghouls do. Karen (Kyra Schon) kills the parents who would kill to protect her and who have probably only stayed together for her sake. Johnny presumably kills and eats the sister who continually insists they must go rescue him. The list of those culpable in the deaths of Tom (Keith Wayne) and Judy (Judith Ridley) include Ben (Duane Jones), Harry (Karl Hardman), and even Tom and Judy themselves.

Night is a study in irony. Johnny (Russell Streiner) does an impression of Boris Karloff (who himself made a living playing living dead men), playfully warning Barbara (Judith O'Dea) about the man in the cemetery.[1] Johnny turns out to be right: the man in the cemetery (now known as the "Cemetery Zombie" [Bill Hinzman]) was, in fact, coming to get Barbara, as well as

Johnny. Harry, hated by everybody in both the house and the audience, insists the cellar is the only safe place in the house where they might survive the night. He turns out to be right, and, after arguing with and then killing Harry, Ben goes down into the cellar and survives the night.

The overall structure of the film is also a study in reversals and ironies. Gregory A. Waller points out that the film begins with one of "them," the Cemetery Zombie, mistaken for a human by Barbara and Johnny, and ends with one of "us," Ben, "mistaken for one of them by the posse" (*The Living*, 295). Ben, having survived the night — indeed, the only person in the farmhouse to do so — is killed not by the living dead but rather by humans who shoot him in the morning. One of the "rules" of *Night* is that the annoying jerk is probably right, even if we do not like him.

Two of three dominant sociocritical modes of reading *Night* are to read it through the lenses of Vietnam and/or the Civil Rights movement. Kim Newman sees *Night* as "a Vietnam apocalypse, with documentary-style sequences of flesh-eating ghouls being snuffed by cheerfully professional National Guardsmen" (176). Although the Kent State Massacre did not occur until two years after the release of *Night*, the Civil Rights riots in the American South had already shown posses of local law enforcement working with private citizens to beat, shoot, hurt and kill fellow citizens, primarily of color. There had been plenty of televised footage of the National Guard of various states fighting against groups of citizens, from the Civil Rights movement to the 1968 Democratic National convention in Chicago. Adam Lowenstein, interviewed in *American Nightmare*, speaks of the final sequence of *Night*: "These images tell the truth, the painful truth about those struggles in ways that not many films of the time have been able to." There is more of Vietnam and the Civil Rights movement in *Night* than in period films about those struggles.

The third mode, of course, is to see the film in economic terms, as outlined in this volume's introduction. David J. Skal sees *Night* as "an allegory of haves and have-nots (the 'living' and the 'dead') struggling over the control and occupancy of an emblematic house" (357). The problem with this (Marxist, though he never calls it that) reading of the film is that the dead are completely uninterested in the house for its own sake. The dead want what is inside it. They want to consume the living. Once the house is (seemingly) empty of the living, the dead abandon it. Once Ben wakes up in the morning and emerges from the cellar, he does not have to fight the dead who "control and occupy" the house. They have already left. Although consumption is the name of the game for the dead, they only consume human flesh and are not interested in the acquisition of material goods in any way. Thus the allegory is an incomplete one at best, especially since our sympathies and sensibilities are with the humans.

Co-writer John Russo says that the social commentary was unintentional, going so far as to tell a *Vanity Fair* reporter, "All that [political] stuff's bullshit" (qtd. in Zinoman 306).[2] Romero has agreed, stating, "I don't know if we meant to have any kind of political subtext in the film, but certainly it's there, the times we were living in. I mean, I was driving the film to New York City on the night Martin Luther King was assassinated, for crying out loud. It was eerie" (qtd. in Alexander 12). Even if unintended, *Night* is emblematic of the period and portrays much of the sociophobia of late-sixties America.

All of these criticisms are valid and interesting, and I list them here to indicate the different ways the film has been read by critics, and the different sociophobics engaged. For the rest of this chapter I will focus briefly on six areas: one, the zombies of *Night* as uniquely American monsters; two, how concern over the rural cemetery movement, the funeral industry and changes in American death rituals can be read in the film; three, how concern over the changes in the relationship between the younger generation and its elders is presented in the film; four, how concern over race relations and especially young African American men manifests itself in the character of Ben and the other characters' relationships with him, especially as read through the film *Guess Who's Coming to Dinner*; five, how concern over the media is made manifest in the media available in the farmhouse; and six, the film's ending.

All American Monsters

If you are reading this book, I must assume that you are at least familiar with and interested in *Night of the Living Dead*. Yet to truly begin, a brief summary of the plot may prove useful. At their mother's request, Johnny and his sister Barbara drive "200 miles" from Pittsburgh to a cemetery where their father is buried in order to place a wreath on his grave. Most notably, the credits are imposed over an American flag flying as they enter the cemetery. They are attacked by a man (the "Cemetery Zombie"), and Johnny is killed. Barbara flees and is pursued by the Cemetery Zombie.[3] She takes shelter in a seemingly-abandoned farmhouse and is joined shortly by Ben, an African American man also fleeing the dead.

Barbara grows more catatonic as Ben boards up the house, and it is revealed that five more people were hiding in the cellar: Harry Cooper, his wife Helen (Marilyn Eastman) and their daughter Karen (who was "bitten by one of those things"), and Tom and Judy, a young couple. Together they finish fortifying the house and then watch television, which explains that the dead are rising and eating the flesh of the living. Harry wants to hide in the cellar, Ben wants to defend the house or even make a run for help. When Ben, Tom and Judy attempt to gas up Ben's truck at a fuel pump in the yard, an accident kills Tom and Judy, and the dead begin to eat them. Ben escapes back to the house but must battle Harry in order to get back in. The dead attack while Karen, who has died, revives and kills her mother with a trowel and then attacks her father. Barbara is seized by the reanimated corpse of her brother, and Ben hides in the cellar, shooting the reanimated corpses of Harry, Helen and Karen. In the morning, Ben emerges, only to be shot by a posse marksman who mistakes him for a "ghoul." Ben's body is thrown on a fire as the end credits roll.

Ben Hervey, in the BFI Film Classics volume of *Night*, links Romero's film to numerous, specifically American horrors of the period: the Tet Offensive, which began in January of 1968; the My Lai Massacre in March; the clubbing and gassing of peaceful demonstrators outside the Democratic convention in Chicago in August; the Tate-LaBianca murders in 1969; not to mention the assassinations of Martin Luther King, Jr. and Robert Kennedy in 1968 (22–3). Hervey quotes Arthur Schlesinger after Robert Kennedy's assassination: "We are today the most frightening people on the planet" (23).[4] The zombie, the frightening monster of *Night*, is an all–American monster.

Kyle William Bishop reminds us that, unlike the vampire, werewolf, ghost, and other monsters, the zombie is "fundamentally American in its origins" (*American Zombie*, 5). Whereas the vampire, werewolf, ghost and Frankenstein's monster are all European in origin (at least as they are shown in cinema — admittedly, all world cultures have ghosts, blood-drinking monsters and humans that transform into animals), the zombie is, as noted in the introduction, a Caribbean creation and a monster original to Hollywood without the benefit of a literary forebear.

Romero's directing credit appears over a reversed American flag, perhaps suggesting a nation in which the reality is now backwards of the ideal. Army Regulation 670-1, which dictates proper military insignia, indicates that the American flag patch is worn reversed on the uniform, with the star field on the observer's right, so as to appear that the flag is waving in the breeze. Romero literalizes this uniform flag on the screen, also indicating a nation at war — not just in Vietnam but also with itself.

Robin Wood was one of the first to comment on the American flag in the opening sequence: "The metaphor of America-as-graveyard is central to Romero's work," he wrote (103). Visually, the film displays a dead or dying world. Although Barbara clearly states that it is "the day the time changes" (in other words, mid–April in the Eastern United States), the trees are still devoid of leaves. In fact, the visual world of the film suggests Fall, not Spring: the landscape itself is dead, and unlike the human corpses, it is not coming back to life. As the flag is the foremost symbol of the United States, its presence at the beginning of *Night* not only establishes the United States as the site of the film, it also, *pace* Wood, informs the audience that what we are about to witness is a comment on American society—that it is dying or dead.

The zombie is, therefore, the all–American monster. Created in the Americas and developed as a monster by Hollywood, the zombie is American by birth. Unlike in earlier zombie films, such as *I Walked with a Zombie* and *White Zombie*, in *Night* the zombies are literally all American: the dead first rise "in the Eastern third of the United States." All of the zombies that attack the farmhouse are local people risen from the dead. Those attacked are not attacked from without but by their friends, neighbors and even family members. In response, they are confronted by all–American people. There are no heroes or higher-ups here, no scientists or magicians, no one who knows what is happening initially. Dillard sees the occupants of the farmhouse as "ordinary" (17). Ben, Barbara, the Coopers, and Tom and Judy are all "regular Americans"—everyday people trying to survive in a crisis they did not create.

Where the Bodies Are Buried

Why do Johnny and Barbara have to drive three hours from Pittsburgh to their father's grave, especially if they still live with or near their mother? It seems very strange to bury someone three hours away. Johnny even states they are "two hundred miles" from Pittsburgh.[5] The opening scene, however, is indicative of a serious change in the American death ritual.

During the colonial period in America, cemeteries were originally next to churches right in the hearts of towns and cities. As cities grew, the cemeteries were moved outside into the rural areas. Beginning in the last quarter of the nineteenth century, with Mount Auburn Cemetery in Cambridge, Massachusetts, the "Rural Cemetery" movement transformed the urban way of death.[6] Despite its name, the Rural Cemetery movement was actually an urban movement, eliminating family and church graveyards and replacing them with large civic cemeteries on the outskirts of cities, landscaped to provide a park-like feeling. As Thomas J. Hannon observes, the Pittsburgh equivalent of Mount Auburn was Allegheny Cemetery, which "has gained both regional and national acclaim as one of the most beautiful and interesting concepts of the movement" (254). The cemetery at the opening of *Night* is a prime example of a rural cemetery: away from the city, landscaped and made to resemble a park.

Furthermore, because of the social migrations in the wake of the Second World War, families often no longer occupied the same geographic area. The combination of the separation and migration of families, and the changing nature and location of cemeteries, meant that it was quite possible to be buried away from one's family. Instead of extended family plots, individuals were buried all over. Simply put, families were no longer buried together, and frequently were not buried nearby. Large numbers of random individuals are now buried in the same cemetery. This burial practice now marks the end of family or community.

The film also engages late twentieth-century ideas of death, including the Cold War phenomenon of "acceptable losses," and mass or "megadeaths."[7] Lindsay Prior argues that the attempt to quantify, qualify and scientifically calculate death is a twentieth century phenomenon: "The premodern portraits present a vision of a random, unpredictable and untamed death; of a death which can strike anyone, anywhere, at any time whatsoever and with equal possibility (178)." The Cold War brought about "estimated casualties" in the millions: deaths per kiloton were estimated by government scientists. The hospice movement and the expansion of end-of-life care have further depersonalized death: "For death has indeed become a predictable and in many respects a technically controlled event" (Prior 189). Early in the twentieth century, many individuals still died at home. By 1968, death had been distanced and separated from the lived experience of most Americans.

Conversely, *Night* separates its characters (and its audience) from the carefully constructed death rituals designed to allow the living to grieve for and say goodbye to the dead. Death, in *Night*, comes suddenly and unexpectedly again. The suddenness of Johnny's death and the pursuit by the Cemetery Zombie leaves Barbara with no opportunity to mourn her brother. Tom and Judy do not even have words said over them or a prayer offered up after their unexpected demise. *Night* shows a world in which there is no opportunity to grieve or carry out comforting rituals. And while "it takes time to let go of a loved one" (Thursby 134), no such time is allowed during the events of *Night*. During the television broadcast, a doctor states, "The bereaved will have to forego the dubious comforts that a funeral service will give. They are just dead flesh and dangerous." While this passage is cited by Kim Paffenroth as a "dismissal of religion," it is also the reality of a society in which the rituals were used to hide or at least cope with the reality of death (41). We will see this dismissal of rituals of the dead amplified in the opening of both the 1990 remake of *Night* and the original *Dawn*.

The specific elements of death rituals are further transformed in *Night*. Prayer does not work. When Barbara prays at the grave of her father, Johnny tells her, "Church was this morning." Minutes later he is dead, and Barbara is so shocked she does not pray for him, as she cannot even bring herself to believe he is dead. Funerals are for the living, but the film now states they are "dubious comforts." Jacqueline Thursby reports that food "as a giver and sustainer of life has been a symbolic part of the festive ritual behavior of mourning and funerary traditions," and that post-burial ceremonies in many societies features both food offerings for the dead themselves and gifts of food for the family of the deceased (8). In *Night*, the irony is that the living become the food offering to the dead. The living dead consume the bodies of Tom and Judy; they neither pray for them nor carry out any rituals. They simply eat them.

Conversely, as the living become the food of the dead, the dead become visual poison to the living. "Don't look at it," Ben snaps angrily at Barbara, when they see the corpse at the top of the stairs. His tone is not gentle, or out of concern. It is an order, barked. Ben does not want Barbara seeing the corpse and becoming hysterical. But Barbara has already seen a few living corpses and her brother killed. Ben's commandment, however, is born out of fear of seeing the dead and fear of seeing the truth of the dead: "It is not some medusan ugliness that makes looking at these 'things' dangerous; it's because they're too like us" (Hervey 47). Certainly the fact is that the living dead are a mirror of the living, but there is also concern because they are also not like us. There is a fundamental wrongness to the dead: how they move, how they sound, not to mention the fact that they are not supposed to move or make sounds at all. Perhaps the biggest problem is that the dead are not behaving as we expect the dead should.

The removal of death from life in the twentieth century has also sanitized death. After one dies, the body is removed and a funeral director embalms the body and then uses makeup, wax and other skills to attempt to imitate how the body looked in life. Any injuries or blemishes are covered up and hidden. The living dead do not look like sanitized corpses. The ones that surround the farmhouse display injuries, have bloodstains, or are otherwise horrific looking. The body in the farmhouse shows all the trauma of death. It is not like the bodies one sees at wakes or funerals. It is disturbing.

Yet there is something about the sight of death and destruction that is inherently dangerous. Martin Harries links the story of Lot's wife in the Bible with the images of 9/11, arguing "destructive spectatorship" indicates that looking at things can hurt us (1). Both Lot's wife in Genesis and those fleeing the falling towers in New York City were told not to "look back," as though witnessing destruction might bring about our own. The dead body at the top of the stairs in *Night* becomes a synecdoche for all dead bodies from this point on. It is clearly not someone who passed away peacefully — the individual's skull has been bashed in, the eyes are sticking out. This death was neither peaceful nor welcome. It is an oracle of what is to come for all in the house: they will not die well or peacefully.

Another possible influence on Romero's film, or at least how *Night* was received, was a new cynicism toward the funeral industry prompted by the publication of *The American Way of Death* in 1963. Jessica Mitford, a British investigative journalist known for left-wing politics in the fifties, at the suggestion of her husband, civil rights attorney Robert Truehaft, began probing the funeral industry. After an initial article on the topic in *Frontier* magazine, her further explorations resulted in the bestselling book, which subsequently resulted in congressional hearings and the passing of legislation to protect consumers from unscrupulous funeral homes. All of this was occurring around the time of *Night*.

Mitford noted that the funeral is third after the house and family car in terms of the "largest expenditures ... in the life of an ordinary American family" (28). She observed that "the trappings of Gracious Living are transformed, as in a nightmare, into the trappings of Gracious Dying," and that the language of American death "is now the language of Madison Avenue" (16). Her observations on the funeral industry are echoed in Johnny's complaints about the wreath he and Barbara have brought to their father's grave:

JOHNNY: Look at this thing: "We Still Remember." I don't. You know, I don't even remember what the man looks like.

BARBARA: Johnny, it takes you five minutes.

JOHNNY: Yeah, five minutes to put the wreath on the grave and six hours to drive back and forth. Mother wants to remember so we trot two hundred miles into the country and she stays home.

JOHNNY: I wonder what happened to the one from last year. Each year, we spend good money on these things. Then, we come out here and the one from last year's gone.

BARBARA: Well, the flowers die and the caretaker or somebody takes them away.

JOHNNY: Yeah, a little spit-and-polish could clean this up, sell it next year. I wonder how many times we bought the same one.

Johnny objects to the expenditure of time and money — he states that the simple act of placing the wreath is not for him, nor for their dead father, but for their mother, who is neither there nor would know if they did not do it.

Johnny's complaints concern the business aspect of death in America. He believes he is being ripped off because he is forced to purchase something neither he nor his deceased father need, which will be removed soon after it has been placed, and that could be cleaned and sold again and he would never know. He is forced to "consume" something he does not want, with no benefit to anyone except the person who sold it to him. Funerals and the accoutrement of remembering the dead are expensive, yet are not needed by the dead. Johnny argues that they really are not needed by the living either, but that he is pressured by family members who have bought into the "American way of death" to spend money "remembering."

Johnny's complaints also raise many of the major themes of the work: the failure of family, intergeneration conflict, and a need to lose reverence for the dead and for tradition. Religion, especially, comes under fire with his request to Barbara to hurry up her prayer ("Church was this morning"); his own admission, "There's not much sense in my going to church"; and his fond memory of his grandfather telling him, "Boy, you'll be damned to hell." Johnny has no place or time for the American way of death or for religion. Funerals were already of "dubious comfort" for him, but his cynicism is a reflection of American cynicism toward the death industry and the epiphenomena of it.

The Kids Are Not All Right

Johnny's complaints are also generational. His elderly mother makes her children drive 200 miles to honor their late father. Religion, burial rituals, and the laying of wreaths are all things valued by the older generation, not by the younger. The sixties, of course, were a turbulent time, with much of the conflict intergenerational. Ira Levin's *Rosemary's Baby*, about the birth of the Devil's child, was published in 1967, the year before *Night* was made. The film version of Levin's novel, directed by Roman Polanski, was released the same year as *Night*. That same year, right after the so-called "Summer of Love," the nation elected Richard Nixon to the highest office in the land in a sign of a growing conservatism after eight years of Democrats controlling the White House.[8] The older generation was growing very concerned about the counter-culture. David Flint reminds us that 1968 was "the year of revolution — student uprisings in Paris and anti-war protests in the USA and UK as ascendant youth culture began to sweep away old attitudes" (7). At heart, both Romero's film and Levin's story display a very real fear of the young.

Middle-class parents were terrified and confused by the behavior of their children, who neither wanted nor valued their parents' values. Whereas Levin presented the child of Satan, literally a devil baby, Romero offered a child who was hurt, fell asleep, then murdered her mother. Harry dies after being shot by Ben and falls down the stairs. An awakened Karen begins to eat her father. Karen then kills and eats her mother, who responds with incredulity. She cannot believe her child would hurt her and keeps repeatedly calling her "Karen" and "My baby" as Karen first pursues her across the cellar, then stabs her with a trowel, her father's blood obviously visible around her mouth.

While there is an obvious Oedipal/Electra complex occurring in the hostility of the dead child toward her parents, there is also a sociophobic on display, as much as the psychology of the moment. Karen's eating of her father and killing and eating of her mother is, in some senses, a literalization of the generation gap. Children are eating their parents. It is a literalization of the often-heard line, "You'll be the death of me." The parents stayed together for the sake of the child, and both clearly love her. She repays them by killing and eating them. She not only rejects everything her parents stand for, she literally destroys her parents and consumes them. She is the generation gap personified.

When Harry's corpse reanimates, it is clear that his right arm has been removed. He has literally been disarmed. Helen has been stabbed repeatedly in the breast with the trowel, which Karen then leaves sticking out of her. Karen has rendered her father unable to perform basic tasks and destroyed the breasts which suckled her. Again, we can certainly read this psychologically, but also contained in this familial violence are literalized metaphors of the younger generation of America. The same impulse that is celebrated in the Broadway musical *Hair* is shown to be murderous, disruptive and cannibalistic in *Night*. The Age of Aquarius has a body count, and the first corpses are those of the older generation.

Guess Who's Coming to Dinner?

Everyone involved in *Night* asserts that Duane Jones was cast not for his race but because he was the best actor who auditioned. Regardless, the casting may have been colorblind, but the viewing in 1968 America (and, for that matter, twenty-first-century America) is not. Audiences read into Ben's race and, as noted earlier, read the Civil Rights struggle into *Night*. Many scholars and genre fans read *Night* as a film about the Civil Rights movement, or, at the very least, that Ben's ethnicity shapes our understanding of the social dynamics of the group within the farmhouse and therefore serves as a metaphor for America.

According to Tony Williams, Ben's story about Beakman's Diner "evokes African American experience of post–Reconstruction days in the American South" (26). The simple act of eating at a lunch counter in the rural area of the farmhouse resulted in Ben confronting violence, some of which was directed against him. He describes the gas truck going past him as a "moving bonfire," and expresses fear that the truck might explode. He is truly haunted as he says, "I can still hear the man screaming." He describes the diner as being "completely encircled." He ends up "alone, with fifty or sixty of those things standing there, staring at me." His only response was to plow through them: "I just wanted to crush them, scatter them through the air like bugs." He describes a kind of wish fulfillment: surrounded by what could be described as a lynch mob, he drives through and away, killing many of those who would harm him and escaping with his own life.

The violence of the diner was just one example of mob violence in the film. Isabel Cristina Pinedo reminds us, "*Night* denounces white violence, whether it issues from the sheriff's (white) posse or the (white) living dead" (113). She further notes that the posse's "actions are indistinguishable from the rampage of the zombie mob" (113–4). Every single large group in *Night* (zombies, mob, crowd at Beakman's) consists of white Americans perpetrating violence against fellow citizens. Ben is at the center of every mob attack in *Night*.

It may also prove useful to place *Night* in dialogue with other films from the period. Kevin Heffernan states that horror was popular with African American audiences, and many inner city theaters played *Night* (207). Heffernan links *Night* with *Black Like Me* (1964), the adaptation of John Howard Griffin's autobiography about his experiences as a white man traveling through the American South disguised as a black man, which was also distributed by Continental and Walter Reade, *Night*'s distributors (205–6). Annalee Newitz sees *Night* as "an updated version of *Birth of a Nation*," except an "upwardly mobile black man" is the hero rather than the villain (109). Newitz also observes that all members of the posse and all the zombies are white.

Simultaneously, it may be possible to read *Night* in the light of the previous year's Academy Award–winning drama *Guess Who's Coming to Dinner*, which featured Sidney Poitier and Katharine Houghton as an interracial couple in contemporary America dealing with the discomfort her parents, as played by Spencer Tracy and Katharine Hepburn, feel over their engagement. At the time, interracial marriage was still illegal in seventeen states in the American South and was frowned upon in much of the rest of America. After the death of Johnny, the first real relationship seen in *Night* is that of Barbara and Ben. He pulls her back inside the house as she attempts to run out, and they begin what might be considered to be a very odd courtship.

The next half hour of film time features Ben and Barbara alone.[9] For twenty-seven minutes Ben and Barbara interact, share each other's stories, and work to stop the initial zombies and understand what is going on. Theirs is the chief relationship in the film — Ben as protector of the catatonic white woman. Harry, upon emerging from the cellar, fights with Ben not only over the wisdom of hiding in the cellar and the material possessions in the house (radio, guns, etc.), but about who will possess Barbara. Despite hearing and ignoring her screams (because he did not want to risk his life to rescue a stranger), Harry now wants to take charge of Barbara: "I'm taking the girl with me." Ben responds, "You leave her here. Keep your hands off her and everything else that's up here, too." While Ben also equates Barbara with the material possessions and prizes of the house, such as the radio and food, he will not allow Harry to take her down to the cellar. Ben and Barbara have established a relationship, and Ben now posits himself as her guardian and protector — in this case, against a white man.

Ben tells Harry to go to the cellar: "You can be boss down there. I'm boss up here." In sixties America, "boss" is a loaded word, and for Ben to tell a white man that he is now "boss" and then turn his back on him cannot be read in any other way than an assertion of black power. Previously Ben told Harry that "if I stay up here, I'm fighting for everything up here, and the radio and the food is part of what I'm fighting for." Ben is fighting the living dead to preserve the house and what he has, but he is also fighting Harry.

Ben becomes an aggressive version of Sidney Poitier's Dr. John Prentice. Whereas Prentice is polite to a fault and makes sure that he does what is proper (to the point of leaving money on Spencer Tracy's character's desk for a long distance call he made), Ben is rude to Harry, asking him, "Is this your house?" and then dismissing him and claiming that everything upstairs is his and that Ben is in command. It is a remarkable moment in the film, and one that both displays Harry's powerlessness and Ben's dominance. It also firmly establishes Barbara as belonging in some sense to Ben, at least more so to Ben than any other man in the house, now that her brother is dead.

Ben is also established as the one with the answers. At the beginning of the film (and the night), the characters are in a bad situation: it is dark, dangerous, and no one knows what is going on. Ben's actions initially reverse the situation, which is why we in the audience also trust him: he provides light, boards up the house and kills a few ghouls, providing safety; and he turns on and tunes the radio, and subsequently finds and sets up the television, providing all with information. All of the raw materials to do these things were present; anyone could have done them. But the Coopers and Tom and Judy hid in the cellar, and Barbara went catatonic. Ben is the problem-solver. Except that his subsequent answers are wrong and, as a result, people get killed.

Harry Cooper is the antagonist to Ben in the classic sense: he opposes the protagonist. R.H.W. Dillard notes that Harry's "response to the situation is to hide in the cellar and wait until the problem goes away by itself or is handled by someone else" (20). When confronted by Ben stating that there are other options and that the group must be proactive, Harry not only rejects these ideas but believes Ben to be "crazy." In Robin Wood's words, he "rages and blusters impotently, constantly asserting a discredited authority" (103). In other words, the film depicts a young, proactive African American man confronting (and, in some senses, besting) a middle-aged, status-quo–preserving white man. Ben is clearly not working class. He wears a sweater over a literal white-collar shirt; nice, clean slacks; and dress shoes. When he reaches for the phone we see he is wearing a rather expensive-looking class ring. He resembles nothing so much as a graduate student or professor on a day off. He is articulate, decisive and sure of himself. Harry, on the other hand, has his tie loosened; he looks disheveled and overwhelmed by the situation. Offering no constructive plan of his own, he is reduced to critiquing Ben's, primarily through *ad hominem* attacks ("You're crazy!").

Harry represents the status quo. Ben represents youth, intelligence, and change. Ben refuses to listen to Harry simply because he is older and white. Ben displays initiative, concern, compassion and control. Harry has none of these qualities. Ben is emblematic of the younger generation of African Americans, inspired by the Civil Rights Movement to change the world, from Dr. King to the Black Panthers. Harry easily stands for those who wish to maintain the status quo, segregation and oppression. But the film places Harry in a position where he is unable to maintain any authority beyond his immediate family, and this makes him dangerous, as he seeks not to work with the others to the benefit of all but to attempt to get the gun from Ben and reassert his will over all the others. When he succeeds in doing so, if only for a moment, the end result is the deaths of all in the farmhouse. As the title of this chapter indicates, although the line is spoken by Helen, it applies to all the different relationships presented in the film — young and old, men and women, black and white: "We may not enjoy living together, but dying together isn't going to solve anything."

"The Television Said It Was the Right Thing to Do."

Romero's work frequently comments on the role of the media in both our lives and the destabilization of society. Romero himself has said, "As far as the people on television not really answering questions and making it more confusing, that's been a conscious part of the zombie films" (qtd. in Gagne 27). Both *Night* and *Dawn* (and, decades later, *Diary*) demonstrate the irony of the need for media to tell us what is happening while simultaneous obfuscating the story, becoming self-serving and self-perpetuating, and even purposefully misleading the audience.

Ben finds a radio in the house and turns it on immediately. When Harry and Tom emerge from the cellar, Harry is less enthusiastic about the arrival of other living humans than he is about the existence of a radio. When the television is found, the entire artificial family gathers around the electronic hearth to watch the news together. Peter Gutiérrez, in an essay included with the DVD of *Night of the Living Dead: Reanimated*, cannily observes that the characters "live the zombie crisis firsthand but can't understand it until they consult the mass media" (n.p.). The radio and television not only frame the experience, they allow the characters to make sense of it and understand it. Gutiérrez argues that all the "crucial information" in this film is mediated.

This presentation of mediated existence and the news making life real very much reflects the cultural situation in America at the time. As Glenn Kay observes, the nightly newscasts and "breaking news" alerts were part of the Vietnam experience (55). Most Americans did not experience either the Vietnam War or the Civil Rights marches and riots first hand. Instead, they were all mediated through Walter Cronkite and other newsmen.

Even more troubling in the film are the statements of both the military figures and the scientists interviewed by the reporters, who give conflicting information, downplay the danger and significance of the information, and who, in the end, offer no actual useful information. We learn that radiation from the Venus probe may be the cause of the zombie outbreak, but this information does not help. What does it matter if the dead are returning because of radiation, a virus, a voodoo curse or a sale at Kaufman's? Later on the television will report that the bodies of the deceased should be burned, and the living dead can be stopped by shooting them in the brain, but Ben has already discovered this on his own when a zombie at the window grabs his rifle. He shoots it twice in the chest, but it only goes down for good when shot in the forehead. It is only later that the television report confirms what Ben has already learned from experience.

Hervey reminds us that the American media coined the term "credibility gap" to point out the disconnect between government declarations about Vietnam and the observable facts (77). *Night* merely demonstrates both the credibility gap of the military and the scientists who speak with the reporters, and the credibility gap of the media itself, which offers conflicting reports, out of date information, and can only confirm what the viewers and listeners have already experienced.

There Has to Be a Morning After

Night ends in morning, not mourning (or, for that matter, fear and horror). In the cold light of dawn the ghouls are not scary at all. Romero shows them easily killed. What seemed like an inescapable situation the night before is revealed to be less horrific by dawn's early light. Sheriff McClelland (George Kosana) reports that they found "three of those things" trying to break into an empty shed. His contempt for them is obvious, as is his assessment of them as a threat: "Beat 'em or burn 'em — they go up pretty easy."

The night of the living dead was terrifying, but the morning after displays the dead as less than threatening, especially when confronted with firepower and organization. The very thing that destroyed the community inside the farmhouse saves the larger community: the citizens are organized and work together under a chain of command. Sheriff McClelland leads a posse of citizens to round up, re-kill and burn all the ghouls. Dillard's summary of this: "The dead, unlike death itself, can be stopped and become a more ordinary horror, one to which there can be a practical response" (21).

Night cautions that we must learn to recognize the difference between real danger (the conflict between people) versus potential danger (when dead). Alive, Harry is a genuine threat to Ben. When he reanimates, he could be a threat, as his intent is to kill and eat Ben, and he carries the zombie plague. Harry, dead, is a potential threat, but one easily dispatched. Before he is even done sitting up, Ben shoots him in the head. Real danger comes from the violence and counter-productivity that erupts when society, even a society as small as seven people in a farmhouse, breaks down.

The ending of the film clearly exhibits the "purposeless" nature of Ben's death. Gregory A. Waller argues that the close proximity of the posse, which arrives at dawn and eliminates the zombies (and Ben, by accident), demonstrates that no one needed to die (*The Living*, 295). All of the adults, had they remained in the cellar and dealt appropriately with Karen, would have lived. The deaths are due to a serious miscalculation on the part of the group and the crises which erupt as they squabble over who is in charge and what the best course of action may be.

Dillard sees the film as showing "the ordinary world revealed for what it dangerously is" (28). We do not need a zombie plague to screw the world up and over—we can do that ourselves. Under the surface of everyday life lurks a dangerous world of neighbors, children and strangers who can and will kill. Furthermore, behind the surface of everyday life lies the potential for unlimited megadeaths—the Cold War results in the potential for the United States and the Soviet Union to destroy the world and everyone in it many times over. Armageddon is only a button push away, and hiding in the cellar will not save you.

The film ends with a bonfire upon which the corpses are thrown, "an unsophisticated means for the disposal of refuse," in Waller's words (*The Living*, 297). The last corpse to be thrown on is Ben's. Even the hero, who has stood for all that we believe in and who has fought the good fight against oppressors both living and dead, is, in the end, "refuse," as are we all. In this chapter I have considered how changes in the American way of death and understanding dying and memorials are traced in *Night*. By the end, however, there are no memorials or funerals or rituals, only another one for the fire. That,

1. Night of the Living Dead (1968) 45

perhaps, is the last sociophobic of the film: that in the end, all of our lives end, we will be completely gone and forgotten, and our lives are meaningless.

Although at first it was not seen as anything other than drive-in fare, *Night* has grown in popular and critical estimation to become one of the most significant and influential horror films (if not just films) of all time. It has spawned five direct sequels from Romero (*Dawn, Day, Land, Diary* and *Survival*), another five indirect sequels in the form of the *Return of the Living Dead* films, three direct remakes and several cinematic remixes which use direct elements of the original (images, soundtrack, etc.), and even live stage versions. The rest of this section will consider the variety of *Night* remakes and how they use the same narrative as the original, yet radically transform the sociophobics to reflect their own periods (instead of Vietnam, Civil Rights, and *The American Way of Death*).

NOTES

1. Ben Hervey reads this opening sequence as a cinematic exorcism — Johnny dies imitating Karloff, symbolizing the death of the old Universal horror/American horror film and the rise (pardon the pun) of a new, non-gothic, more domestic type of horror (34–5).

2. In fairness, however, Romero's subsequent work has obviously embraced political content and social comment, while Russo has made films like *Santa Claws* (1996), *Scream Queens' Naked Christmas* (1996), *Midnight* (1982) and *The Booby Hatch* (1976). As Ben Hervey states, "Even Russo's better work, though, aspires to little more than straight-ahead scares and chuckles" (25). Despite the lack of intentional social commentary, Russo's work still exhibits sociophobics, as will be demonstrated in chapter three.

3. A larger question that has always troubled me is why doesn't the cemetery ghoul eat Johnny after killing him? Why does he pursue Barbara?

4. Hervey's BFI Film Classics book on *Night* really is the definitive study of the film, which I fully concede almost renders my chapter here redundant. There are a few things which I believe Hervey misses, and a survey of *Night* is necessary for my larger purpose in reading the remakes of *Night*. I do admit, however, that Hervey's volume is essential reading on *Night*.

5. This figure must be hyperbole on Johnny's part, because two hundred miles from Pittsburgh places them in either Ohio, Virginia, three quarters of the way to Philadelphia or almost to Canada.

6. For information on the Rural Cemetery movement, its origins and Mount Auburn as archetype of the movement, see Stanley French's "The Cemetery as Cultural Institution: The Establishment of Mount Auburn and the 'Rural Cemetery' Movement," in David E. Stannard's *Death in America*.

7. The term "megadeath," now perhaps better known through the misspelled use by a thrash metal band, originated in the 1960 book *On Thermonuclear War* by Herman Kahn, although he had coined the term in 1953. It refers to one million deaths, and entered common currency in discussions of global thermonuclear war, as in "the outcome would be ten megadeaths, instead of twenty or thirty." It was a way of reducing mass death to comprehensible numbers.

8. The films and the politics of the time were interlinked in the minds of the period. After his election, bumper stickers began to appear proclaiming "Richard Nixon is Rosemary's Baby," implying that the new president was the Antichrist and the devil incarnate, yet another example of the use of horror film as allegory for the American political landscape (Bloch xix).

9. Ben arrives around 14 minutes into the movie, and Harry and Tom don't emerge from the cellar until 41 minutes into the film. It is the longest period of any sustained relationship in the film. Johnny dies within minutes, and after the cellar door opens, the configurations of characters change as they go up and down the stairs into the cellar, and in and out of the house. Ben and Barbara spend almost a full half hour together.

2
"I'm fighting; I'm not panicking": Night of the Living Dead (1990)

The first remake of a Romero zombie film came five years after the release of *Day of the Dead*. Romero himself wrote the screenplay, based on the original screenplay he co-wrote with John Russo, with his long-time collaborator and special effects wizard Tom Savini directing the remake. In this remake there is not very much new or different from the original. The same narrative follows the same story structure. No new major characters are introduced or cut. The living dead and the epiphenomena remain the same. Thus, the small differences from the original are the things which transform the meaning and source of horror. The remake was also an attempt to regain copyright of the original film and allow the original investors to perhaps finally make a profit.[1]

There was also the new context of *Return of the Living Dead*, *Thriller*, and "Bub" from *Day*. The dominant mode in zombie cinema at this point was comedy, with serious political and cultural commentary left to more serious dramas and filmmakers such as Oliver Stone. It's important to remember that the 1990 remake came only three years after *Wall Street*, Stone's opus on corruption and the ethically challenged nature of the financial sector. The film's tagline, as well as the most famous quotation from *Wall Street*, was "Greed is good." The film critiqued motivated self-interest versus doing what is best for the community. In the Reagan/Bush era, with its commitment to getting government off your back and promoting rugged individualism, the community is not as important as self-interest. Greed is good. Look out for number one, number one being yourself. This tension between self-interest and communal need is also reflected in other films of the period, including the remake of *Night*.

The second cinematic context of the new *Night* was the evolving motif of the strong female protagonist. Sigourney Weaver in *Alien* (1979) and *Aliens* (1986) became the model for strong female characters. Joining her was Linda Hamilton in *The Terminator* (1984) and (much more obviously) *Terminator*

2: Judgment Day (1991). Barbara in the new *Night* becomes an assertive, confident action hero in her own right, fighting and defeating zombies and patriarchal living humans.

In addition, by 1990, horror had been trending juvenile again, or at least become seriously rooted in youth culture. Exemplary horror films from the period include *Child's Play* (1988) and *Child's Play 2* (1990), in which the killer is a possessed "Good Guy" doll; *The Monster Squad* (1987); *Gremlins* (1984) and *Gremlins 2: The New Batch* (1990); *Goonies* (1985); and *Ghoulies* (1985) and *Ghoulies II* (1988). Many of which were rated PG-13, the rating created by the Motion Picture Association of America in the wake of complaints about *Indiana Jones and the Temple of Doom* in 1984. PG-13 is an intermediate rating between PG and R, suggesting that some material might be inappropriate for individuals under the age of 13, usually graphic violence and gore, but that it's missing the sexual content which guaranteed an R rating. Much horror fell into the PG-13 demographic, and thus was aimed at a demographic between 13 and 25. The *Night* remake, however, was rated R and thus aimed at an adult audience. Like the original *Night*, attacked by Roger Ebert for being shown to children (the dominant audience for horror in 1968), the remake of *Night* was an adult horror film in a market saturated by horror comedy and horror aimed at the PG-13 crowd.

Given that one of the primary intentions was to establish copyright and not vary too far from the original film, significant differences appear in the remake. The radical transformation of the character of Barbara is responsible for most of the changes in both the narrative and meaning of *Night*. There are also significant differences in some of the other characters, in the opening sequence, and in the ending. First, I shall consider the opening sequence from the graveyard to the arrival of Barbara and Ben at the farmhouse, and how the film demonstrates a new context and hence a new set of sociophobics. I will then focus on Barbara as a character. Related to the change in Barbara are the changes to the male characters—Ben, Tommy and Cooper—and the women who love them, Helen and Judy Rose. Of particular concern is how the film represents social class and the rural/urban divide. The discovery of a television, as in the original, creates commentary on the media, albeit one different from the original. Lastly, I shall consider the radically different ending, and what it tells us about sociophobics of 1990.

"Doesn't Take Long for the World to Fall Apart"

The graveyard scene which opens the film is both familiar and different. Before any images are shown, Johnny's voice says, "They're coming to get you, Barbara"—one of the most recognizable lines from the original. This line both establishes the opening situation of the movie (the conflict between Barbara [Patricia Tallman] and Johnny [Bill Moseley]) and acknowledges the remake. It demonstrates an awareness of the audience's awareness, or at least of Linda Hutcheon's "knowing audience" (120). Tom Savini, the director of the remake, uses the opening to pay homage to the original, but then immediately begins playing with the tropes of what the "knowing audience" knows.

The familiar and the different mix in the film from the opening shot. The siblings are placing a wreath on the grave of their mother, not their father, resulting in another cinematic reference (after the Boris Karloff of the original). Johnny drags himself down behind a tombstone, crying, "No, Mother!" which echoes *Psycho* as much as it does the original *Night*. The remake also features a different motivation. In the original, Johnny and Barbara's mother insist they visit the grave of their father. In the remake, Johnny asks Barbara, "You're still scared of her, aren't you? That's why we're here, isn't it?" Barbara is afraid of their dead mother, so Barbara is the one who insisted on the long drive to the cemetery. Their mother "damn near drove [Barbara] into a convent." It is implied Barbara does not have much of a social life, even with both her parents dead.

This is not the respectful Barbara who loves her parents of the first film — this is a Barbara put upon by, and frightened of, her own family members. She is neurotic, repressed and uncertain of herself. Johnny calls her display of parental devotion "a charade." He also mocks her own repressed, virginal status, continuing to use the Boris Karloff voice: "They're horny, Barbara. They've been dead a long time!" From her reaction, it is clear that Barbara is uncomfortable with the discussion. In other words, the film establishes from the beginning that Barbara is mousy, unassertive, nervous, and easily dominated. Her costume of blouse, skirt and sweater also accentuates her delicate femininity while de-emphasizing any sense of sensuality or sexuality. The film does this to establish Barbara's character as a timid wallflower so that her transformation to confident, even brash, self-assured woman is a more defined character arc.

There is no visual explanation for the Cemetery Zombie in the original *Night*—no open casket, no hearse, and no indication as to why this recently dead individual is wandering through the cemetery.[2] *Night* 1990 makes up for this by giving the audience three men in the cemetery and all the accoutrements of a funeral: an open casket (ominously empty), a hearse, and a mound of dirt. The knowing audiences expects that the individual approaching Johnny and Barbara whom Johnny pretends is some sort of monster, will, in fact, be revealed to be a monster. As the old man (Pat Reese) approaches them, the expectation is that he is the new Cemetery Zombie. There is blood on him, and he looks decrepit; but after stumbling into Barbara, he speaks, apologizing. He then continues walking away, clearly not a zombie. This character is an inversion of Bill Hinzman's Cemetery Zombie of the original. As he moves away, Johnny and Barbara grow concerned, and as he turns around they are then attacked by the real Cemetery Zombie, a visibly aggressive rotting corpse (Greg Funk).

The cemetery zombie's attack can initially be seen as an attempted rape. Reynold Humphries sees it as "clearly sexual" (134). The zombie pushes Johnny out of the way to get to Barbara. He pushes her down and climbs on top of her, pulling off her glasses and clawing at her blouse and legs. He pulls her sweater off as she screams and virtually ignores Johnny's attempts to pull him off Barbara, remaining focused on her. His attack on her is an attack on not just a human he wishes to bite and eat, but an attack on a female.

The tropes being echoed at this moment are not just from the original *Night* but also from exploitive feminist empowerment films, such as *I Spit on Your Grave* and *Ms. 45*, in which women are initially sexually violated by a small group of men and then seek violent revenge. Although not successful in his attack, the Cemetery Zombie is the first catalyst in the transformation of Barbara into an avenging woman. Barbara will fight back, and even eventually kill the Cemetery Zombie in a later scene. She will also seek revenge against and kill Harry in much the same way, and for much the same reason.

Already the comic (even slapstick) violence of the original *Dawn* is present here. As the Cemetery Zombie shoulders Johnny out of the way to grab Barbara, the fight grows increasingly silly. Everything Barbara and Johnny do to stop the zombie ends up hurting Johnny. As Johnny grabs the zombie, Barbara kicks its head, which then collides with her brother's. His hand is accidentally punctured by Barbara with the wreath they plan to leave on their mother's grave, as she repeatedly stabs the zombie with it. Thus the stark terror of the original is replaced with a paradoxically humorous yet more graphic and violent fight between the Cemetery Zombie and the siblings.

Johnny is once again killed by the Cemetery Zombie, and Barbara again flees to the safety of the car. She sees a man in a suit (Tim Carrier) walking toward the car and calls out to warn him and ask for help. A reverse shot from behind the man reveals that the suit is completely open at the back, common practice for morticians putting clothes upon the body of the deceased. The man's suit begins to peel down, revealing an autopsy Y-incision sewn shut. This man is the one from the casket. His funeral was interrupted by his reanimation. Barbara is now threatened by two aggressive male zombies.

This moment is the next step in the transformation of Barbara. She tries to warn the man, whom she calls "Mister," but she also hopes to receive help from him. Instead, he is revealed to be another assailant. The sexual threat from this zombie is also blatant, as his clothes are falling off and he begins to smear his naked chest on the car windows. While there is obviously a "gross-out" aspect to this action, it accentuates the corporeal nature of the zombies, not to mention the sense that their assault on her is a sexual violation as well as an attempt to eat her flesh. In fact, neither of the zombies seems interested in biting her, nor are they at all interested in Johnny's nearby corpse. They seem interested in attacking her and her alone.

Barbara will not receive any help from the men in the cemetery. She must escape on her own, and, as her predecessor did, she rides the car backwards down a hill out of the cemetery and then runs through the woods to a property on the other side of the forest. She first passes a barn (more on that later) and, as in the original, enters a home that is a scene of carnage, with more than one zombie lurking about.

As in the original, Barbara exits the home only to see Ben (Tony Todd) arrive. Unlike the original, where she is blinded by his headlights, night has not yet fallen in this *Night*. She (and we) sees Ben's truck coming down the dirt road in the distance. His arrival, and how it differs from the original, gives more indication about the concerns of this *Night*. Ben does not just pull up and get out of the truck. He purposefully hits a zombie walking up the dirt road to the farmhouse, flipping it up over the truck cab and causing it to fall to the ground, mangled and with a broken spine. He drives past this zombie and pulls up in front of the house. He wears a suit and tie. He carries a crowbar, not a tire iron.

This is Ben as middle manager. He is clearly some sort of businessman who is making do with the items he finds. Neither the truck nor the crowbar match the outfit he wears. He is clearly grabbing and using and keeping things he finds as the zombie outbreak begins. He is informed enough and scared enough himself to run down the zombie on the dirt road, but as he does not see the zombie from the front, he cannot be certain the man stumbling in the road is dead. This Ben is less self-assured, less in charge than Duane Jones. He is panicking and fleeing to safety.

Ben believes Barbara is hysterical when he tries to pull her inside the house, saying "Come on," and she repeatedly screams, "No!" But she knows what Ben does not: there are ghouls inside, and therefore the inside is no safer than the outside. This idea will become a recurring theme in the film and echo, albeit subtly, the debate in the original. Instead of Harry (Tom Towles) and Ben arguing over whether or not the cellar is the safest place, Ben and Barbara will argue about whether entering the house or making a run for it is the wisest course of action.

Ben drags Barbara into the house, where he confronts the first zombie, whom we might assume is Tom's cousin, Satchel, mentioned by Tom as having been killed by Uncle Rege. Ben smashes the first zombie with a frying pan, then impales its skull with the crowbar, shattering the door window in the process. He is panicked and frightened as he locks the door. Simultaneously, Barbara grabs the fireplace poker. The large zombie sneaks up behind her, but she senses its presence and repeatedly hits it in the head with the poker. Remarkably, Barbara and Ben kill their respective zombies at the same time. She is not catatonic and does not need rescuing. In fact, she is more aggressive and less fearful in her fight than Ben is in his. It is only after the fight that she draws into herself and becomes not catatonic, but quiet and horrified.

Upon seeing the large zombie on the floor, Ben asks, "Who is he?" This question then leads to a series of questions—"Do you know any of them?" "This isn't your house?" "Do you live here?" "Do you have a car?" Barbara does not answer. We will only learn later that, unlike in the original, the people in the house are known to some of the characters. Tommy was visiting his uncle and his cousin at this house. Uncle Rege had a heart attack, died, reanimated and killed Cousin Satchell. These are not an entire group of complete strangers gathering by chance at an isolated farmhouse. The Coopers and Ben and Barbara were passing by and sought refuge at the farm; Tommy and Judy Rose, however, are local. The film sets up a rural/urban divide among its characters.

The sequence at the house continues, with Ben seeking to kill other zombies in the area in order to make the environment of the house safer. This series of actions serves to show Ben as less secure than in the original and to further continue the development of Barbara as independent heroine. When Ben kills the second zombie on the porch, Savini centers him in the shot. His expression is one of disbelief and regret. This is not Duane Jones' surefooted, secure and certain character. Tony Todd initially plays Ben as lost, and possibly horrified at his own violent actions. He moves backwards from the kill and falls against the porch wall. Savini follows this with a single long shot from behind the mangled zombie near the road, as Ben walks down from the porch to the still-moving corpse—not with a direct purpose but with a weary resolution. He pushes the zombie's head down into the dirt so that he will not have to look this former human in the eyes when he kills it.

After he pushes the crowbar into the zombie's head, he looks up and screams, "God damn you!" as if he is screaming at God himself. This line, however, is immediately followed by Ben's looking down at the corpse and continuing, "God damn all of you!" This Ben is angry not just at the divine, but also at the zombies themselves for simply existing. The zombies must be put down if the humans are to be safe, but Ben does not want to have to do it. He is a reluctant hero that will rely on bluster, machismo and aggression to confront the zombies and the other men in the house. But masculine aggression will not save the day or defeat the zombies. Romero's script focuses much more this time on the women in the farmhouse.

An Apology to Women

As noted above, the larger theme running all the way through the film is the transformation of Barbara from scared, mousy little sister to heroic woman who survives the events that kill everyone else. The film begins with Barbara being defined as subservient to, and terrified of, her own family. Her own mother terrified and browbeat her. When she tells Johnny he is being mean, he responds, "I'm your older brother. Being mean and heartless is part of my job." By the end of the film, she alone is alive in the farmhouse, and, unlike Ben in the previous film, she survives the posse and even recognizes them for what they are. It is she and not Ben who kills Harry.

Romero stated that Barbara, in the form of Patricia Tallman, was "his apology to women" for the catatonic Barbara of 1968 (qtd. in Blumberg and Hershberger 259). This Barbara fights off the seemingly sexual assault of the two zombies in the cemetery and begins to transform. Later in the film, when the group goes outside to search Uncle Rege's body for keys to the gas pump, Barbara sees Cemetery Zombie and shoots it in the head as revenge against the ghoul who killed her brother. After this moment of vengeance, however, she also has a realization: "We can get away." The zombies move slow. Rather than masculine aggression, which encourages confrontation, protection of the house and violence, she realizes they can simply walk away from the zombies.

Observing the zombies out the window, Barbara states, "They're so slow. We could just walk right past them, we wouldn't even have to run. We could just walk right past them. [To Ben] We have the guns. If we're careful we can get away. You told me to fight. Well, I'm fighting; I'm not panicking. This place is not safe, not upstairs or down. We should leave before it's too late." Ben's response is empty cheerleading in support of the status quo: "I'm fine. You're fine. We're all fine." But they are not fine. The noise of fortifying the house has brought an increasingly large number of zombies to surround the house and try to get in. Savini shows a female zombie walking past the house at a distance. The hammering is heard in the background and she turns from her path to walk toward the noise. The very activity designed to make them safer is actually increasing the danger.

Barry Keith Grant offers a very canny observation. As the film progresses, there are fewer and fewer reaction shots of a frightened Barbara, and more and more POV shots from her position (208–209). The film literally begins to shift to her point of view. Isabel Cristina Pinedo also observes, "Throughout the course of the film, she sheds her impractical pumps and skirt for the hardier boots and pants she finds in the farmhouse" (145). She also begins carrying one of the rifles.

It is through the rifle that she first proves to the others that the individuals surrounding the house are, in fact, the living dead. When none of the other people realize the reality of the situation, she demonstrates that she not only knows the true nature of the threat, but also how to overcome the situation and avoid being killed. She repeatedly shoots a zombie in the chest, asking, "Is he dead?" She does this to demonstrate to the others that the attackers are, in fact, living dead. Only a headshot kills the attacker. Although fantastic, it is true. Barbara not only figures it out, she attempts to conclusively prove it to the others, who, sadly, are more interested in fighting over territory. After she shoots the zombie in the head, Ben accuses her of being unstable:

> BEN: You are losing it girl, you are losing it.
> BARBARA: You think so? Whatever I lost, I lost a long time ago and I do not plan on losing anything else. You can talk to me about losing it when you stop screaming at each other like a bunch of two-year-olds.

Judy Rose asks Tommy if Barbara is crazy. None of the other characters see what Barbara sees. While they doubt her sanity, it is, in fact, *they* who are wrong and she who is right.

This assessment is also held by Barry Keith Grant, who argues that Barbara

> not only survives, but does so by deducing the correct strategy in response to the zombie attacks: neither to defend the house (Ben) nor to retreat to the cellar (Harry) but to flee, since the zombies can easily be outrun [203].

Barbara is proven right again and again by the film, but none of the men listen to her. Because she is a woman, even when she speaks sense the men, busily involved in territorial disputes, ignore her. She leaves a fight between Ben and Harry to go outside, looking for the keys to the gas pump, and it is only when they perceive her actions to be a threat — she opens the door and goes outside where the living dead are — that they stop fighting and pay attention to what she is doing. Barbara stops panicking and begins fighting, as the quote used for the title of this chapter suggests, but none of the men pay attention to her, despite this fact. Instead, Barbara becomes part of what the men believe they are fighting for.

Early in the film Ben takes off his jacket and puts it on Barbara — a kindness, but also a gesture of gender. His coat wrapped around her marks her as weak and in some ways as his property. She needs his protection to survive. She will eventually shed the coat. Subsequently, she will also shed her shoes and her dress in favor of sensible boots and overalls. The change of clothes indicates a change in status. She does not stop being a woman, but she stops accepting the gender roles that her mother, brother, Ben and even society attempt to put her in. By the end of the film she holds her own against the good old boys who are leading the zombie roundup.

This use of coat as marker of male territory occurs again in the cellar. Ben, looking for stronger wooden doors to seal off the house, sees Sarah and tells Helen, "You ought to keep her covered. Some blankets from upstairs or something." Harry's response is to take off his jacket and cover his daughter with it while glaring at Ben. The move is protective and caring, yet also territorial. As with Ben's jacket on Barbara earlier, it is a marker of territory and male property. Although Barbara is, in the words of Peter Dendle, "the most multidimensional character" and thus "ultimately the most capable of survival," the other three women in the film are defined entirely by their relationship to the men in their lives (123).

Patriarchal Males and the Women Who Love Them

The placing of the jacket on Sarah marks the ambiguity of Sarah and her relationship with her father. We never actually see the two of them interact. Helen (McKee Anderson) is much more involved in the care of the sick daughter. Yet Harry seems to have both genuine concern for his daughter and a willingness to use her to get his way with the others. The two are not mutually exclusive. Harry can love his daughter on one level while still exploiting her to engage in a contest of wills with Ben:

BEN: Look, from now on, you leave that door open! We may want to get down there. We may *need* to get down there if those things break in!

HARRY: Yeah, sure! You want the best of both worlds, you get caged in up here, you wanna be able to run downstairs. Well that's not the way it's working, pal. You want to get in that cellar, you get in there now! Or you can forget it!

BEN: I'm not boxing myself in down there, until there's absolutely no other choice!

HARRY: Yeah, well I'm not gambling with my daughter's life! Look, if you wanna stay upstairs, go ahead, but don't count on me to help you!

BEN: I'm not counting on you for shit, Cooper!

Harry will "not gamble with his daughter's life" and seems genuine in this concern. Yet he'd rather let his daughter lie under his jacket (not a very good covering) than accept Ben's help.

After Tom and Judy die, Harry uses their daughter as a reason for Helen to get back in the cellar rather than help: "Get in that cellar, Helen. Your daughter needs you." This statement is, of course, a ruse to get Helen out of the way so that Harry can take the rifle from Barbara and prevent Ben from returning to the house. Harry knows that Helen will not listen to him for his own sake but will do things to protect her daughter. When she reanimates, Sarah does not attack her father, but rather is drawn to attack Ben. The final conflict between the two men is over whether or not to stop Sarah-the-zombie. "Shoot her, Cooper," Ben begs. "She's my daughter," is Cooper's response. When Ben shoots Sarah, Harry's response is to shoot Ben. While they each sought guns a moment ago in order to be able to declare dominance over the other, the actual gunplay occurs when Cooper's daughter is hurt by Ben. Even in death, Harry's desire to protect his daughter is genuine but still ambiguous. He needed no other prompt to shoot Ben, but the shooting of Sarah removes any reason not to shoot Ben.

Even Tom and Judy are not immune from the aggressive, assertive masculinity that requires women to be subservient to the men and the men to protect their women as little more than territory or property. He gives her orders. When she balks at fortifying the house out of fear, he barks, "Come on, do what I tell you!" When she wants to go with Tommy on the gas run, he tells her no. She does not make her case directly to Ben but asks Tom to plead for her: "Tell him I know how to drive. Tell him, Tommy." Only when Tom confirms her ability to drive does Ben allow it. By this point in the film, a male order has been established. Ben is the alpha male, Tommy will do what he says (as the use of a juvenile form of the name indicates: he is not "Tom" but "Tommy"). Judy, Helen and Sarah must either do what the men say or make their case to their man, who will appeal any decisions by the alpha male. Only Barbara is immune to this social order, and only Barbara survives it.

Ben himself is not immune to hyper-masculine posing and fights Harry at every turn, even when it makes no sense to do so. Harry carries the television down to the first floor, and Ben attacks him, believing Harry will take it to the cellar. The television is destroyed in their struggle, but, as Harry points out, he was not taking the television to the cellar, as there is no reception down there. Ben's aggressiveness destroyed their one opportunity to learn more about what was happening.

Tony Todd sees Ben as a "reluctant hero" who "feels like he failed his family during the crisis.... He didn't or couldn't save his immediate family, so he doesn't want to fail his new 'family'" (qtd. in Maberry, *Zombie CSU* 339). If Ben sees this group as his "new family," then he and Harry are going to have conflict over who will be *pater familias*. Whereas Duane Jones' Ben was younger than Harry, and obviously in conflict with an older white man who resented a younger black man not listening and obeying, Todd's Ben is almost the same age and social status as Harry. This is not a conflict between generations but between two alpha males in a situation that does not require them to fight each other.

In the original *Night*, the characters have some nuance, and although the film gears us to be predisposed more toward some characters than others, there is room for ambiguity. Ben, although heroic, often behaves unlike a hero, shooting an unarmed Harry at point blank range, for example. Harry, though craven and selfish, is no villain. He displays concern for Barbara and especially for his daughter. We may not like him, but the film proves him repeatedly correct in his pronouncements. In the 1990 remake, Ben's less-heroic qualities are amplified, as is Harry's unlikableness. Both men ultimately prove themselves to be, in short, jerks.

Barbara has the answers in the 1990 *Night*, and they are actually correct. Unlike the original's Ben, who survives the night by luck and force only to die by the same reasons, and Harry, who is right but dies anyway, Barbara is right, does the right thing, *and* survives.

Working Class Stiffs

In his review of the remake of *Night of the Living Dead* for *Sight and Sound*, Steve Bard criticizes director Tom Savini and the film for failing to link zombies to the masses of unemployed and the recession under then–President Bush (30). Yet, rather than critique the film that was not made (and certainly Bard has a point in that the zombies are not used as an overt metaphor in this film), I hope to critique the film that is. In this case, the zombies are not the focus, the humans are. The zombies, as always in Romero's films, represent a threat from outside, and frequently they also represent some form of social change.

Night 1990 serves as a fish-out-of-water narrative for many of its characters in that it is set in a rural, working-class location (farmhouse in Pennsylvania), but five of the seven survivors in the farmhouse are urban middle-class elites. In the farmhouse they are very threatened by the rural population around them. Interestingly, Tom and Judy die by accident, and the other people in the house are killed by each other. The rural folks kill their own and the urban folks kill their own, but the urban characters (let us remember, Johnny and Barbara have driven two hundred miles "into the country") are much more afraid of the rural ones outside. Although it may be reading a bit much into it, ten years into the Reagan/Bush administrations, this film indicates a concern for "Reagan Democrats"—working class (and often rural) voters who normally would vote Democrat but who supported Reagan. On a much more general level, this film asserts a fear of the countryside. We might link *Night* 1990 with such films as *Deliverance* (1972), *The Texas Chainsaw Massacre* (itself with sequels released in 1986 and 1990), and

The Hills Have Eyes (1977): rural horror in which people from urban areas passing through rural ones are terrorized by the indigenous people. In *Night* 1990, the indigenous rural dwellers are now zombies.

Bard is quick to observe that the zombies are "heterogeneous," and thus "the implication is that nobody is immune from the social restructuring of post–Fordism. Everybody's job is potentially at risk" (30). Yet Romero has said, "Zombies are the real lower-class citizens of the monster world and that's why I like them" (qtd. in Bard 30). The first zombies we encounter were in suits because they were buried in them, but at the farmhouse the next zombies encountered are Rege and Satchell, both farmers. Those who gather around the farmhouse are a variety of social classes, but predominant among them are flannel-and plaid-wearing locals. Mr. McGruder, a neighbor of Rege who comes through the window to frighten Judy Rose, is in overalls and a work shirt. Most of these zombies are lower class and from the area.

Night 1990 divides its characters by class and geography. One is either working class, middle class or wealthy; likewise, one is either rural, from the country, or not. Johnny drives a BMW, wears leather driving gloves and is well dressed. Barbara seems to be wearing off-the-rack, inexpensive clothing. He is upper middle class, she is lower middle class, but both are clearly suburban or urban. Tommy is local and working class — Steelers hat, Iron City beer shirt, workboots and jeans. Judy Rose matches him in a workshirt and jeans.

Harry Cooper, on the other hand, is in a tuxedo, with a lot of gold jewelry. Helen is in a very nice dress with expensive jewelry. Even Sarah wears an expensive-looking dress. They are obviously upper-middle class to wealthy. Cooper carries himself with a sense of entitlement. He is used to being listened to. Even more than his predecessor, this Harry comes from privilege. Cooper helps himself to a beer in the fridge and wanders around the house looking at things. He is not used to being questioned or challenged. When discussing the situation, Cooper swears up a storm, calling things "bullshit." He finally challenges Ben, who questions Harry's assertiveness in a house obviously not his own: "You don't exactly look like neighbors, yourself!" Ben is in a suit, driving a borrowed (stolen?) pickup truck and carrying a crowbar. He is also not local, nor working class. He is middle class.

Further distinctions between class are made as Barbara begins to trade her middle-class garments for working class clothes. She dresses like a working class, rural individual, and she survives. Within the house itself, Ben, Barbara, Tom and Judy Rose seal up the house while Harry and Helen hide in the basement. The lower and middle class do the work while the upper class benefits from their efforts.

Judy (Katie Finneran) becomes "Judy Rose," thereby making her even more rural. This *Night* further refines its setting as rural. Before she runs into the house, Barbara runs into a barn with hay bales. Uncle Rege is in bib overalls. The posse is not merely a gathering of locals under local law enforcement, it is a mob of good old boy rednecks, drinking and shooting and throwing the heads and bodies of those they kill into the rear of an old pickup truck. It is the first day of zombie-hunting season, and the hunters are having a fine time. This is zombie horror as rural horror.

The Zombie Uprising Will Be Televised

As in all Romero films, media are suspect. Television is no longer trusted to deliver information, despite more ownership of more sets and even more hours of programming. The significance of the television set in the farmhouse is much less important than it was in 1968. By 1990 the United States had entered the age of cable television, although the farmhouse television is clearly an analog broadcast model without cable. For the audience, however, television features multiple news sources. CNN (Cable News Network) was launched in 1980 and ten years later was an active presence throughout the country. In 1989, NBC launched its own cable news channel, the Consumer News and Business Channel (CNBC). By 1990, news is national rather than local.

In *Night*, the media provides no real answers — it reports attackers in a "trance-like" state and obviously psychologically damaged. The newscaster laughs at the news from Stockton, California, that the recently deceased are returning to life, "driven by an unknown force that enables the brain to continue to function." Immediately following that report, another states that the doctors at the Centers for Disease Control "reject that theory, calling it preposterous beyond belief." They posit a mind-altering germ that is affecting the victims, although they cannot explain how a germ spread so quickly across the entire nation.

Harry watches the television alone upstairs, unlike in the original, where all the characters in the living room see it. This scene immediately follows Barbara's demonstration that the attackers are already dead. In other words, the reporter and the CDC are demonstrably wrong — a reversal of the original, in which media made the experience real, while experience did not. *Night* 1990 seems to suggest that personal experience should outweigh media reports and expert opinions. The media is not seen as a source of information or a bulwark against government or corporate malfeasance. Instead, corporate culture appropriates the counterculture, and the media itself is corporate-controlled. In 1970, Gil Scott-Heron proclaimed, "The Revolution will not be televised"; by 1990, MTV was announcing, "The Revolution Will Be Televised." Even "the revolution" is now controlled by corporate America, which uses it to sell products to the supposed revolutionaries.

Ironically, the television is smashed as part of the fight between Ben and Harry. "That was our only way to find out what was going on and you smashed it. I wasn't taking it downstairs. You can't get any reception in a basement, dickhead!" Harry screams. And yet the information the television was offering was incorrect. The film repeatedly demonstrates that Barbara, through the process of observation and deduction, understands the threat to the farmhouse community more than the media does. The loss of the television is no loss — the group would be better served by listening to Barbara.

Barbara ends the fight between Harry and Ben by suddenly opening the back door of the house and going outside. While they desire to spend time, energy and effort fighting each other, she seeks the keys that would allow them to unlock the gas pump and escape. Judy Rose and Helen search the dead bodies for keys while Barbara stands guard and the men do nothing. Barbara is again proven right as they watch the approaching zombies. The dead move very slowly, and are no threat if one takes proper precautions.

"That's Another One for the Fire"

Arguably, other than the treatment of Barbara, the greatest difference between the original *Night* and this remake, both in terms of narrative content and sociocultural meaning, can be found in the ending. Ben and Harry shoot each other. Ben hides in the basement, Harry in the attic. Barbara tells Helen to lock the family in the basement, and she, Barbara, will go for help. Barbara leaves the house armed with a handgun and makes her way through the living dead to search for help.

Barbara eventually runs into a blind zombie woman, who obviously is not a threat. The woman can only follow Barbara, based on sound. Older, carrying a doll, she wanders slowly in circles trying to find Barbara. Barbara simply pushes her away twice, then shoots her in the head. There is no struggle. Barbara, for the last time, is proven right. "Oh, God!" screams Barbara, echoing Ben's cry at the beginning of the night. It is not clear if she is upset at shooting the woman (although that is unlikely, as she has shot many living dead tonight), or if she is giving voice to frustration that she has been proven right and nearly everyone in the house she just left is dead because they would not listen.

In the original, a living dead Johnny enters the house to take Barbara away. This Barbara finds Johnny already killed again, his unreanimated corpse in the back of a pickup truck. The ending reasserts the rural/urban divide, as a group of redneck hunters, clearly not the deputized posse of the original, are out hunting zombies and taking their corpses as bizarre trophies. The scene then rapidly transitions to dawn at an encampment of hunters and law enforcement, where, in a makeshift arena, a drunk fights a zombie with a club while others cheer him on. Zombies are hung, some by the neck, some upside down, from a large tree and used as target practice by the crowd. The image is one of lynching, and it is striking that, like the posse of the original, the crowd at the gathering is all-white. Furthermore, there are not just men but women there, too, and the whole event feels a bit like a redneck carnival.

In addition to the coffee truck, there is also a hotdog truck, which Barry Keith Grant sees as suggesting the "brutish, insensitive phallic culture" (208). We might also note, however, that hot dogs are not merely phallic symbols (although they certainly are)—they are also emblematic of lower class and working class cuisine, and symbolic of the nature of the event. This gathering is not merely a celebration of insensitive masculinity, it is a carnivalesque American jamboree suggestive of NASCAR, county fairs, sporting event tailgating, and the first day of hunting season in certain parts of the country (including the rural areas surrounding Pittsburgh). It is this last that echoes most strongly in this scene, with everyone dressed in hunting clothes and carrying guns and knives. One might counter Grant's assessment with Romero's and Bard's: these are working class people treating the zombie apocalypse as they would any major civic event that allows them to bring guns. The urbanites forced to take shelter in the farmhouse developed no sense of community and by the end were trying to kill each other, despite the zombie apocalypse raging outside. The rural folk at the zombie fair demonstrate a considerable sense of community and pleasure. They are enjoying themselves and celebrating together.

Barbara's conclusion as she watches the rednecks beat and shoot the zombies for fun: "They're us. We're them and they're us." Throughout much of the original *Night* and the 1990 remake, zombies are dehumanized through language. They are called "them" (obviously in opposition to "us") and "those things." They are not people or human in any senses of the word anymore. Yet Barbara recognizes at this moment that living humans and zombie humans function in very much the same way, and the living do not come off looking so well by comparison.

Barbara joins the posse clearing out the area. She returns with a group to the farmhouse. As they cut through the cellar door, it opens and Ben emerges as a zombie. As in the original, he is shot by the posse, but this time there is no irony or shock in it. He died and became another zombie; the only sensible thing to do is shoot him in the head. As the other hunters drag Ben's body out, Barbara remains behind, and a hand falls on her shoulder. Harry is alive, having survived in the attic. "You came back!" he says to her, the gratitude and joy clear in his voice and eyes. Barbara raises her gun and shoots him in the head anyway. "That's another one for the fire," she tells the two good ol' boys who come running back at the sound of the shot, the same line Sheriff McClelland speaks in the original about Ben.

Barbara's killing of Harry satisfies the audience (the audience I saw it with in 1990 cheered), but the fact that what shocked audiences in 1968 (the accidental shooting of the lone survivor, Ben) not only failed to shock but was celebrated by audiences in 1990 evinces a cultural shift. In fairness, she would have probably done the same to Ben by that point, had he lived and she had the opportunity. Jamie Russell reads the scene as an embodiment of militant feminism: "Barbara executes Cooper because his behavior represents everything that is wrong with the dominant patriarchal order" (164). Barbara kills Harry and knows she will get away with it, as the circumstances require all zombies be shot in the head and their bodies disposed of immediately. For the social change needed, the patriarchy must be overthrown, but Barbara's shooting of Harry is also personal.

As in previous female-empowerment revenge films, *Night* 1990 shows a transformation of Barbara from the timid victim of the cemetery scene to the female avenger in this last scene. She killed the Cemetery Zombie in revenge for killing Johnny. She kills the blind female zombie out of frustration, not necessity, and is clearly overwhelmed by emotion in the moment. Yet in the killing of the Cemetery Zombie she takes grim satisfaction. And like Jennifer Hills (Camille Keaton), the heroine of *I Spit on Your Grave* (which was also released under the title *Day of the Woman*), Barbara mercilessly slaughters those men who would violate her and who oppress women. *Night* 1990 is an exploitation movie transformed into reactionary feminist film: the ends justify the means if it brings about social change and female empowerment. Her cold killing of Harry, and even colder intoning of, "That's another one for the fire," demonstrates that Barbara has completely transformed from mousy girl frightened of her mother and brother to a woman who can kill a man in cold blood for being oppressive to women. She kills Harry not only for what he has done to her over the past night (which was obnoxious, but not ever truly evil), and for what he has done to the others in the farmhouse (which was admittedly far more problematic), but also for what the other men in Barbara's life have done to her. She kills Harry because she cannot kill Johnny or her father. But killing Harry ends her old life and starts her new one.

Notes

1. Several sources argue this fact, but both John Russo and Tom Savini directly state it in "The Dead Walk," a DVD extra on the *Night of the Living Dead* (1990) DVD. The 1990 remake

was designed to stop another proposed remake, to make money for those who had not profited because of the original *Night*'s lack of copyright notice, and to attempt to establish copyright ownership over the term "the living dead."

2. As will be examined in the next chapter, in the 30th Anniversary Edition of *Night of the Living Dead*, John A. Russo's "expanded and enhanced" version of *Night*, a very full explanation for the Cemetery Zombie is given, which effectively robs it of its power. The 1990 remake of *Night* merely uses an open casket instead of giving an entire backstory to the Cemetery Zombie, as Russo does.

3

"This has got to be the strangest load you've ever hauled!": *30th Anniversary Special Edition* (1998) and *Children of the Living Dead* (2001)

In 1997, George Lucas released a twentieth anniversary "Special Edition" of the original *Star Wars* films. While the films offered much cleaner digital prints with more special effects, there were also narrative and character changes to which many fans and critics objected. A year later, John Russo released the *Thirtieth Anniversary Special Edition* of *Night of the Living Dead*, using a similar production and promotional strategy: current technology allowed for both the restoration of the film to a pristine, sharp, clear condition, and the transformation of the film into something the original filmmakers would have made if they had had the technology, time and budget. For Lucas, it was restoring and adding certain scenes to his original trilogy, sometimes substantially altering the story, much to fans' discontent (the most famous being the "Greedo fired first" addition). For Russo, it was adding a wraparound narrative to the original *Night* featuring an executed child-killer, a fundamentalist Christian minister and a reporter, which completely reframed the story to make it both much more religious and much less serious.

As chapter 2 indicated, the original *Night* offers no visual explanation for the Cemetery Zombie. We have no idea who he is, where he came from or why he is in the cemetery. Initially Johnny and Barbara mistake him for a living person. John Russo gives an explanation and then some in the "30th Anniversary Special Edition" DVD of *Night of the Living Dead*. He was a child-killer who had just been executed in the state of Pennsylvania, and his corpse was being driven to the cemetery to be buried in front of the parents of his last victim. When he reanimates, he climbs out of his coffin and attacks the men charged with burying him, who flee. He then stumbles through the cemetery until he meets Barbara and Johnny. A very doughy and obviously much older Bill Hinzman, who has aged considerably in twenty-five years, results in scenes that do not blend as seamlessly as the filmmakers claim in the DVD commentary. His presence now explained, some of the horror and mystery are now removed, although, as noted below, this explanation is rooted in the sociophobics of late twentieth century American fears of child predators.

Not a remake per se, *Night 30* is a reimagining that completely reshapes the original through the use of new characters, additional scenes, a new encompassing narrative, and a new soundtrack by Scott Vladmir Licina (who also plays the new character the Rev. John Hicks). I will, however, consider this project as a remake of sorts, since it uses the original film but adds enough material to reshape the entire meaning, as a remake does. After describing and analyzing the new scenes, I shall consider the zombie as child molester and then explore how the film constructs fears of the millennium, apocalyptic thinking and fundamentalist preachers. Lastly, I will consider *Children of the Living Dead*, Russo's unofficial sequel to *Night*, which further deconstructs and rearranges the meaning of *Night* and is the first film since *Return of the Living Dead* and its sequels to use "Living Dead" in the title.

"Expanded and Enhanced"

The new material consists of four new scenes. The first is a prologue that begins outside a prison and ends in the cemetery, explaining the origins of the Cemetery Zombie. The second is inserted in the middle of the film and consists primarily of zombies feeding on the aftermath of a car accident. The third scene is an addition to the arrival of the posse near the end of the film, featuring an attack on the Reverend Hicks by a zombie. The fourth and final new scene is an epilogue that shows the aftermath of Hicks' zombie bite.

The film begins with new material: outside a prison, the aftermath of an execution. The body of a child killer who has been electrocuted is picked up at a prison by two men hired to bury the body, and brought to a cemetery for burial. Waiting at the cemetery are the parents of the dead child, Arthur and Hilda Krantz (George Drennen and Julie Wallace Deklavan), and the Reverend Hicks. The men who are driving the body are uneasy. One reassures the other, "He's dead, he can't hurt you." The audience is already aware of the irony of this line in a film called *Night of the Living Dead*. The dead can and will hurt you.

The parents of the murdered child engage both the men assigned to bury the body and the clergyman in a strange theological and political debate, both about the propriety of burying the executed man in the cemetery ("He doesn't deserve to be buried next to decent folk") and whether he deserves the comforts and trappings of ritual and religion ("Some sins should be beyond repentance"). They stay only to make sure the man is dead, asking to see his body in what can only be described as a contrivance to get the casket open so the executed man can become the "Cemetery Zombie." They leave before any prayers can be said over the man.

The Reverend Hicks prays for the dead man, stating, "I do not ask for mercy, I ask only for justice." This moment of prayer introduces the sociophobic of conservative religious beliefs — not a loving, forgiving Jesus, but an angry, judging warrior Jesus who will throw all of His enemies into eternal fire, the Jesus of *Left Behind*, not the Sermon on the Mount. It also reminds us of the sociophobic of child abduction. The parents of the murdered child, and the Reverend Hicks, want "justice" for a murdered child and punishment for the child's killer.

The second new scene consists of the aftermath of a car wreck. Dead bodies are seen in the wreckage of a car that hit a tree. Three of the bodies in the car reanimate and exit the car. A group of living dead begins moving past, including a waitress from Beakman's Diner. The passing zombies eat the body of the driver, even before the radio reports that the murderers are eating the bodies of their victims. Seeing the zombies eat the driver of the car undercuts and even removes the power of seeing the eating of Tom and Judy later.[1] The scene is odd, especially when one considers that Tom and Judy die when the truck explodes, and we see the zombies pulling their remains out of the vehicle in order to consume them. It is as if Russo has put a very similar, if not nearly the same, scene in the film forty minutes before the original zombies-eating-the-corpses-from-the-vehicle scene.

The third addition is an extended posse scene, with men with guns running around the cemetery shooting zombies. The slow-moving zombies flee from people slowly walking behind them, shooting. The Reverend Hicks speaks to Darlene Davis (Debbie Rochon) in the cemetery as the posse moves through. He compares the events of the past twenty-four hours to the Biblical flood or the destruction of Sodom and Gomorrah, claiming, "We are being punished for our sins. The dead are rising and judgment day is at hand." This prophesy is ironically undercut by the next scene in which dozens of the risen dead are shot down.

Suddenly, reporter and cameraman are gone, and the Reverend is confronted by the Cemetery Zombie. "By the power of the Holy Ghost, I condemn thee to eternal death and damnation. May the beasts of hell that inhabit you leave your body so that your soul may burn in everlasting fire. So your soul may burn in everlasting fire." He kneels down and holds up his Bible, but the Cemetery Zombie bites his face. He is saved when Arthur Krantz hits the zombie repeatedly with a shovel, and then another member of the posse shoots the zombie in the head.

Russo, then, has created an epilogue that radically changes the story but also transforms the meaning of the entire film. One year later, the Rev. John Hicks is in the "Ormsby Medical Center."[2] The fact that it is a year later and there is no reference to an ongoing crisis of the living dead, and that things appear to be "normal," goes against the narrative of the larger trilogy of films. The dead are no longer rising, or at least they are under control.

The Reverend Hicks is being interviewed by reporter Darlene Davis. A year later his zombie bite is now healed, leaving a visible scar. His immune system is being studied in order to see why "there doesn't seem to be a difference between [his] body chemistry and someone who is not infected." The Reverend keeps a pet, a dog named "Moshu," so that if he does suddenly become a zombie his instinct will be to attack the dog and not the people around him.[3] As Darlene exits, he cries after her to, "Spike the dead to prevent them from rising before judgment day." Oddly enough, the film then cuts back from the Reverend Hicks to the fire outside the farmhouse and the burning of bodies a year earlier, to allow for the original end credits.

Strange though some of these additions are, the new wraparound story of *Night* plays with sociophobics very much pertinent to the late nineties, on the verge of the millennium. They also radically transform the original *Night* into a very different story and a very different *kind* of story, one tinged with religious overtones and reflecting the concerns of the late nineties, not the late sixties. This is a *Night of the Living Dead* as shaped by *America's Most Wanted*, *The 700 Club* and the *Left Behind* books. The siege of a small Pennsylvania farmhouse is now encased in a much larger millennial narrative of the forces of genuine evil held at bay by the forces of God.

"I Ask Only for Justice": The Zombie as Child Molester

In the original *Night*, the Cemetery Zombie was a mystery. His origins and how he came to be in the cemetery are unknown. These mysterious origins are part of what makes the figure so terrifying. Also, despite the title of the film, we initially assume he is not a zombie or one of the living dead. The *Night 30th Anniversary Edition* gives an entire backstory to this character. We know before he emerges from the coffin that he is dead. We know he was executed. We know he is a child killer. The daughter of Arthur and Hilda Krantz was killed by the Cemetery Zombie. The implication is that he is not mere child murderer, but also child molester.

The child killer is an old cinematic trope. *M*, Fritz Lang's masterpiece starring Peter Lorre as a killer of children in Germany, is the quintessential model of the horror film rooted in child-killing. In the first half of this expressionistic drama, the killer is a genuine source of fear, as we never see his face, only his body, and we hear him whistle "In the Hall of the Mountain King" from Grieg's *Peer Gynt*. When he is discovered and chased, he becomes a pathetic figure, no longer the monster of our imagination but a sad, little man who preys on children and is justly punished by the community.

Night, on the other hand, gives us the child killer after death. He has been executed by the state for his crimes and is about to be buried. When he rises out of his casket as a zombie, it is a larger metaphor. His execution did not stop his evil. He has returned to attack and kill again. Although we only see him attack adults (Barbara, Johnny, the Reverend Hicks), the film offers the image of child predator as literal predator, one which execution does not stop.

In 1998, *America's Most Wanted*, hosted by John Walsh (father of Adam Walsh, who was kidnapped and murdered in 1981), was celebrating its tenth year. The zeitgeist of America in 1997 and 1998 reflected growing concern over missing and exploited children, and with the adults who preyed on them. Numerous states and municipalities moved to make it easier to find missing and exploited children, capture and punish those who preyed upon children, and to use the public to locate abducted children. "The Jacob Wetterling Crimes Against Children and Sexually Violent Offender Registration Act," part of the *Federal Violent Crime Control and Law Enforcement Act of 1994*, perhaps better known as the Federal version of "Megan's Law," required states to register sex offenders and release information about registered sex offenders to the public.[4] It was amended in 1996 and 1998. Thus, in the four-year period before the *30th Anniversary Edition* of *Night of the Living Dead* the public discourse in the United States was full of debates and discussions about sexual predators, sex offenders and especially those individuals who preyed on children. There was a great deal of concern about protecting society and children from predators. "Megan's Law" was named after Megan Kanka, who was kidnapped, raped and murdered in 1994 in New Jersey. Her killer was a convicted sex offender who had been paroled, despite the fact that one of his therapists believed he would commit another assault.

The Cemetery Zombie never gets a name, but he does get an extensive criminal history. He was executed by the state but reanimated by the zombie outbreak. Barbara and Johnny were not only attacked by an early example of the living dead, they were attacked by a zombie child molester. His instinct to attack Barbara instead of Johnny is thus rewritten in this version as an impulse, even in death, to prey upon the weaker and more child-like of the siblings. He also attacks and bites the Reverend Hicks before being shot dead a second time in the graveyard. Whereas the fate of the original Cemetery Zombie remained unknown, this Cemetery Zombie finally receives the justice for which the Reverend asks. Mr. and Mrs. Krantz do not want the man who killed their child to receive any service or Christian burial. He receives none of these. Instead, after attacking several people, he is killed again and his body presumably thrown on the fire and burned as refuse. Justice against the child killer is finally achieved.

Millennial Fears and Apocalyptic Preachers

Romero's films are apocalyptic and millennial. They propose an end of human history and the beginning of something new.[5] Christian apocalypticism features the rise of the dead: "So will it be with the resurrection of the dead. The body that is sown is perishable, it is raised imperishable" (1 Corinthians 15: 42), and "The trumpet will sound and the dead will be raised imperishable" (1 Corinthians 15:52), to offer up but two examples. The Book of Revelation contains numerous instances of the dead rising, being set in judgment, and other horrific and catastrophic events occurring as God brings an end to the world and prepares a new world, one without sin, for the faithful. The Book of Revelation also contains the seeds of millennialism, the belief that Christ will have a thousand-year reign on Earth. In the years immediately before the year 2000, much public speculation and many, many books were written about whether or not the world would end in 2000.

Y2K fears, as they were called, took many forms. There was concern about the computers that ran society not being Y2K compliant, causing planes to fall from the sky, the economic system to plunge into chaos and even home computers with personal records to stop working. Even louder were the voices asking if 2000 would usher in the Christian apocalypse, the final battle and the return of Christ. It was a period of millennial and apocalyptic tension.

Feeding into society's fears were deeply apocalyptic religious groups, such as David Koresh and the Branch Davidians in Waco, Texas. From February to April 1993, the Branch Davidians, under their leader David Koresh, were held under siege by the federal government, most notably agents of the F.B.I. and the Bureau of Alcohol, Tobacco and Firearms (A.T.F.). The Branch Davidians believed in a coming apocalypse, and the government was concerned for the safety of the children of the group (it was also reported that children at the compound were being abused), and the amount of firearms and explosives that the group had acquired and maintained in their compound (Kirsch 239–243). When federal agents attempted to serve a warrant, a firefight broke out between the Davidians and the federal agents, resulting in several deaths on each side.

The government was concerned that, as happened in Jonestown with the People's Temple Cult, the Davidians might plan a mass suicide. After a prolonged standoff, the government attempted to end the siege after fifty days by storming the compound. The Branch Davidians set fire to their own compound and fought back. Seventy-five members of the Davidians (fifty adults and twenty-five children under the age of fifteen) were killed in the raid; only nine survived. Paradoxically, in the aftermath, both the government and the Branch Davidians came under heavy criticism. The government was criticized for the use of extreme force before all other options had been exhausted, and was seen to be overstepping its bounds. The Davidians, on the other hand, were perceived as a dangerous millennial cult.

The siege in Waco demonstrated a growing resentment on the part of the religious right toward contemporary American culture and society, and a desire for Christ to come and destroy the world as it was. Apocalypticism is rooted in a doctrine of separation: God will come and "separate the sheep from the goats — in other words, the believers from the non-believers (Matthew 25:32). Believers will be rewarded with eternal life; non-believers will be punished eternally in some kind of hell. This religious resentment provoked concern over millennial preachers and their concern about the coming apocalypse. There is a fine line between hoping the world ends soon and working to bring about that end.

Millennial and apocalyptic preachers were not just limited to the extreme groups and the "cults." Mainstream Evangelical Christianity embraces millennial expectations. Indeed, the last decade of the twentieth century featured a veritable explosion of millennial and apocalyptic culture, much of it rooted in Evangelical Christianity, as the year 2000 approached (see Shaw 205–210). Televangelists and Christian broadcasters, such as Pat Robertson, Jack van Impe, Charles Taylor, Chuck Smith, Ray Brubaker, Paul Crouch and James Dobson (better known now for his organization Focus on the Family), were all popular ministers who actively preached Armageddon theology in the late nineties on America's airwaves (see Halsell 3–9). All of them and others asked if the world might not end and Jesus might not return in the year 2000.

Numerous non-fiction and fiction works filled bookstore shelves about the supposed coming apocalypse. Hal Lindsey, whose *The Late Great Planet Earth* (1970) was the gold standard for apocalyptic prophesy, contributed *Planet Earth 2000 A.D.* in 1994 and *Apocalypse Code* in 1997. In 1995, however, the most widely read apocalyptic fantasy was created. In that year, Tim LaHaye and Jerry B. Jenkins wrote *Left Behind*. "Thus began a sensationally successful media enterprise that demonstrates the power of the apocalyptic idea in its purest and simplest form" (Kirsch 244). A volume a year followed, up to and after the 30th anniversary of *Night*: *Tribulation Force* (1996), *Nicolae* (1997), and *Soul Harvest* (1998). LaHaye wrote in 1972, "I believe the Bible teaches that we are already living in the beginning of the end" (qtd. in Kirsch 243). The *Left Behind* series, a collection of novels that begins with the rapture and ends with the defeat of the antichrist many volumes later sets the Biblical apocalypse in contemporary America. Readers watch the end of history unfold through the eyes of a small group of individuals who were not raptured themselves, but, by virtue of coming to understand what happened to their Christian friends and relatives, have now converted to Christianity and lead the fight against evil. It is this model of contemporary Biblical apocalypse that infuses the *30th Anniversary Edition* of *Night*.

The Reverend Hicks compares the events of the past twenty-four hours to the Biblical flood or the destruction of Sodom and Gomorrah, claiming, "We are being punished for our sins. The dead are rising and judgment day is at hand." Although this prophesy is ironically undercut by the next scene in which dozens of the risen dead are shot down, and the apocalypse seemingly ends, it does give voice to genuine Christian apocalyptic belief. Hicks asserts in the epilogue, "God has chosen me as he chose Saint Paul. Through me a miracle has been worked." Hicks sees himself as the embodiment of some divine plan.

Indeed, by the end of the film Hicks is miraculously alive. In the original version (and, for that matter, in this one), when Karen is bitten by "one of those things" she sickens and dies and reanimates, which is the fate for every character bitten by one of the living dead. The Reverend Hicks, however, does not die, but has a scar and seems to be fully healed. Hicks explains that Arthur Krantz hid the reverend from the authorities and bathed the wound in holy water and "prayed while I was delirious for seven days and seven nights." Subsequently, Krantz was put in jail for hiding Hicks. This brief explanation inserts two tropes into *Night*. The first is the power of traditional religion, prayer and ritual. David Flint reads this story as "suggesting that a Christian belief can somehow cure the infected" (92). Christianity has efficacy, and calling on the power of Christ while using religious tools (holy water, prayer, etc.) has the power to stop the otherwise inevitable death and reanimation. In other words, Christian beliefs can stop the zombie apocalypse and leave the Christian prepared for the real apocalypse.

Second, we can see the echoes of *Left Behind* in this story. In that series of books, Christians are persecuted, despite repeated demonstrations that their faith accurately represents reality. Reading between the lines, Arthur Krantz has been put in prison for hiding the reverend, ostensibly because his actions threatened the public. However, none of that is stated explicitly. Instead, it is implied that Krantz is jailed for the actions he undertook because of his faith. The reverend is imprisoned as well, albeit in a medical facility. This film confirms the Christian worldview and the power of Christianity and Christian belief while also confirming the correctness of Christian paranoia: the government, given the opportunity, will persecute and incarcerate Christians.

The epilogue continuously reasserts this theology. The scientists are all atheists and agnostics, claims the Reverend Hicks, and do not understand the true nature of the living dead: "Those things were demons, creatures of Satan inhabiting the bodies of our dead." In other words, the living dead were not reanimated by radiation from the Venus probe. Instead, God allowed demons and evil spirits to take over the bodies of the recently deceased and use them to attack and kill others. This fact also explains why the reverend did not perish from his zombie bite: the condition of being a zombie, not being caused by radiation or a virus but rather demon possession, means that the pouring of holy water, the use of prayer and the repeated rituals (which more or less describes an exorcism) kept the Reverend Hicks from becoming demon-possessed himself. The threat in this film is not from reanimated corpses but from the demons and evil spirits reanimating them. And, of course, the first and most significant zombie is the Cemetery Zombie, a child killer and executed criminal who becomes the first corpse to be reanimated by the demons. Russo's additional scenes radically transform *Night* from secular zombie film into theological nightmare of demon possession, and highlight the saving power of Christian faith.

Zombies as demon-possessed human bodies also echoes Hal Lindsey's oft-cited belief that UFOs were actually "deceptive ruses by demons," who were out to convince people of the existence of life on other planets and thus ostensibly lead them away from a literal belief in scripture.[6] The demon-possessed living dead serve to drive people to sin and despair, rejecting God and thus ensuring they will go to hell when they die. What has often been read as a liberal critique of the American middle class, the family, the Vietnam war and society in general is radically transformed into a conservative critique of secular society which does not recognize the very real threat of demons and the Devil.

The Reverend Hicks' final words on the matter are: "Spike the dead to prevent them from rising before judgment day." This statement does not make much sense either in terms of the film or in terms of theology. It seems to suggest the living dead need to be "spiked," presumably in the head, in order to prevent this false resurrection, which is only a reanimation and not a true return to life. Only the eternal life promised by Christ, which will be granted after judgment day, can be considered a true resurrection. In order to prevent demon-possession of dead bodies, the reverend seems to be suggesting that the bodies be spiked. "Spiked" might also refer to nailing the dead into their coffins so the bodies cannot rise, a practice historically associated with preventing vampirism.

Russo, in any case, plays fast and loose with both the story of *Night* and fundamentalist theology. The overall effect of the new footage is to transform the original film's secular apocalypse into a pre-millennial religious one, and to (perhaps unintentionally?) assert an extremely conservative, fundamentalist Christian view of reality. *Night 30* is a Christian horror film in which the horror no longer comes from fear of the dead but from fear of demons and evil spirits and what they can do to you while alive, and what they can and will do with your corpse after you die. This construction is nowhere to be found in the original. Two years before the year 2000, John Russo and company remade *Night* into *Left Behind: The Zombies.*

Strange Geneologies, or Why Children *Do Not Always Resemble Their Parents*

Three years after the *30th Anniversary* version of *Night*, and one year after the millennium, John A. Russo executive produced *Children of the Living Dead*, purported by some to be a sequel of sorts to *Night*. Sheriff Randolph (Martin Schiff) explains the current zombie outbreak by explaining that there had been a zombie outbreak in rural Western Pennsylvania "back in 1968": "Some people claim that it was a Venus probe that crashed back to Earth and released radiation. The dead began to walk."[7] There was another outbreak, he reports, in 1986, which is shown at the beginning of the film.

Children of the Living Dead opens with the ending of *Night*: a redneck posse is shooting and destroying free-range zombies, piling up the corpses and setting them on fire. A helicopter overhead references both the original *Dawn* and the 1990 remake of *Night*, especially through the use of point-of-view shots from the helicopter to show fields full of the living dead. The opening sequence features extensive carnage and shooting, including a one-man rampage by Tom Savini that dispatches a number of zombies in innovative ways. Deputy Hughs (Savini) and Sheriff Randolph then rescue children from a barn, but Hughs is attacked by a powerful zombie, one different from the others, and hurt badly; he must be shot in the head before he turns.

The film then advances to "14 years later," when Candy (Heidi Hinzman), Steve (Justin Kraus), Denise (Jennifer Karazian), Gary (Chris Mowod), and Jesse (Barrett Hackney), a group of teens in a van on their way to a concert, stop by the barn from the opening in order to party and provide a backstory about Abbott Hayes, a rapist and murderer whose body disappeared from the morgue right before the zombie outbreak previously shown began.

They stop to party on the grave of Abbott Hayes' mother (named Alberta Hayes) but are frightened off the road by his zombie and crash, killing all. After their funeral, Hayes' zombie appears again to bite their corpses and reanimate them. They then form the first new soldiers in Hayes' seeming zombie army.

Meanwhile, Matthew Michaels (Damien Luvara) plans to raze the Hayes homestead and build a car dealership. "That's great," proclaims the sheriff. "This side of town needs new, anything new just to bring life back into this community." Michaels, in his early twenties, has been put in charge of the project by his father, who owns a series of dealerships. The father wants the son to drop out of college and learn how the real world works, so he gives his son the new car dealership to learn the family business. Behind his son's back, however, the father gives ex-con foreman Gregg Peters (Tom Stoviak) directions to cut every corner in building the dealership over the old graveyard. Michaels Senior and Peters decide to relocate the town's graves, but only by moving the headstones to the new location and throwing the actual caskets in a trench on the car dealership's property. "No one can find out," says Peters. "I can understand that," responds his assistant Brad (Robert Oppel). "It'd make me mad as hell if my loved ones were relocated to a mass grave."

This scenario already is taken directly from the plot of *Poltergeist*. It is "cost prohibitive" to move the actual graves, so the evil businessman will only move the headstones. In doing so, have been violated and, in a traditional horror story like *Poltergeist*, the dead will return to seek revenge against the living. Here the dead are not ghosts but zombies. This scenario also anticipates *Night 3D*'s concern over mishandled burials and the removal of loved ones' remains. The film indicates that the building of the car dealership will result in the return of the repressed, so to speak. The dead who were put down in 1968 and 1986 will return again.

Matthew Michaels, however, first meets local waitress Laurie (Jamie McCoy), who tells him the local ghost (or zombie?) story. She explains that Abbott Hayes' trouble started with his mother: "She dressed him up as a girl. Sent him to school as a girl, took him around town as a girl." He was raised as "Alana," and everyone thought of him as a female until it was revealed he was male. He then killed his mother and began abducting teenagers and young girls. In a raid on his house, authorities found two decaying corpses in his living room. He was tried and sentenced to prison, and murdered there by another inmate. His body, however, vanished from the morgue and was last seen as a zombie in the 1986 outbreak.

This story, ostensibly set in the same township as *Night*, effectively serves as an erasure of *Night*, in that, as noted in the introduction, Romero removed the zombie master — the person controlling and animating the zombies. *Chil-*

dren reintroduces the zombie master, who is also a zombie, in the form of Abbott Hayes (A. Barrett Worland). Like *Night* it offers the Venus probe as the cause of the original outbreak, but the outbreaks in 1986 and the present are direct results of Abbott Hayes, who kidnapped a group of children in 1986, all but one of whom (Laurie) are killed by him in the present. Much of this plot does not make much sense, but, as with *Night 30*, the new material completely changes the original story with its additions.

Children also anticipates *Night 3D* in another manner: it is ultimately a slasher film, with Abbott Hayes (who is a third-rate Jason or Freddy) as a supernatural serial killer. His primary skills seem to be making faces at the camera and moving slowly but with a great deal of panache. It is apparent, however, that he is not a typical slow-moving zombie that seeks to eat the living. He is, instead, a hyper-intelligent, plotting zombie who creates other zombies to do his bidding. His first kills are the teenagers whom he had kidnapped as a young zombie in 1986. After reanimating them, he uses them as mindless killers to attack Brad, Peters and Michaels Senior.

Considering the tropes of the slasher genre, as outlined by Carol Clover in *Men, Women and Chainsaws*—an evil killer, a terrible place, weapons that don't work, a final girl, and victims that are transgressors—*Children* is a slasher film (26–34). Abbott Hayes as a child suffered forced transvestitism by the mother he eventually killed. He then became a killer of women. Now he has returned from the grave as a zombie master. He is the epitome of a slasher film killer.

Deputy Dusty (Sam Nicotero) tells Michael the cemetery is "a bad, bad place," and he should "never go there alone." The cemetery and the adjoining Abbott Hayes property are presented as the "bad place" of Clover's schema. The physical location has a history of violence and evil, and now that violence and evil have returned. Similarly, the victims of the slasher zombies are not innocent. They are transgressors. Transgressions can involve drinking, drugs and sex (the teens), or economic injustice (Michaels and Gregg). Joseph Michaels (Philip Bower) and Peters do bad things to their workers, the environment and the communities they work in. The teens killed initially in the film set the slasher mode, as they are going to a concert but stop to drink at the bad place—Alberta Hayes' grave. They plan to do all the things that teens do at a concert, and, as a result, they are killed by Abbott Hayes. The only member of the social circle who does not die in the accident is Laurie, who does not go to the concert (despite being the one who bought the tickets) because she has to work. She waits tables at the local diner and is clearly trusted by its owner, as she had to go to work instead of the concert because he became sick. Her work ethic, combined with the good deed, saves her life. She is not a transgressing victim and instead will serve as the "final girl."

The final siege at the diner shows the construction crew, some of the local townspeople, and Matthew and Laurie fighting the zombies, killing them. Some of the living die, but Abbott Hayes' army is defeated, though he himself slinks away to return again in the future when an opportunity presents itself. The sheriff, for his own corruption, is bitten by a zombie, and Laurie must shoot him in the head before he can turn. The ending, however, is remarkably conservative: the authorities show up, all the zombies are destroyed and their bodies burned, order is restored, and Matthew and Laurie are free to begin their lives as a young, heterosexual couple committed to their small town.

In better hands, this might have been a narrative of economic exploitation, the death of small-town America, a critique of corruption in rural municipalities or even a simple study of the legacy of evil handed from generation to generation, sliding from 1968 to 1986 to 2000. It contains the seeds of a critique of small-town life, the role of business in circumventing the community's good and pre–9/11 concerns about quality of life. Instead, the filmmakers reduce the legacy of *Night* to an occasionally nonsensical slasher film with zombies.

Both the additions to the special edition of *Night* and *Children of the Living Dead* suffer from poor writing, poor acting, and banal and pedestrian direction. The larger issue for this volume, however, is what these films tell us about what frightened our culture when they were made. In that sense, the idea that the *30th Anniversary Edition* of *Night* is "expanded" is not entirely accurate. It is expanded only in that the running time is longer and more scenes have been added. The effect of these scenes, however, is a reduction. Romero's zombie films, to paraphrase the bumper sticker, were observed locally but developed globally. The audience is shown the effects of a global zombie apocalypse on a small, local population. One never loses the sense that the human race is undergoing this experience collectively.

In these two films, however, global horror is reduced to the local. Both films locate the living dead outbreak to a single small town in rural Pennsylvania. The terror comes not from realizing that the horrible events affecting you are taking place all over the planet, but from a zombie child molester and a local preacher, from a transvestite serial killer turned zombie master hiding in the woods by the highway. These films reduce the horror to a local phenomenon and one that is fairly easily defeated. They are reactionary horror films, conservative in their outlook. God, guts and guns will defeat zombies, and then the town can return to normal. In a sense, the greatest fear demonstrated by these films is shown by its absence. Russo and company want to avoid any larger catastrophe or deal with any global terror, so the horror is kept to farmhouses and local criminals, as they can be easily dealt with. This is horror for global warming deniers, so to speak: the bigger problems are not the ones that affect the world, but the ones that trouble me in my own backyard, a zombie apocalypse writ very small and very local indeed.

Notes

1. His head is also hollow, with no explanation as to how a car accident would cause this injury. In addition to dozens of zombies walking past the car crash, the initial zombie is "Rosie," dressed as a waitress from Beakman's Diner. Ben mentions that he had been there in the original, and Russo runs with the Beakman references in the 30th Anniversary edition. Dan (Grant Cramer), one of the men who delivers the body from the prison to the cemetery, is dating a waitress at Beakman's, and he and Mike (Adam Knox), the other delivery man, decide to go to Beakman's after they drop off the body. It makes one wonder about the symbolism and significance of the diner to Russo, as it figures so prominently in the additional footage, while only meriting a passing reference in the original.

2. This name is also an inside joke. Alan Ormsby is the co-writer and star of *Children Shouldn't Play with Dead Things* (1973), another film about the living dead. The same joke reference is made in *Night of the Living Dead: Reanimated*.

3. I must confess, on a personal level, although the idea of giving him a pet as a precautionary measure could be interesting, the name "Moshu" and the idea that should the good reverend zombify he will attack this tiny dog and not another human, or that the dog will buy those around him enough time to escape, reduces this element to the ridiculous and transforms what should be the suggestion of danger into a bit of silly business.

4. See "Jacob Wetterling Crimes Against Children and Sexually Violent Offender Registration Program" at *Cornell University Law School United States Code Collection,* http://www4.law.cornell.edu/uscode/html/uscode42/usc_sec_42_00014071----000-.html (accessed 15 August 2009), for a full description of the law.

5. David Pagano sees them as "meta-apocalyptic"—"that is, although they enact a prophetic attempt to claim a true perspective on the present by looking back from the conclusion of history, they emphatically, violently, and gleefully refrain from separating inside and outside, space and time, in the fashion of apocalyptic prophets" (74).

6. Interestingly, in the zombie boom of the first decade of the twenty-first century, different authors of fiction have used the same idea—that zombies are actually animated by demons—to explain a zombie plague and sometimes to offer a theological moral along with zombie action. In the case of the former we have the series of books by Brian Keene, such as *The Rising* and *City of the Dead,* which imagine zombies as dead bodies inhabited by spirits and demons; and in the case of the latter, there is Mark Rodgers' *The Dead,* in which the zombie milieu is incorporated into an overtly evangelical Christian understanding of the end times. The zombies are demon-possessed.

7. Except, of course, that the Venus probe did not crash to Earth in the original *Night.* It was destroyed before it could crash.

4

"Hey, are you, like, freaked out about zombie movies?": *Night of the Living Dead 3-D* (2006)

Paul R. Gagne reports that *Day of the Dead* was originally conceived as a 3-D film in the wake of *Jaws 3D*, but ultimately Romero did not pursue that idea (149). Thus, the 2006 adaptation of *Night* is the first 3D film in the Romero family, so to speak, with the soon-to-come *Night of the Living Dead: Origins 3D* also using the emerging 3D film technology to create a more experiential zombie film. The idea behind 3D is to make the film viewing more realistic and experiential. Unfortunately, *Night 3D* does not use the 3D effectively to enhance the effect of the zombie attacks, instead focusing on a character offering the audience a joint and Ben's fist as he drives his motorcycle toward a zombie, punching it in the face.

It is a shame that the most interesting and intelligent moment in *Night of the Living Dead 3-D* occurs in the first thirty seconds of the film and promises a fascinating reconstruction/deconstruction of the original. In a roadside shed with a television on, the original *Night of the Living Dead* opening is playing. As the title credit appears, with Johnny and Barbara's car driving across the television screen in the background, the words "Night of the Living Dead" leave the television screen and fly through the space to the window, where we see another car driving past, this one containing this film's Johnny and Barbara. The image is startling and surprising, and seems to promise a shift from the original, using the new technologies available. It also suggests a connection to the original which will be honored but deconstructed throughout the film.

Alas, such was not meant to be. Apart from this playful moment and all the insight it promised, the film was universally despised by critics and fans, and with good reason.[1] Although I said in the introduction I would not judge these films, I do want to state categorically at the beginning of this chapter that *Night of the Living Dead 3-D* is a terrible film, not just a terrible remake.

Badly acted, badly filmed, poorly written and illogical, it is a failure as a piece of horror cinema, as a remake of Romero, and as time and money spent on human endeavors. In theaters it carried the disclaimer, "This is a new motion picture filmed in 3D that is a re-imagining of the 1968 public domain motion picture *Night of the Living Dead*. George A. Romero is not affiliated in any way with this new film." In other words, the filmmakers had to disavow any connection to Romero, though they were remaking his seminal work. Having said all that, let us examine how *Night of the Living Dead 3-D*, however poorly, still reflects the social phobias of the period in which it was produced.

Building off this opening image, I propose to first examine the metacinematic approach to the original *Night*, and then consider the shift in scale to a local, rather than global, national or even regional apocalypse. I will then look at how the film constructs the idea of the twenty-first century family, consider the film as reflecting the mortuary scandals of the early twenty-first century, and then, finally, following Carol J. Clover, read *Night 3D* not as a zombie film but rather as a post–9/11 slasher movie.

The opening shot sets a motif that runs throughout the film: the continual presence of the original. While all remakes are haunted by the original, this remake features the original as an active presence on every television screen, from that opening shot to the movie that the Cooper family watches later on in the film. The family in *Night 3D* watches the original *Night* on television. This conscious acknowledgement of the original both highlights the differences from it and accentuates the influence of the original on all horror (especially zombie) cinema since.

This metacinema of *Night* also occurred in *Halloween II*. In that film, *Night* plays on television screens in the background of various scenes, making it apparent that several residents of Haddonfield are watching the movie. The progress of the film-within-the-film matches the progress of the events of Halloween night in Haddonfield. *Halloween II* thus forms an intertext with *Night*, taking a slasher narrative and suggesting the siege of the household in *Night* is echoed by Michael Meyer's continued attacks on the town of Haddonfield. Michael also transcends mere serial killer to become, like the dead in *Night*, an almost supernatural force of nature that cannot be stopped. The best one can hope for is to survive one's encounter.

Night 3D does the same thing, except as a remake. The presence of *Night* on all televisions in the film reminds us of genre and the "rules" of Romero, and sets the ignorant characters of this film in opposition to the knowing ones of the original. Furthermore, just as in the original, the television becomes a means of learning about the truth of the characters' situation; the characters in the remake remain woefully ignorant of the danger, even when the television presents many of the same situations, and cautions the characters, in a sense, not to repeat the mistakes of those in the original. Unfortunately, while the film is self-aware, the presence of *Night* reminds us that the characters are not, and all will once again die. The original *Night* is thus not mere horror film or antecedent in this case, but a prophetic historic text. History does not repeat itself, but historical situations do, and this film constructs *Night* as a cautionary tale that is ignored by its viewers, who subsequently find themselves in peril for doing so.

Rescued by Ben (Joshua DesRoches), Barbara (Brianna Brown) runs into the farmhouse living room, yelling, "You have to believe me, they're coming back to life; the dead are coming back to kill us all!" As she says this, she walks past the television where the original Barbara and Ben fight the hands coming in through the windows at the climax of the original *Night*. It is another self-referential moment, like the opening, in which the other characters do not believe Barbara's zombie story even as they watch it play out on the television screen in their own living room. As she passes the television set, Barbara pauses and looks back, seeing her namesake being grabbed by zombies. Owen (Adam Chambers), the stoner farmhand, slurs, "Oh, shit, she's right." He then looks from the Barbara on television to the one in his living room and asks her, "Hey, are you, like, freaked out about zombie movies? Because you were, like, freaking me out for a second." The moment is meant to be humorous, but it actually reflects a profound change from the original.

In the original *Night*, the characters, even though they have all lived through zombie assaults themselves, do not understand what is happening until the radio and the television make sense of it for them. In this remake, even when the zombie narrative is playing out in front of them, it does not make sense, they do not believe it, and they doubt the sanity and sensibility of Barbara. Owen, as the only one not in the original film, is a character who stands in for us, the audience. And he cannot distinguish between reality and a film. He is the only one who says Barbara is right, but he says so because he is too stoned to know the difference. We, the audience, likewise no longer know the difference. This is *Night of the Living Dead* as reality television.

Barbara warns the Cooper family about "zombies," and they laugh. She wants to call the police, and they will not let her. First, Ben tells her that she cannot tell the police she was "attacked by zombies," as "they won't believe you." Second, Henry Cooper (Greg Travis) is a marijuana farmer and does not want the police on his property. These are not the concerns of people facing an apocalypse that they themselves have experienced.

Later, Owen, delirious from a zombie bite, tells Ben and Henry that they "should not have watched that movie. It cursed us. It's like a premonition." Henry tells him, "Owen, that's the stupidest fucking thing you've ever said." Viewers might be inclined to agree, but Owen responds, "We're in the shit," which we can take to refer to both the trouble the characters are in, but also Owen's awareness of being "in" the movie, or at least in the same situation as the original *Night*, which they just watched. While not quite Pirandellian self-awareness, the film does reflect an interest in, and an attention to, how we understand zombie narratives. In doing so, it also comments, however unintentionally, on the human ability to ignore reality in favor of the narrative we want or hope is actually occurring, and the human ability to ignore the dangers we are specifically warned about in order to focus on our own fears and concerns.

Small Apocalpyses

Night 3D reduces the zombie apocalypse into a local event. The original *Night* initially states that the "Eastern third of the United States" is affected by the crisis, and subsequent broadcasts imply a growing crisis. The suggestion is made that the destruction of the Venus probe above the atmosphere might flood the entire Earth with the "strange radiation" that appears to be reanimating the dead. In short, it is at least a national crisis. *Dawn* is also at least a national crisis, and the *Dawn* remake makes clear in the opening credit sequence that it is a worldwide crisis. The 1990 remake of *Night* implies that all of the United States, if not the world (it is never specified), is affected, as the film is set in the Pittsburgh area but the television newscaster speaks about the dead rising in California. In short, when the dead rise, it is a national or international phenomenon which spells the eventual end of humanity.

Night 3D, on the other hand, is very local — just one cemetery. In a sense, this is faithful to the original in that even though the original features a national crisis, it is only experienced by the audience locally at the farmhouse. Similarly, the 1990 remake also focuses on the crisis within a single township. Just as all politics are local, all zombie uprisings are local. It is the local dead we fear — not that of those in other states or countries. *Night 3D* returns to what actually lies at the heart of *Night*—local horror. The most dangerous dead in *Night* are family members — Karen and Johnny.

In addition to local horror, *Night 3D* also, like the *Thirteenth Anniversary Edition*, engages millennial and apocalyptic fears. Although the millennium had passed, and with it any and all concerns, secular or religious, about Y2K, the events of 9/11 reawakened American apocalyptic concerns. *Night 3D* specifically raises the issue of the rapture and the end of days in a conversation between Hellie and Barbara. After Hellie wonders out loud, "Why is this happening?" she expresses her fears of the end of the world to Barbara:

HELLIE: Have you ever read any of those *Left Behind* books? You know, 'cause I was starting to think that this might be the beginning of...

BARBARA: What, the end of the world?

HELLIE: I mean, I really don't believe in any of that stuff, but when something like this happens, you gotta think ... you know? I mean I always thought of myself as a good person; but am I really?

BARBARA: Whatever's doing this — I don't think it's God.

Hellie expresses fear that it might be the end of the world, although she herself states that she "really doesn't believe any of that stuff." She is not a believing Christian, but she does fear what she has begun to perceive as apocalyptic signs.

As her statement "I mean I always thought of myself as a good person; but am I really?" demonstrates, this local apocalypse becomes a source for self-reflection. There is an inherent tension in the United States in Bush's America, which simultaneously praises individual freedom (to the point of stating that our enemies in the war on terror, themselves religious fundamentalists, "hate us because of our freedom") and embraces a fundamentalist, rigid and judgmental framework of belief that similarly denies freedom. Organized religion promotes specific frameworks of acceptable behavior and divides the world into the in-group and the out-group. The in-group is saved, the out-group is damned, and there is no exception for people who think of themselves "as a good person." One either believes and follows the mandates of the religion, or one does not and risks rejection and damnation if the religion proves correct.

This fundamentalist schizophrenia (freedom/rigid code of behavior mandated by authority) is reflected in the house in *Night 3D*. A family of pot farmers is attacked by zombies and tries to survive. Their income is derived entirely by illegal means, but they are a nuclear family, arguably in much better shape than the more bourgeois and mainstream family of Barbara and Johnny. It is this family that will suffer for their transgressions, but their transgressions hurt no one. One might argue that they are farmers and entrepreneurs — they are following the American dream, except that their crop is morally unacceptable.

Furthering the religious schizophrenia of the film is the fact that the crisis has not been precipitated by God, but by one of His misguided followers. Gerald Tovar, Jr. (Sid Haig) accidentally spilled chemicals on the dead; now they are reanimating. He chooses to interpret this within a religious framework. He chooses to see himself doing the work of the Lord: "I don't kill — I give life," he tells Barbara. When she expresses not only doubt but condemnation, he declares to her in religious language that what he does is a form of salvation: "I won't hurt you — you'll be born again." The deliberate use of the phrase "born again" refers not only to the return to life of the dead but also the Christian belief that one must be "born again" by accepting Christ as one's personal savior in order to be saved. For Tovar, zombies represent a literalization of salvation: we live again after death.

The film makes clear, however, that this belief is a religious delusion that is far more dangerous than the chemicals which initially reanimated the dead. At the finale, we learn that Tovar killed his father, and that his motivations for not cremating the corpses were religious ones. "I saved them. My father wanted to burn them, but I redeemed them and gave them life eternal," he tells Barbara. She asks him if he thinks he is Jesus, and he laughs and says, "Well, I did bring them back to life." Tovar just might think he is some sort of divine being. Whereas the original film's crisis was the result of multiple problems, from NASA to local errors, *Night 3D* demonstrates how one misguided individual, operating under religious beliefs, can create a local disaster. This experience has been borne out from the Branch Davidians at Waco to the fundamentalists who carried out 9/11. In the first decade of the twenty-first century, religious fundamentalism is at the root of our sociophobics. Gerald Tovar, as a result of his actions rooted in his religious beliefs, ends up killing far more people than he could do on his own.

Tovar does not bring about the rapture. There is no one left behind wondering where the believers went.[2] Jesus does not return. The sheep and the goats are not separated, and the Day of the Lord does not arrive. This is not *the* apocalypse. This is *an* apocalypse, a local revealing of hidden things that brings about the end — not of days, but of the characters. As an apocalypse, this is horror as event rather than action. Unlike the slasher film, in which the horror comes from the actions of Michael Meyers, Jason Vorhees, or Freddy Kruger, *Night 3D*, like many post–9/11 films, posits horror as an event, a happening that then unleashes death and destruction on a wider (yet still local) population. In this case, as in 9/11, the event and the horror are both sparked by a delusional religious belief and an apocalyptic sensibility.

A Death in/of the Family

At the opening of the film, Johnny (Ken Ward) and Barbara are again in a car headed toward a cemetery. This time, however, they are not going to visit the grave of either parent but to meet their mother at the funeral of an aunt they have "seen maybe twice in the past ten years," according to Johnny. The relative was not worth visiting or spending time with while alive. The characters, however, begrudgingly attend her funeral. Death makes one momentarily more important than when one was alive, and this idea forms a recurring theme in the film, most notably in the actions of Gerald Tovar, Jr.

Dead bodies are more important (if only briefly) than the living person that body once was.

From the beginning, this Barbara is no wallflower. She is not the younger sister being put upon and mocked by her older brother. There are no Boris Karloff impressions here. The only reference to this key line from the original is that Barbara receives a text from her brother after he drives off without her, having been attacked by zombies. Reduced to text-speak, the screen reads "Coming 4 U Barb." Although Johnny still resents having to drive to a cemetery, this relationship is fundamentally different than the other two. This Barbara will not become catatonic at the threat of danger, as in the original, nor go on an arc of self-discovery and empowerment, as in the 1990 remake.

While Johnny drives, Barbara texts back and forth with her mother, who wants to know if Johnny was late picking her up. The siblings do not live together, nor does either live with (or perhaps even near) their mother. When Barbara reads the text from their mother, Johnny responds, "Of course, Mom, Johnny's always to blame, just like his father." Behind this line is the implication of family strife, an absent father, and a disconnect between the siblings and their parents, reflecting not only the reality of the high number of divorces in the first decade of the twenty-first century but also the fragmented nature of family life. We learn later in the film from Barbara that Johnny and his mother "hated each other."

Furthermore, the only "nice" thing Johnny can say about his aunt is, "At least she never had any kids, so I don't have to deal with a bunch of jerkoff cousins." In the original, Johnny and Barbara drive two hundred miles at the request of their mother to leave a wreath on the grave of their father. This Johnny wishes he didn't have any family so that he would not even have to go to a funeral. A group of people who only see each other once or twice every ten years is gathering in a cemetery, even though none of them actually wants to be there. Familial bonds have devolved to familial obligations.

Johnny mockingly imitates his mother, whom he claims never even liked her sister: "Oh, my family's all gone. What am I going to do?" The mocking dialogue demonstrating the lack of both sincerity and affection between family members. These people do not love each other. In fact, they do not even like each other. And the zombie outbreak literalizes the strife and nonexistent bonds between them.

Johnny is attacked at a distance from the camera and gets into his car and flees, abandoning Barbara. Although Johnny was attacked by two zombies, the 2006 remake's "Cemetery Zombie" is actually Barbara's mother (Marcia Ann Burrs), who attacks her as she turns from the two zombies who went after Johnny. With the attack of the mother zombie, this film completes what was suggested in the original: the complete dissolution of the family and the literalization of a metaphor — families either fall apart, abandon each other or try to kill one another. Unlike in the original and the 1990 remake, in which the Cemetery Zombie attacks are filmed in close shots and are presented very personally, in this version we see two zombies (not very clearly) grapple with Johnny at a distance, and then he flees. Barbara's attack by her mother, however, is filmed in close-up. The events that lead to Johnny's death are no longer close to Barbara. She does not experience the attack nearby but sees it from far away. His death is not a part of her life. Nor is the attack on her by their mother part of his. He simply leaves. Barbara has no family anymore, and from the opening conversation it seems like she did not have much of a family to begin with, since they are so disconnected from one another.

Later on in the film the corpses of Johnny and his mother will return. As Barbara, Ben and Tovar make their way back to the mortuary from the farmhouse, Mother and Johnny emerge from the woods. Seeing them, Barbara throws a rock and calls out, "Go away! I've had enough of you!" The film seems to imply she does not recognize them immediately, but rather thinks she is speaking to zombies in general. One might, however, read a complete lack of grief or sympathy when she does realize who they are, and Ben and Tovar move to kill them. Barbara thought her mother and brother were dead. When they rise from the dead and move toward her, her reaction is not one of mourning but one of aggression. She has "had enough" of her family and wishes to live her life without them.

Tovar attempts to comfort her, telling her, "Sometimes an act of God is the only thing that brings a family together." It sounds like one of the trite things a funeral director of his caliber would say, but Barbara simple rolls her eyes and walks away. The "family" is not brought together — two of the three are zombies, and they are killed a second time. If they had not been shot by Ben, they would have attempted to kill Barbara. The family hated each other in life, and now they hate each other in death.

Barbara is pursued through the woods by the two zombies who initially attacked Johnny. Instead of running to the farmhouse, Barbara runs to a mortuary. A sign identifies it as "Tovar & Son Crematorium and Mortuary." As she runs past the outside of a building, a large, naked man (Mark Sikes) sprawls on top of a man who is revealed to be a priest (Robert DiTillio), biting him. The image is supposed to be shocking, one supposes, although it is also absurd.

The mortuary, in addition to being filled with bodies and body parts, is full of zombies. Barbara is surrounded by zombies in what seems to be a garage when she is rescued by Sig Haig, as comic relief in the form of Gerald Tovar, Jr. After hitting a zombie in the head with a shovel, he tells her, "You can't be in here Miss, employees only. As a matter of fact, you're going to have to leave the ground immediately." Unlike previous *Night*s, in which none of the characters know what is happening or why, Tovar does. He is neither confused nor frightened, only nervous that the situation at the mortuary is getting out of control. Once the actual situation of which he is aware is made known to the audience, both his lines here and the naked man astride the priest make more sense.

Later on in the film we will learn that this zombie outbreak is not from radiation or a virus, nor is it occurring anywhere else. This horror is completely localized to the neighborhood. Unlike the other zombie films of the period, which reflect 9/11 sensibilities, *Night 3D*'s sociophobics concerns the growing scandals in the United States surrounding the mistreatment of corpses at cemeteries, mortuaries and funeral homes. The funeral industry, by 2006, had developed an even worse reputation than it had after the publication of *The American Way of Death*.

Where the Bodies Aren't *Buried*

Two thirds of the way through *Night 3D*, at about the same point in the original where the television broadcast explains the situation, Gerald Tovar, Jr. explains why the dead began rising:

> They started coming back to life about two weeks ago. First it was just a twitch here, a twitch there. I thought it was my mind playing tricks on me. And then some of them got up and started coming and coming. And I knew I couldn't avoid it any more. I had to deal with it.

Ben asks him, "Are you saying the dead have been coming out of the ground for two weeks?" At this, Tovar replies:

> No, no, no. No, not out of the ground. They're not strong enough to get up out of buried coffins. As a matter of fact, I don't even think that most of them that are in the ground are alive. At least, I don't like to think so.

The dead that are coming back are "the ones that were supposed to be cremated."

> Now you know my daddy handled all the cremations. He wanted me to help with it, but I couldn't help with it. I tried. I tried. I tried to do everything exactly the way he wanted. I learned how to do the embalming. And I got real good at that. And I always tried to act right with the families. I just couldn't stand the fire.

It is then revealed that Gerald Tovar, Sr. died two years before and that the bodies that were supposed to be cremated have been stored at the mortuary for two years, hundreds of them. Medical waste and body parts were also supposed to be cremated and were not.

Tovar also reveals that he was unlicensed. To add insult to injury, people "would bring us things that they wanted us to cremate, things that they didn't want to have to report," including medical experiments. Because of "leakage" from the medical experiments, the dead began to reanimate. He is responsible for all of the reanimations and the subsequent zombie-caused deaths.

This exchange establishes several things. First, the theme of the broken family continues with the Tovar family. "Junior," as Henry calls him, tried to please his father, but the death of his father spells his failure as a mortician. Likewise, his duty to his dead father further complicates the situation, as he continues to take in bodies and not dispose of them properly.

Second, the cause of the zombie outbreak is not due to radiation from a Venus probe but because of leakage from medical waste onto stored cadavers. Tovar is an incompetent mortician, and his business is a danger to the community. Rather than warn the local community or work with others to stop the problem, the problem is exacerbated by the cover-up. As seen many times in the period preceding the film (Enron being perhaps the best known example), corporate malfeasance causes problems, but the cover-up makes the effect far worse.

In the case of *Night 3D*, the idea of corporate incompetence, malfeasance and cover-ups within the funeral industry was taken directly from recent news reports of actual mortuary scandals. In 1996 it was revealed that at Paradise Memorial Park in Santa Fe Springs, California, a small city just southeast of Los Angeles, workers dug up old graves and resold plots, stacking six or seven bodies in a single grave (Ramos A7). Over 7000 legal claims were filed, which took six years to resolve (Ramos A7). What followed was a series of unrelated (but similar) scandals at cemeteries in which bodies were not properly disposed of. In Florida, for example, at the Menorah Gardens Cemeteries in 2001, "managers at cemeteries near West Palm Beach and Fort Lauderdale oversold and misplaced plots and dug up and scattered remains to make room for others," eventually resulting in at least 350 bodies being removed, dumped, misplaced or crowded (Kleinberg). That same year also saw an illegal embalming scandal in Houston, Texas.

In February of 2002, as the Sante Fe Springs claims were being settled, another cemetery scandal broke out on the other side of the country—one that attracted much more national attention than those in Texas, Florida or California. In Noble, Georgia, police initially found over eighty decomposed corpses scattered around the grounds of a crematorium at TriState Cemetery ("Corpses Scandal"). The operator, Ray Brent Marsh, was arrested and told police that the incinerator had not been working, so he simply kept the bodies in storage. Tests, however, showed that it *was* working (Roach 252). Some of the bodies may have been left to rot for years. Eventually, three-hundred-

and-thirty-nine different corpses were identified, "stacked in sheds, dumped in a pond, crammed in a concrete burial vault" (Roach 252).

Police had been alerted when a woman walking her dog in the woods nearby found a human skull. The BBC reported that "the local coroner in the town of Noble described the scene as 'the worst horror movie you've ever seen — imagine that 10 times worse'" ("Corpses Scandal"). It is this imagery that seems to have inspired *Night 3D*.

Tovar knows personally the bodies he is handling. They are his friends, neighbors and, mostly, clientele. He takes money from bereaved families in order to prepare the bodies for burial and cremation. Instead, he stores them, accidentally exposing them to some sort of medical waste, which reanimates them. When he first encounters Barbara in the mortuary, he is attacked by the naked zombie. "Mr. Dellamo, please," he pleads with the animated corpse. Tovar is not frightened by the zombies and treats them as misbehaving children who are a disappointment to him. We do not fear the living dead in this film, we fear the individuals who created them and do not take them seriously. Because of Tovar, several people have died. The threat here is not the masses of zombies, the threat is an incompetent businessman in the funeral industry.

Since *Night of the Living Dead 3-D* was released, more cemetery scandals have come to light, including a major scandal at Arlington National Cemetery. In its own poor way, *Night 3D* capitalizes on these scandals but also addresses the very real concern that one's loved ones may not receive the best treatment postmortem, and that one can never be certain if what is buried in a grave or placed in an urn are the actual remains of one's relations.

A Post–9/11 Slasher Film?

After fleeing the mortuary, Barbara continues to run through the woods. She encounters more living dead. These corpses are not fresh, like those of the original or 1990 remake. They have clearly been decomposing for a while. She wrestles with them and is saved by a helmeted man on a motorcycle. She jumps on the back of his bike and they ride away from the corpses. We have just met Ben. Flipping up his helmet mask, he is revealed to be a very young, ostensibly good-looking Caucasian man. Ben is no longer the African American outsider but instead looks like a character from the cast of *The OC*, *One Tree Hill*, or any other WB or CW teen angst drama.

He drives Barbara to the farmhouse, which has no corpses in it, nor anyone hiding in the cellar. Instead, a multicultural, multiethnic family is inside, watching the above-mentioned original *Night*. Cooper, now named "Henry," a pot farmer, his wife, now called "Hellie" (Johanna Black), their daughter

Karen (Alynia Phillips), and "Owen," the stoner farmhand, are unaware that anything unnatural has been happening in the neighborhood.

This situation is not a crisis in *medias res*; it is the beginning of the event for this group. Unlike the original, the Coopers and Tommy and Judy Rose are unaware of the erupting crisis of the reanimated dead. Like the characters in slasher films, they are unaware of the true danger. Unlike the original, the characters in this remake exhibit behaviors traditionally seen in a different subgenre of horror: the slasher film. In a slasher film, a group of individuals, usually representing different and specific types, are in an isolated location where they are stalked and killed off one-by-one in a variety of fashions. Examples include everything from the original *Halloween, Black Christmas* and *Friday the 13th*, to the more recent remakes of those three films, to recent original slasher films like *Urban Legend, Scream* and *Hatchet*.

Slasher films are also morality tales. Teenagers or twenty-somethings go into the woods or some other liminal place in search of illicit activities. They drink, they smoke dope, and they have promiscuous sex. As a result of participating in these activities, they are punished by the killer. The one person who survives is the "final girl," as outlined by Carol J. Clover in *Men, Women and Chainsaws*.

According to Clover, the generic components of the slasher film include: a killer or set of killers (who are often sexually confused, and for whom killing is a sexual substitute), a "Terrible Place" that may seem like a haven but which has a history of "human crimes and perversions," weapons which do not work, and victims who are transgressors (26–34). The survivor is the "final girl" who might be "chased and cornered," but by virtue of not participating in the debauchery and displaying intelligence, creativity and the resourcefulness to survive, either defeats the killer(s) or at least escapes him or them (for now), such as Laurie Strode, Jaime Lee Curtis' character in *Halloween*, or Alice in *Friday the 13th* (35–6).

While not truly focused on punishing sexually active women, this version of *Night* displays all these tropes of the slasher film. The zombies themselves are not Romero's zombies and, truth be told, do not represent much of a threat in this film (although, ironically, they are more directly responsible for the deaths in this version than the original). The "killer" in this film is Gerald Tovar, Jr., who has daddy issues and whose sexuality is undermined and infanticized by his dedication to his father and his belief that he is giving the dead new life. Called "Junior," by all who know him, itself a marker of child not yet become a man, and subsumed into his father's identity, Tovar tricks Ben and Barbara into coming with him so he can feed them to his father. That plot point alone completely transforms this film from a *Night* remake into a standard slasher plotline.

In the slasher film (at least in the first in a series), the killer's identity is not known until the final reel: Mrs. Vorhees in *Friday the 13th*, Angela in *Sleepaway Camp*, etc. Tovar seems to be a simpleton who is overwhelmed by trying to live up to his father's business legacy. Instead, he is revealed to be an insane religious zealot who consciously chose to unleash the zombies in the area. He is the killer; they are victims and tools. When he is finally overwhelmed, killed and consumed by them, it is the righteous justice of the slasher film: he is killed while trying to kill others, and his death is seen as moral comeuppance.

The mortuary is a "Terrible Place" where Tovar's mishandling of the dead resulted in their rising to kill the living. This is not Romero's *Night*, in which a scientific explanation is given for the reanimation of dead tissue all over the world. This film is a tale of vengeful, wronged killer corpses that, rather than being cremated were exposed to medical experiments that reanimated them. Tovar subsequently imprisoned the corpses, believing he was giving them life. "Human crimes and perversions" at the Tovar Mortuary has resulted in the dead rising and attacking the living, as embodied in the previously described image of the naked fat man astride the priest. Tovar's twisted religious views find a metaphor in the image of a naked dead man ravaging a priest — traditional religion is perverted and violated by Tovar's beliefs. The mortuary is a place of human evil. These are not Romero zombies, they are slashers in the service of a slasher.

Guns, especially rifles, were very important in the original and the 1990 remake, but not so much in this one. Ben carries an old revolver which he aims at Henry but actually uses on a reanimated Karen, and later on Barbara's mother and brother, leaving him with one bullet, which Barbara must use on him when he becomes a zombie. Gerald Tovar, Jr. carries a shovel as his weapon of choice, and it is far more effective than the gun at stopping the undead. Clover observes of the slasher genre: "Victims sometimes avail themselves of firearms, but like telephones, fire alarms, elevators, doorbells, and car engines, guns fail in a pinch. In some basic sense, the emotional terrain of the slasher film is pretechnological" (31). *Night 3D* fights a zombie outbreak with pretechnological weapons.

The victims are a diverse group, representing different types. They are also transgressors in the slasher film sense. A young, good looking couple (Ben and Barbara) are at the center, and they keep themselves from the transgressions. Henry, Hellie and "Owen," their stoner farmhand, grow and sell pot.

Tom (Max Williams) and Judy (Cristin Michelle) are the definitive proof that we are not watching a zombie film but a slasher movie. Tom and Judy are not even in the farmhouse with the rest of the group in this film. They are not part of the group. They are out in the barn, listening to rock music, smoking weed and having sex. The first shot of them shows the couple making out while leaning against hay bales in a dimly lit barn, with a pitchfork jammed into the ground in the foreground. This shot could have been lifted directly out of any of the *Friday the 13th* films. Judy's first line is "I'm still hearing that screaming," to which Tom replies, "They're still watching the horror channel." He is intent upon having sex, and they ignore the obvious danger signs.

Like the first *Night* remake, the noises of the living are what draw the zombies. Initially they had surrounded the farmhouse, but when they hear Judy's screams during lovemaking, they leave the house for the barn. It is because they are high and distracted by their lovemaking that the living dead killers can surround and sneak up on them. Tom is torn apart trying to get Judy out of the truck that she has run to. She does not die in a fiery explosion in this *Night*, however. In her fear and negligence (admittedly, she is naked and surrounded by zombies), she leaves the rear window of the truck cab open. The zombies are able to grab and kill her, devouring her remains. They both die in the truck, but unlike in the original, Tom and Judy's deaths are neither tragic nor an accident. They die because they are transgressing the moral code of the slasher film: have sex, do drugs and you die.

Karen in this film was not bitten by a zombie before she is introduced to the audience. Instead, she is a bratty tween who wants to know what is going on, and when not allowed to be part of the adult conversations, she escapes first to her bedroom and then out her window. She is presented as a disobedient child who sneaks out of the house, which in slasher films is a behavior that always gets the killers' attention. She sneaks out to eavesdrop on the conversation about zombies and, as a result, is attacked by a zombie herself, the first person at the house to be attacked. She will return to the house as a zombie, biting and killing Henry. Her literal transgression (she "moves outside the boundaries" of the house) results in the death of herself and her father. Whereas the Karen of the original and Sarah of the remake are innocent victims, this Karen, in a sense, deserves what happens to her.

Owen is the biggest stoner of the bunch, and it is implied he also regularly tries to seduce Hellie. Thus, it is no surprise that he is the first to be bitten inside the house. He is bitten by a zombie that is quickly dispatched by Barbara, who garbs a knife and stabs it in the head. While the others panic, she closes the door to prevent further entrance by other zombies and tries to organize the group to lock the doors and secure the house. Ben performed this function in the original, but here he is just as confused as the others. Barbara, acting as a resourceful final girl, is the one who knows how to resist the evil.

The finale features Barbara as a literal "final girl." Ben, bitten himself, becomes a zombie at Tovar's mortuary and is killed by Barbara with the final bullet in the one gun they have. Immediately the garage door opens, unleashing a horde of zombies, who begin moving toward Barbara. She simply stands there, facing them as they move closer; and although we hear her scream, the film never actually shows her being eaten or attacked. The ending is suggestive of the typical slasher "false death of the killer" and "return of the killer for a sequel" tropes ironically discussed at the end of *Scream*. Unlike the ending of the original, which was unambiguous in its deaths, or the ending of the *Dawn* remake, which, while slightly ambiguous, does imply the deaths of all surviving living characters, this ending shows a defiant Barbara facing the zombie horde with an empty gun but not running away. It is a slasher film ending complete with literal final girl.

Slasher films are indicative of a reactionary morality. There is a good reason why they flourished in the eighties under Reagan. This fact would also explain why *Night 3D* in 2006 re-envisions the narrative as a slasher film. President Bush's administration could be seen as being to the right of Reagan's, and the resurgence of slasher films is indicative of the return of a reactionary morality after 9/11. Under President Clinton, Hollywood gave us ironic and self-aware slasher films, such as *Scream*. Post-9/11 horror cinema returned to the eighties-style slasher: the *Texas Chainsaw Massacre* was remade in 2003. Two thousand and six, the same year *Night 3D* was released, saw a remake of *Black Christmas*, arguably the first slasher film. Rob Zombie's remake of *Halloween* came out in 2007. Nineteen-eighty's *Prom Night* was remade in 2008. Subsequent remakes include *Sorority Row* (2009), *My Bloody Valentine* (2009) and *Nightmare on Elm Street* (2010). *Night 3D* was right in the center of the second slasher film boom.

This trend of remaking slasher films is, as noted previously, primarily economic. There is a built-in audience for a known title, and marketing is much easier. Furthermore, there is also a nostalgia for these films. We are not only post–9/11, we are post–*Scream*. Interestingly, many of these remakes ignore *Scream* and rely on the same trite tropes that trilogy made ironic. And that is their very appeal.

The slasher film creates a simple world and a simple worldview. Those who are smart and avoid transgressing the moral law of America live. Those who break the rules die. Unlike 9/11, which demonstrated that anyone, regardless of behavior or actions, could die simply by going to work or by being in the wrong place at the wrong time, slasher films assert a morality and a meaningful cosmos. There is a comfort in knowing the rules of behavior that lead to death or life. In short, nostalgia for a simple time results in nostalgia for the slasher film, which not only reminds us of a simple time, but also offers a simple and safe worldview. We need not fear a zombie outbreak because that sort of thing only happens to a pot farmer and his family because of the religious delusions of the local mortician. What is missing from this film is Romero's grand worldview. The sociocultural shift demonstrated is one from the fears of the original to an almost infantile desire to control and limit the horror, and explain it through slasher film morality. While reflecting concerns about an untrustworthy funeral industry and the dangers of delusional religious belief, the film ultimately seeks to domesticate Romero's apocalypse into a much more local, comprehensible and controllable one.

None of this analysis, however, is an apology for *Night of the Living Dead 3-D*. The fact that one can see sociocultural concerns embedded in the film does not mean they were put there consciously by the filmmakers, nor does it erase the negative qualities of the movie. Instead, we might note that even poor films whose purpose seems mainly to make money off of other, more talented peoples' visions are still a reflection of the culture and period that produced them. If the film is a horror movie, then the fears reflected, no matter how poorly the film does so (and no matter how little actual fear, terror or horror is generated), are still a reflection of the fears of that society and that time.

Notes

1. Michael Ordofia's review for the *Los Angeles Times* is typical for the film. Entitled "A Waste of Time, Zombies and Plastic Eyeglasses," the review notes, "Even for ultra-low budget, grade-Z horror movies, this is a truly incompetent film ... resulting in food-poisoning-like symptoms in the viewer" (E2).

2. In fact, the film's one true believer, Gerald Tovar, Jr., also dies at the hands of the dead, as a direct result of this small apocalypse. The believer is not saved, just as the unbeliever is not saved. We might read into this a rejection of fundamentalist and literal religious belief. At the very least, the film shows the danger of religious belief with no proof of correctness of efficacy.

5

"Now you better watch this and try to understand what's going on":
Night of the Living Dead: Survivor's Cut (2005)
Night of the Living Dead: Reanimated (2009)
Night of the Living Dead: Origins (2011)

Bunnies!

Arguably the most faithful remake of *Night* is a cartoon. *Night of the Living Dead (in 30 seconds and Re-enacted by Bunnies)* is a highlights reel that compacts the narrative into 30 seconds of 2–3 second sound bites as performed by animated rabbits.

Starz on Demand commissioned that piece from Angry Alien / Jennifer Shiman.[1] Like all of the "30 Second Bunny Theatre" pieces, it is both an amusing tribute to the original and an animated remake that reduces the film down to component images and recognizable lines, including a bunny sheriff telling a bunny reporter, "Yeah, they're dead, they're ... all messed up." A few additional lines are necessary in order to convey the plot of the film as well. At the end, Ben announces, "I'm alive," and then is shot.

Bunny *Night* serves as a synecdoche for *Night*. It reduces the film text down to component moments, images and lines, removing subtlety, nuance and all the other material. The events staged in the cartoon include the Cemetery Zombie attack, the arrival of Ben, the arrival of Harry and Tommy, immediately followed by Harry in the cellar insisting he is right and Karen saying, "I hurt." Ben announces they must get out, and Harry tells him he's crazy. Tom and Judy die; Karen eats her parents; and Barbara is dragged out by zombies all in the space of five seconds. Ben simply comments, "Darn it." He then goes down to the cellar, and, as noted above, gets shot after announcing he is alive.

Though not a remake in the technical sense, it does reduce *Night* down to a series of specific images and sound bites that are not only emblematic of the film but also summarize all of the fears and concerns discussed in the introduction and first chapter. To reduce is to make smaller and simpler, and transform the narrative into a series of references. While one can follow the story without having seen the original, the pleasure of viewing comes from knowing the original and seeing how the entire story can be told in half a minute.

Nor is this *Night* intended as horror. It is parody. No one, apart from Anya on *Buffy the Vampire Slayer* and children traumatized by *Bunicula*, is frightened by bunnies. With the exception of the last film discussed in this chapter, *Origins*, none of the other remakes and remixes discussed here actually seem intended as horror. Instead, they are ruminations on *Night* itself, appropriating parts of the original in order to comment on it or make a new text that amuses, or both. This chapter explores reimaginings of *Night* that use animation and experiments in using the original film footage in new ways.

Survivor's Cut

Like the *30th Anniversary Edition, Night of the Living Dead: Survivor's Cut*, also known as *Benefit of the Living Dead*, is a recut version of *Night*— or, more accurately, a remix of *Night*. The title (both of them) is a play on words, as the project was intended to raise money for the investors who made no money from the original Night due to the loss of copyright. "Survivor's Cut" not only refers to a new "cut" (i.e. edit) of the film, but also the cut of money given to the surviving investors. Like with any good remix, even the title is a playful twist on words, presenting simultaneous and multiple meanings. While originally offered free on Prelinger's Archive website, the film was subsequently released as a DVD as well. "*Benefit of the Living Dead*" suggests that the remix was done not only for the benefit of the story but also to make money for the original artists.

A remix is a non-linear reinterpretation of a work of art, adding and subtracting elements and rearranging original elements into new configurations. While invented in the world of hip-hop and popular music, the remix as a conceptual understanding of texts based on the rearrangement of other texts is now present in film, literature, visual art, and other media. Artist Dean Lachiusa samples *Night*, adding a new introduction (like the *30th Anniversary Edition*), recoloring, new music and sounds. Perhaps most importantly, the events of *Night* are recut in a new order. Thus the film does not begin with Barbara and Johnny; instead, the cemetery scene is presented as a flashback.

Survivor's Cut is therefore technically not a remake but a remix. The remix is interesting to be sure, but it neither introduces a new sociophobic nor emphasizes any of the ones already present. Instead, by rearranging the elements and changing the emphasis from narrative to understanding a known narrative in a new way, the focus moves from fear to *Night* itself. In that sense it falls into the same category as *Reanimated* and even videos which replace the original soundtrack with a comedic one: the original material is rearranged, and the added material is more comment on the original film than it is an investigation of what scares us.

Scary as a Cartoon in MOMA: Reanimated

Night of the Living Dead: Reanimated is a project organized by Mike Schneider, whose screen credit reads "*NOTLD:R* Curated by." The choice of terminology is interesting and indicative of Schneider's intention. In the commentary he notes that he wants to simulate "the gallery experience," and that *Night* was his first "museum." Rather than attempting to remake *Night*, or use it as the raw material for something new, Schneider took the original soundtrack and asked artists to create new visual footage, inspired by the original. The end result included 125 artists (out of 500 who submitted). The final product is a visual remix that might be seen as *Night* meets hip-hop culture — participatory, remixing and mashing up original texts, resulting in a "new" text that is both a version of the original and a fragmented new thing.

The variety of "animations" is remarkable. Some, in fact, are not even animated but rather comic book and manga-style still images. In some of those moments, Schneider or the artist utilize camera movement, not image movement, so that the camera pans across or up or down a still image, giving movement to what is otherwise static, a blend of film and photo. The beginning of the film is mostly still images. The overall effect is to create a sense of stillness and of Barbara's life as static and two-dimensional. Other styles of animation include stop-action with real people, stop-action with figures, stop-action with Lego figures, and even claymation stop-action, rotoscoped images, puppets and video game–style imagery. There is no internal consistency in terms of which style of animation is used in each scene, and the style can shift within scenes and even within a single shot.

As Peter Gutiérrez remarks in the DVD commentary, *Reanimated* is not so much an adaptation of *Night of the Living Dead* as a visual commentary on it. I would argue that it is not just a commentary on *Night*, but on its cultural influence. Several of the animations reference the larger world of zombie culture beyond the original *Night*, but also connect that zombie culture with the original film. When the zombies begin beating on the walls of the house, for example, the living are animated as mice and the dead are cats. The violence is cartoonish, and the overall visual aesthetic is more reminiscent of *Ren and Stimpy* and "Itchy and Scratchy" from *The Simpsons* than any zombie film. Yet the use of a very specific cartoon style both comments on the original as being cartoonish and comments on *Night* as influencing cartoons (*Ren and Stimpy*, *The Simpsons*, and *South Park*, among others, have all done zombie episodes).

Night's tropes also have dominated the development of zombie-based video games. Feedback then occurs in the loop, as *Night* and its children influence games such as *Resident Evil* and *Doom*, which then become films in their own right, not to mention how their visual aesthetic subsequently influences films such as *28 Days Later* and the remake of *Dawn*. *Night: Reanimated* is filled with video game–like moments: Ben killing the zombie with a tire iron when he first arrives at the farmhouse looks like a video game, employing the same animation style as *Resident Evil*.

Later on in the film, while Ben talks to Barbara, another animator transforms the screen into the image of an old-style computer game. The screen is divided into five boxes. Written in the box across the top of the screen is "STATUS: Boarded up pretty solid." Along the left hand side of the screen is a box with the character's name "Barbara," and a second box below it with a pixel character image, clearly Barbara sitting on a couch. Next to this is a box with a list of options: "Examine, Give, Talk to, Use, Open, Push, Close, Pull, Take and Exit," with an arrow pointing toward "talk to." In the box on the bottom of the screen is written first "BEN: This place is boarded up pretty solid now," followed by "BEN: We outghta be all right here for a while," then "BEN: We have a gun, bullets, food and a radio," and finally "BEN: Sooner or later someone's bound to come and get us out"—all while Duane Jones says these lines on the soundtrack. They are then replaced by "BARBARA:..." as there is silence on the soundtrack. The aesthetic here is of very early video role-playing games. Ben and Barbara are characters in which one may type in suggested actions or comments. Their statistics and attributes are also displayed, so that one might know what one is capable of and what the situation is. When Ben's hit points reach zero, he will die. This sequence does for early role-playing video games what other sequences do for cartoons, graphic novels, and first-person shooter games.

When Ben is shot, the film cuts from a still drawing of the chief and Vince to a view of Ben through a videogame-style gun sight. The sight moves slightly back and forth, and then bucks, and we see the figure in the distance drop as if shot. On the one hand, the viewer is implicated in the shooting of Ben. On the other hand, by showing Ben shot dead video-game style in a first-person shooter game, the viewer is linked to the player of the game who just shot Ben. Whereas in the original Ben's death is meant to be shocking and horrifying, the reduction of his death to the shooting of a video game character (for which no one is sad, horrified or mourns) both trivializes his death and simultaneously questions the pleasure one receives from shooting characters in video games. Conservatives may complain about the violence in video games, but this moment in *Reanimated* actually requires that one thinks about the repercussions of taking pleasure at shooting characters in the head. It is the closest *Reanimated* comes to linking to a contemporary sociophobic: that video games numb one to violence and numb one's moral sense.

As John Biguenet indicates, there are a variety of allusive forms in cinema: visual, literary, musical, etc., which can point to other films, culture, literature, etc. (132). Allusion only works, however, if one knows what is being alluded to. In this case, the use of cartoons and video game imagery alludes to these forms and ultimately serves to remind us of *Night*'s influence on, and its similarities to, these other forms.

In another telling moment, the scene in the cellar between Harry, Helen and the very sick Karen Cooper is performed with hand-held Barbie-like dolls. They are in a cardboard box, surrounded by small props and elements which reflect both the mise-en-scene of the original *Night* and the aesthetic of a homemade "Barbie's Dream House," transforming the entire scene into a brilliant series of literalized metaphors. The characters are rigid and unbending. They are awkward. Their lives are parodies of domestic bliss and material success, which Barbie promotes. They are empty, soulless individuals now manipulated by the situation rather than their own free will.

Some of the news sequences are done with sock puppets. These also contain numerous references to other zombie films: under the four clocks are the words "Night" "Dawn" "Day" and "Land," and the names of the rescue centers are all references to other zombie films (Pittsburgh: "Fiddler's Green"; and McKeesport: "Ormsby Public Health Department," a reference to Alan Ormsby, the co-writer and star of *Children Shouldn't Play with Dead Things*). Such references are "Easter eggs"— allusions for the knowledgable fan while deconstructing what is actually happening in the film. The sock puppets themselves become literalized metaphors, this time for the media, which are puppets of the government and the corporations that pay for them. They do not offer any real assistance or insight. They are entertainment, and not very good entertainment at that. In another news sequence, the silhouettes of the characters are shown as we circle behind them. We watch the news with them. The viewer is visually united with the characters as we all watch the screen within the screen. Watching characters watching other characters becomes a comment on the echo chamber of the media experience.

Perhaps the biggest thing to take away from *Reanimated* is both the idea of "public domain" and the idea that individuals can transform a text. The dominant forms of American art right now are postmodern reimaginings of other works of art: collage, remix, mashup, remake, etc. The advent of the internet has further transformed how culture is created and disseminated. While film and television continue to dominate the entertainment industry, You Tube and other digital sharing systems allow for anyone who can afford the basic technology to create their own texts. Hollywood no longer solely controls the means of production. Things go viral. We have memes. *Night* can be reproduced with Legos and seen by millions. As a result, *Reanimated* is part of a much larger milieu of fan-created culture. It does not generate fear or refer to any major sociophobic outside of itself, but it does generate insights into how *Night* is seen now. Sadly, for the current generation, it has lost its power to frighten.

Similar to *Reanimated* is a much earlier project. *Reanimated* kept the soundtrack and replaced the images with new, animated (or not-so-animated ones). In 1991, a group of LA-based comedians kept the images and replaced the soundtrack. *Night of the Day of the Dawn of the Son of the Bride of the Return of the Revenge of the Terror of the Attack of the Evil, Mutant, Alien, Flesh Eating, Hellbound, Zombified Living Dead Part 2: In Shocking 2-D* used the film but removed the soundtrack and replaced it with their own in order to radically change the story and the meaning. James Riffel, working under his stage name Lowell Mason, wrote, directed and did many of the voices for the new soundtrack. This version of *Night* removes any intention to scare or frighten or refer to any sociophobic. It is a cartoon which takes the images of *Night*, creates a new narrative with them (aimed at generating laughs, not shivers), and, along the way, points out the ridiculousness of some of *Night*.

Similarly, *Mad Movies*, a late-night television series in the eighties produced by Kent Scov and the L.A. Connection Comedy Theatre, featured a *Night of the Living Dead* episode. Like Riffel, *Mad Movies* would remove the soundtrack of a public domain film and then redub it to tell a new story. Whereas Riffel did it by himself, *Mad Movies* featured a full cast of regular improvisational performers who worked collectively to dub the film. In the *Mad Movies* version, Barbara became "Darlene," who was planning a big house party, and Ben was "Dwayne," her cousin, who was there to help with snacks and music. The zombies cry out "Surprise," only to be told it is not a surprise party.

With both of these redubbed versions, the images of *Night* with a new soundtrack transform the zombie film into comedy. Obviously, in doing so any sociophobic is removed, and the film is not about fear but humor. Although frequently humor and horror are two sides of the same coin, such as in *Shaun of the Dead*, there must be moments when the humor is subsumed under the fear. Not so in the dubbed version, where humor is the sole goal.

A Return to a Beginning That Never Was: Origins

As of this writing, *Night of the Living Dead: Origins* is reportedly in post-production but not yet released.² It should be noted, therefore, that much of what I write here is entirely conjecture based on a few advanced articles, an IMDB page, and the production company's promotional information. The final version might be significantly different, and this section of this chapter should be read with this in mind.

Written and directed by Zebediah DeSoto, and as of this writing titled *Night of the Living Dead: Origins 3D*, the film is a computer-generated animated remake of *Night*, beginning with the start of the outbreak. The actors providing the voices are also a compilation of horror-familiar and recycled Romero: Tony Todd, who played Ben in the 1990 remake, voices Ben. Bill Mosley, who played Johnny in the 1990 remake, voices Johnny. Joseph Pilato, who played Rhodes in the original *Day*, voices Harry Cooper. Thus *Origins* is also an intertextual remake, referencing *Day* and the first *Night* remake especially.

Origins has updated the setting, placing the narrative in a post–9/11 world, not unlike the remakes of *Dawn* and *Day*. DeSoto has also been influenced by the images and "tone" of the 1992 Los Angeles riots, in the wake of the Rodney King verdict (Snellings 9). DeSoto has set the film in a New York City brownstone, which also radically changes the narrative. *Origins* now sets the beginning of the zombie apocalypse in an urban, not rural, setting. Furthermore, New York is not Pittsburgh, a mid-sized city in America's rust belt with a very distinctive identity and sense of self. We might note, therefore, that this version is an adaptation of Romero's characters and some of the story elements into a new location.

The location of New York is very much in keeping with post–9/11 horror. In the wake of the terrorist attacks on America, New York is not only Ground Zero but also Ground Zero for the embodiment of American fears. Films such as *Cloverfield* set horror narratives in Manhattan, and adapted narratives not set in New York are remade in that location. H.G. Wells' *The War of the Worlds* is set primarily in London. The 1953 film version is set primarily in Los Angeles. The 2005 Steven Spielberg version is set in and around New York. Richard Matheson's novel *I Am Legend*, which inspired the original *Night*, is set in contemporary Los Angeles, as was the 1971 adaptation *The Omega Man*. The 2007 film version, however, moves the action to New York City. After 9/11, New York is the face of American horror.

The film also moves the starting point of the narrative to before the dead begin to walk. DeSoto claims an interest in both the characters' backstories and "how they first encountered the zombie plague, and their own personal circumstances" (quoted in Snellings, 9)—hence, "origins" (where did these people come from, what experiences did they have as the dead began to rise?). The original *Night* begins in medias res. Tom, Judy and the Coopers are already in the cellar. Beakman's diner is in the past. DeSoto returns to the beginning moments and backstories. The overall effect might well be to erase the cinema verité of the original in favor of a more traditional style of narrative.

The origin of *Origins*, then, as confirmed by images from the film, is not just the original *Night* but also a video game visual aesthetic. In games such as *House of the Dead, Resident Evil, Dead Rising, Dead Space* and *Left for Dead*, the character's backstory is given as the game begins and then follows a series of situations in which the characters must fight their way through hordes of zombies on the way to achieving a series of smaller objectives, many of which are also first-person shooters. Although the information needed is slight (after all, the point of playing the game is to shoot zombies, not understand a character's persona), the game must require some form of identity for the character and the situation.

April Snellings reports that Zebediah de Soto looks to "expand upon Romero's apocalyptic vision, rather than simply exploit it" (9). The word Snelling uses is "epic," although DeSoto is more specific when he says he "really want[s] to blow up the scope and make this the *Empire of the Sun* of zombie movies" (9). The key to understand the context of *Origins* is this idea of "scope." Romero's original is small in scope: the action predominantly takes place within a single location, a house, and the characters can only tap into the bigger picture through media. This version is much bigger, removing the intimate feel of the original in order to create urban horror which stands for a global apocalypse. Vietnam may have been at a distance, but 9/11 was right here. Though more people died in Vietnam, it was not as spectacular, experienced in real time, nor on home soil. Thus *Origins* uses the tropes and story of *Night* to reframe the 9/11 experience as zombie movie.

In their own ways, all of the projects discussed in this chapter reframe *Night* in various ways. In doing so they rarely embody a new sociophobic and as frequently remove the ones already present in the film, reducing it to comedy or an intellectual curiosity. Even those framed as aiming to be higher art (*Survivor's Cut, Reanimated*) are more comment on the film itself than on society. Perhaps that is why this is the shortest chapter in the book: remaking *Night* by reframing it through changing the soundtrack or the images, or by using animation to narrate the story, ultimately becomes more about *Night* than about the ideas and fears behind night. The iconic lines and images of the film are shifted around, removed or replaced, or reduced to soundbites and freeze frames. What is ultimately reduced to nothing is any sense of horror or fear or what we should be afraid of. This observation is not a criticism, just a fact, and for that reason, *Reanimated* and other remixes are no more about sociophobics than bunny zombies, no matter how much fun or funny they are.

Notes

1. The original animation may be found on the Angry Alien Website at http://www.angry alien.com/0206/NOLDbuns.asp, alongside dozens of other films parodies done in 30 seconds with bunnies.

2. Although Snellings's article lists a 2010 release date for *Origins*, according to the Internet Movie Database, the actual release date is 2011, and the film is now fully titled *Night of the Living Dead: Origins 3D* (see http://www.imdb.com/title/tt1512222/).

Interlude: Living Dead, Live! *Night of the Living Dead* on Stage and in Other Media

Night of the Living Dead has enjoyed a considerable afterlife in other media. It inspired a song by the Misfits (1979), subsequently remade by 88 Fingers Louis and the Troublemakers, and is the title of an entire live album by Southern metal band Jackyl (1996). It was novelized by John A. Russo and has been adapted into a graphic novel. One of the most interesting phenomena is the adaptation of the film for live performance in front of an audience. This chapter is not a comprehensive survey of live stage performances but rather a sampling of the many theatrical performances of the past fifteen years in order to understand *Night* remade in front of a live audience.[1]

Night on stage is not just another remake; it is an adaptation across media, moving from medium to medium — from film to stage. Thus, already it is a different experience. Theater, unlike film, is a social art. Film requires collaboration at the production stage, but one may encounter film alone. Indeed, as I write this I am watching *Night of the Living Dead* alone. With the advent of home theater technology (VHS, DVD, etc.), one need never watch a film in the company of others again. Theater, on the other hand, by definition is live and collaborative. In order for theater to exist, there must be at least two people: an actor and an audience in the same space together.

Theater transforms the filmed image (colored lights on a wall with a soundtrack, or digital images with a soundtrack) into a live presence. The audience is in the same space as the characters in the film. Whether *The Lion King*, *Legally Blonde: The Musical*, or *Night of the Living Dead*, the film narrative on stage is transformed not only by the changes in narrative and character (often required by the medium — theater has no digital effects, jump cuts, montages, etc., though it can simulate them in different, albeit self-aware ways), but by the new medium itself. Theater is live; it is spatially and temporally located. If one wants to watch the 1990 remake of *Night*, one may rent or buy the DVD and watch it as many times as one wants, wherever one wants. If one wants to see the Maverick Theater performance of their adaptation of *Night of the Living Dead*, one must go to the theater in Fullerton, California, at 8:00 pm, Wednesday through Sunday nights in October of that particular year. By 9:45 pm, that particular remake of *Night of the Living Dead* is over and will never exist again, as theater is also ephemeral, since it is live. Even if one returns to the same particular theater to see the same group of actors the very next night, the performance is different.

Given the ephemeral nature of *Night* as live stage performance, the presentation itself can be different, depending on the specific nature of the production and the time of production. The sociophobics will be different than in the film, but they will also reflect those found within the film. Any performance of *Night* is self-aware meta-cinema, especially if the live performance is using the original or commenting on it through the use of film/projection, as some productions do. *Night* live is haunted, in Marvin Carlson's sense, by *Night* the film. Our culture is haunted by our cinema. We remember and compare any and all *Night*s we have encountered.

One may present *Night* on stage as a straightforward adaptation, translating the action of the film to the stage as much as possible, echoing the film and imitating it as close as possible. One may present *Night* with variations — adding, subtracting or changing things. One may also present *Night* as camp, either intentionally or unintentionally. The period-specific nature of *Night* makes many lines laughable. And where the film might still offer genuine scares, what frightens on celluloid, filmed in what appears to be a real cemetery, becomes much less scary and much more laughable when performed in front of styrofoam tombstones and in the same space where a month before one sat through *Annie* or a Neil Simon play. What might seem on the surface to be potentially more frightening — sharing the same physical space as the living dead — does not always scare, especially since the willing suspension of disbelief becomes much more difficult in that same space.

We must also consider the motivations of both artist and audience when *Night* is put on stage. The audience attends more often than not because they are fans of the film, but that very reason creates expectations that are not necessarily met by the live performance (which, of necessity, cannot recreate the film but only a simulacrum of it). The reasons for producing *Night* vary, although money is certainly a major reason. Linda Hutcheon argues that adapting film for the stage is "obviously economically driven" (5). Although she writes of *The Lion King* or *The Producers*, this observation holds true for stage versions of *Night* as well. Hutcheon further argues that those who know and love the original film will seek out a stage version, but, additionally, "new consumers will be created" (5).

Several theaters present *Night* every year around Halloween, as it is clearly a seasonal moneymaker. The Blue Monkey Theater Company in Portland, Oregon, for example, has given multiple productions throughout the first decade of the twenty-first century, using Lori Allen Ohm's script (discussed below), directed by John Monteverde. The Maverick Theater in Fullerton, California, is, as of this writing, in its fifth season of performing *Night* as their "Annual Haunt."[2] For such companies, the repetition is not merely because of artistic satisfaction, but because audiences are virtually guaranteed to attend, raising revenue. Frequently, but not always, these productions are offered at Halloween-time, which makes them a higher-culture version of a haunted house. One goes with the expectation to be harmlessly frightened or engage in the spirit of the season in a manner that watching a genuinely frightening or disturbing film would render unenjoyable.

Yet many other plays always generate a paying audience, and artists usually need other reasons for selecting a particular script or project. I suggest another major reason for the numerous stage productions of *Night* is participatory culture (in Henry Jenkins' sense). The artists that stage *Night* are engaging in the same activity as fans who make their own versions of *Star Trek* or *Star Wars*, or who write fan fiction. Debbie Rochon, defending the additions to *Night of the Living Dead* in 1998 and her presence in the *30th Anniversary Edition*, said, "To any one of my critics out there I ask them this: If you were asked to be cut into your favorite film, would you say no?"[3] *Night* live is a means by which local actors and artists can put themselves into a film they love. It is a means for directors to take what they love, Romero's film, and be part of recreating it. Then an audience comprised of fans of the original joins together with artists who are fans in a participatory performance in which *Night* is recreated and all play a role.

In some cases the audience can literally join in the recreation of the film on stage. The Coterie Theatre in Kansas City, Missouri, in 2007 and 2008 produced *Night of the Living Dead* as an onstage production. In addition to the regular cast of characters, locals could play a zombie in the production. Coterie offered a class in how to be a zombie, and the extras performed each night.[4] Not only did this practice generate a larger audience, as people came to see their friends as zombies, it more fully broke down the barriers between audience and artists, since the theater's patrons could become part of the play.

Night is also very popular among younger generations, many of whom were not yet born when the original was produced and presented. Student productions have proven remarkably popular at universities and numerous high schools.[5] To cite just two, the University of Akron in 2005 and the Rose-Hulman Institute of Technology in Terre Haute, Indiana, in 2008 both presented stage adaptations of *Night*. Assuming an average age of 18–23 (the average age of college students), most of the student artists were all born between 1982 and 1985 (in the case of the former) and 1985 and 1990 (in the case of the latter). All of these students were born after *Night* and *Dawn*, and some were born after *Day*. Yet they want to present a play based on a zombie film released in 1968.

Partly this desire comes out of the above-mentioned participatory culture. Partly it is also a play that allows one to do as one pleases with it in order to generate scares and have fun. As noted earlier, productions of *Night* can also be seen as a higher-culture version of a Halloween haunted house. *Night*, like any local "haunted house" at Halloween, has a built-in audience with built-in expectations. One way that we can view the live *Night* phenomenon is as a narratively-structured local haunted house. One attends for the low-level-to-nonexistent frights. Sally Bosco, for example, reviewing the 2009 Jobsite Theatre Company production in Tampa, Florida, noted that she was not a fan of horror films and did not like to be scared, but that she enjoyed the production very much (Bosco). Haunted houses usually do not get reviewed in the theater arts section of the newspaper, but productions of *Night* do.

In this interlude I analyze a half-dozen productions that presented *Night* in different ways and adapted it using different techniques. Some were straightforward. Some were camp. Some were unintentionally funny; others very specifically were intentionally funny. Some used film or video, some used the original film, some stayed very close to the original film, others offered extreme adaptations. All of them form remakes that comment on the original. The four types of adaptation that we will encounter are metacinematic, straightforward horror, camp and some combination of two or more of the above. Note there is no evolution or teleology here (although the productions are presented chronologically)—just four different ways to approach *Night* for the stage. Other techniques and elements will also be used, but these are the four approaches. Lastly, we should note that unlike in the cinematic remakes, there is no new sociophobic incorporated into the play. While in some cases, like Gangbusters' production in Los Angeles in 2006, the horror culture of post–9/11 is present on the stage, the current social fears are almost stunningly absent from stage productions of *Night of the Living Dead*, in favor of a tribute to the original film.

The first stage adaptation was Squonk Opera's 1995 piece *Night of the Living Dead: The Opera*.[6] Squonk Opera is a performance collective headed by Jackie Dempsey and Steve O'Hearn, based in Pittsburgh and founded in 1992. As the name suggests, it is a blend of high and low culture, employing images, music, humor and spectacle to create self-referential, surrealistic multimedia performance pieces (ten to date). In 1995, Squonk Opera was commissioned by Marc Masterson, then artistic director of Pittsburgh City Theatre, to create *Night of the Living Dead: The Opera*.

Night: The Opera was, first and foremost, not an opera in the traditional sense. Instead, the film *Night of the Living Dead* was projected on a screen in the theater and in front of the screen the company presented a live performance somewhat like, but also significantly different from, "the floorshow" at screenings of *The Rocky Horror Picture Show*. In some sense, the performance deconstructed ideas of high and low culture by blending behaviors and expectations from movie-going and opera-attending. Patrons were given wrapped hard candy and encouraged to unwrap it all at the same time, creating the first sound-piece of the "opera." Live music was then created on stage as the film was projected, with additional visual moments offering counterpoint and juxtaposition. For example, while the living dead ate the remains of Tom and Judy, the members of Squonk Opera sat down and drank tea and ate scones. The civility of the "high culture" event on the stage was in conversation with the cannibalistic orgy projected behind it. One of the first stage productions of *Night*, therefore, was a multi-media event that formed a comment on the film by projecting the movie and offering a live performance in front of it as counterpoint.

This approach has been echoed by other groups and performance collectives, such as the Mayfair Theatre in Ottowa, Ontario, in July 2010, which featured a projection of the film, with live performers in front of the screen accompanied by live music. Rather than a full remake or adaptation, these versions form a kind of commentary on the original. Squonk Opera's version commented on the film as a Pittsburgh cultural property, but also commented on the different natures and expectations of theater and film. In doing so, they also encourage the audience to view the film as a critical exercise and actively participate in the creation of meaning from it. These productions also rely upon the production of live music. Both Squonk and Mayfair used live music to adapt *Night*. The music forms its own commentary and level of reference to the film. Eventually the soundtrack itself would be remade and sampled by 400 Lonely Things (discussed later).

Other productions blend live and filmed elements in the service of narrative, rather than to comment on the original. In Denver, Colorado, beginning in 2008, the Bug Theatre produced a stage version of *Night*, now an annual production. Bug Theatre's production employs metacinema, straightforward horror, and camp to tell the story. They also use video and additional material to shape the narrative. The scenes that take place in the cemetery are shown on television monitors as filmed footage of the outdoor scenes, bridging the gap between live theater and film. Interestingly, the televisions also tell the story of the corpses in the house (something that *Night* 1990 also does) and the backstory of the Cooper family, including how Karen came to be bitten. By reframing the experience with literal cinematic flashbacks and backstory, the Bug Theatre production reframes *Night* as television leading to live experience.

The second major stage production, which has seen its script performed in many places all over the United States, also premiered in Pennsylvania, where, of course, *Night* began. Lori Allen Ohm's adaptation premiered at the Roadhouse Theatre for Contemporary Art in Erie, Pennsylvania, in September of 2000, directed by Ohm. To this author's knowledge, Ohm's version is the only one that has been published as a script for others to perform.

Ohm's script is practically a transcript of the film, with a few additions. The set consists of the farmhouse, with an area set aside to represent the cemetery and the outside of the farmhouse. The script demonstrates clearly how adapting the story to a live stage production, with a single set if one wants to recreate naturalistic cinema (and *Night* is nothing if not cinema verité), requires additional dialogue to replace action and image that would simply be photographed in a film. Actions which take place outside the house once the characters are in the house are described in dialogue:

BEN: They're smashin' out my headlights, man. (*Pause.*) Two of them" [14].

There is no need for such a line in the film because Romero shows it. In other words, Ohm's script results in a cinema of image transformed back into a theater of spoken word.

In theater, language makes reality. When I walk on stage and someone else says, "Our cousin Hamlet and our son," the reality that I am Hamlet is established. When, later in the same play, the English Ambassador enters and says, "Rosencrantz and Guildenstern are dead," the audience has not been shown their execution or their corpses. It is simply the words that have made the reality. In theater, words are privileged; whereas cinema, as a form of photography, privileges the image. When *Night* is live, we do not see, we are told. So, for example, one of the biggest differences in the narrative is the death of Tom and Judy, which takes place off-stage and out of sight. Ben shouts from off-stage that the truck is on fire (we never learn how or why this happened). We hear the explosion and see Helen's horrified reaction. Ben re-enters alone and beats Harry, who, as in the film, refused to open the door. Gone is the explosion itself, Ben's fight back to the door, and the direct reveal of flesh-eating.

Interestingly, at the end of the scene the zombies enter carrying body parts adorned with pieces of Tom and Judy's costumes, and begin to consume the flesh. So the big horrific moment of cannibalism is preserved, even if the moment of accidental death is not. The moment of flesh-eating is presented, but because the explosion is not shown, we do not see the zombies pulling the body pieces out of the truck; thus Tom and Judy must be identified by their costumes. More likely, the audience, being a "knowing audience," knows what comes next and assumes, when body parts are seen, that they are Tom and Judy's. The overall effect, however, is to mute the horror of the moment.

Another radical change in the script is that the television broadcast sequences play out on a side stage. Characters watch the television in the house, which faces upstage, away from the audience. The newscaster and the other characters appearing on television thus represent what they are watching on television on another part of the stage.

Ohm's script, most importantly, represents an attempt to simulate a black and white film in real life:

> With the optional exception of blood, the entire production is staged in black and white, including the main setting, lighting, properties, costumes, hair and makeup [9].

In other words, the script attempts to recreate a black and white film live in front of an audience. The designs are thus all in shades of black, white and gray, making the experience unreal if not surreal. The real world is rendered into black and white. This technique serves as a distancing device, as well as one trying to approximate period film as much as possible. Yet the danger is in rendering the production camp. Not every production follows this mandate — other productions using Ohm's script have been in "full color."

Ohm's script is also reductive, reducing some of the complexity of the film to more simple elements easier to track on stage. Ohm buys the Venus probe theory, as the first scene of the play is one not found in the film:

> A sudden, bright flash of light represents the radiation from the Venus probe. Pause. Lights up in the audience to a late, hazy afternoon in the graveyard. Two unburied corpses rise and trundle over the grounds to exit [9].

Missing from the script, therefore, is any ambiguity about why the dead are reanimating.[7] Two things should also strike the reader immediately: the sociophobics of *Night* performed live on stage are muted. None of the millennial fears one might expect from the year 2000 are present. On the other hand, the profound influence of subsequent zombie films and other, more recent examples of zombie culture are seen in the rising of the dead. We see the dead climb out of graves, which is derived more from *Thriller* or *Return of the Living Dead* and its sequels, or even *Children Shouldn't Play with Dead Things*, than *Night*.

The play then has a very quick denouement. The last two scenes, containing the deaths of Barbara, Harry, Helen, Karen and, eventually, Ben, plays out in three pages consisting mostly of stage directions. As in the film, Ben survives the night. The final scene has "Chief McClellan" and the deputies enter through the audience, just as the zombies did earlier, in order to invade the farmhouse. Both the zombies and the posse move through the audience (the "house" in theatrical terminology) in order to enter the house. Both the dead and the living come from "us." This theatrical moment is an echo of *Night* 1990's "we're them and they're us" conclusion, but it also reflects that everything bad comes from us—the audience. We want to see zombies kill and we want to see zombies killed. Likewise, both zombies and posse consists of everyday individuals now driven to a new purpose. An audience is a group of individuals who come together and exhibit mob behavior. The audience all act similarly, have a code of behavior, and can be lead to have thoughts, feelings and reactions that each person might not have had individually. It is this "mob mentality" that produces both zombies and posses.

Using a strobe effect, Ben is shot in the living room as the deputies enter the front door. Then follows the stage direction:

> ZOMBIES enter from every direction. DEPUTIES cross to BEN'S body, one with a meat hook raised. All ZOMBIES flood the house to envelop the DEPUTIES. Howling, CHIEF MCCLELLAN careens through the front door with a ZOMBIE clinging to him, gorging on his neck. Blackout. Long pause. Lights fade up. All ZOMBIES, including DEPUTIES and CHIEF McClellan [now zombies], rise and turn their attention to the audience. Blackout [45–46].

This ending is much bleaker than the original. Not only does Ben die, the entire posse dies. The posse then turns on the audience and begins moving toward them. It is threatening, but it is also an inversion of the earlier scene.

Zombies have moved through the audience throughout the performance, unnoticed by the audience. The fourth wall is firmly in place, even as the living dead move through the aisles. After the last human dies on stage, the audience suddenly is noticed and becomes a target for the zombies. The audience, while not technically assaulted, is suddenly "seen." While this moment can be, and is, rather amusing, it can also be a truly uncanny one. We have seen *Night* before, but for the first time *Night* is seeing us. It is uncanny in that the audience sees the zombies and sees the zombies seeing them. Although one is always that aware the zombies are in makeup and are merely actors, the sudden breaking of the fourth wall reminds us of the threat posed to us by what we have just seen. Like in a film, however, when the credits roll the illusion is restored, in the theater the curtain call, when the zombies emerge to take a bow and acknowledge the audience it removes the threat and dispells the uncanny moment.

Another version, interestingly termed "Translated by" Leon Shanglebee, was directed by Christian Levatino at the Stella Adler Theatre in Los Angeles in 2006 and produced by the Gangbusters Theatre Company. Shanglebee wrote in the program, "You're about to see suspense, tension, drama, blood, terror, violence and death.... I kept all the juice from the movie and added a couple of things only a true fan would ever notice.... This is a horror play based on a movie."[8] By identifying the production as a "horror play," Shanglebee indicates the production's intention to remain horror and not turn to camp, while still acknowledging the transition from one medium to another (which is, perhaps, what Shanglebee means by "translated by").

The play was performed on one of the stages at the Stella Adler Theatre, with two television monitors showing "live video feed" from outside the house. As the audience watched the play from inside the house, they could also watch the dead slowly surrounding the outside of the house on the television monitors. The noises of the living dead knocking on walls and windows was matched by the video feed of the dead (backstage, presumably) pounding their fists on the walls. The images suggested nothing so much as video feed from security cameras. The monitors also played the television news reports as the characters within the farmhouse watched them. The overall effect was to further mediate the experience in a manner very different from Squonk Opera or Bug Theatre. Whereas Squonk performed other things in front of the original film, and Bug employed previously filmed footage in order to provide the backstory for the live action the audience was about to see, Gangbusters presented live action mediated through video. What was appearing on the televisions was also happening live in the theater at the same time. The audience received a mediated version of a live performance, not a recording of a performance given previously in a cemetery or in a studio. Gangbusters preserved the liveness of the event, in Philip Auslander's sense, but mediated it, simulating how we now experience catastrophe: as it happens, but through a television.

Leon Shanglebee also wrote, "So sit back and watch seven people fuck up any chance of survival." The emphasis in this case, without the zombies in the audience as Ohm had, was on the humans falling apart within the farmhouse. We see live on television what happens outside the house as we also witness the destruction of everyone within the house. In a sense, this is a stage *Night* for post–9/11 theater. Just as America watched things happen on television and worried it might also be happening right outside the window, this *Night* played with the mediation of crisis and the direct experience of crisis, and how it lead to catastrophe within the home. Again, though, the overall sociophobics of *Night* were lost in the translation to the stage. The experience echoed the experience of 9/11 and perhaps was informed by the experience of 9/11, but was not a comment on or an exploration of 9/11 as horrific experience. This *Night* was not about what frightened us, it simply tried to startle or shock the audience into fear using techniques that made the events on stage seem as real and horrific as possible to a 2006 audience.

Squonk Opera created a self-aware, meta-cinematic live *Night* by interacting with the film itself. Ohm and her company attempted to recreate a black and white film on stage. Gangbusters attempted to create a straight horror play through the use of video and live action to recreate a catastrophe that was both mediated and experienced. Other groups, however, reject an attempt to create explicit horror in favor of camp or humor, and still others attempt to blend horror and camp, recognizing the challenge in making a live *Night* effective as straight horror.

The Riverfront Playhouse in Aurora, Illinois, in September and October 2007 presented *Night of the Living Dead: The Musical*, with book by Jack Schultz and music and lyrics by Jack Schultz and Kathleen Dooby. Unlike Shanglebee, who claimed that his "horror play" was full of "suspense, tension, drama, blood, terror, violence and death," Schultz argued for the impossibility of live horror, particularly of this kind of outdated horror in a post–9/11 America and in a more theatrically sophisticated culture:

> Of course the play is campy. There's no way to treat such miserably dire circumstances as these folks are experiencing at the hands of something as ridiculous as reanimated corpses and not incorporate any humor. The music is intended to supplement the campiness.[9]

Schultz also calls the situation "melodramatic," although he also stated that the horror was not "completely neutralize[d]."

Schultz is right. One of the strengths of the original *Night* was that it was able to transcend its own melodrama and drive-in schlock origins and offer a truly terrifying film infused with sociophobics that reflected its time. Schultz's point of view is that the film's narrative does not have a transhistorical horror that is the equivalent of the original period. Its melodrama, transcended at the time, seems hokey and dated now. In order to place this same story on stage now, Schultz's solution is to embrace the inherent ridiculousness of the piece in a contemporary context and play it as camp.

The musical genre is already inclined to camp by heightening the already ridiculous. In musicals, the characters' emotions and thoughts are so large they cannot be contained by speech and so must be sung. The musical lends itself to camp because it relies both on artifice and excess in order to create effect. *Night* lends itself to camp for the same reasons, not to mention that the 1960s performance style now seems very affected and artificial. The arch emotions and gravity behind the character's lines allow sophisticated audiences and artists to treat the material ironically, distancing themselves from the horrific aspects of the narrative and instead embracing it with irony. As a result, productions such as Riverfront Playhouse's *Night* are less interested in capturing the horror of *Night* (and thus exposing the sociophobics behind it) than laughing at the narrative for taking any such concerns so seriously. Unlike metacinematic productions, which use distancing devices, such as video, to enhance and recapture the horror of the film, musicals use the distancing device of music to allow the audience to take an ironic stance and not be frightened at all.

In Tampa, Florida, in October and November 2009, the Jobsite Theatre Company at the Shimberg Playhouse, David A. Straz Center for the Performing Arts performed the Ohm script under the direction of Chris Holcom. Jobsite adds another layer of performance by having zombies in the parking lot and theater lobby. On the one hand, this technique might be seen as camp, as it also creates a "haunted house" or theme park experience, robbing the production of the slow reveal of the living dead. On the other hand, one is attending a production entitled "*Night of the Living Dead*," so the zombies are not only expected, they are demanded. By having the audience encounter the living dead immediately, the production challenges expectations held by a "knowing" audience while making the event more of an experience. The zombies break the fourth wall as one is exiting one's car, an experience Ohm's script reserves for the last thirty seconds of the play; and one is invited to engage the zombie apocalypse as part of the production experience. One does not just watch Jobsite's *Night*, one is an active presence.

Like Coterie, Jobsite also uses "guest zombies." The overall effect of these two techniques is to localize the experience. Whereas the play is set in Western Pennsylvania, having zombies in the parking lot and some of the zombies known to the audience as people from their own everyday experience has the effect of moving the zombie apocalypse to something that is happening *here and now*. Unlike the mediated experiences of Bug or Gangbusters, Jobsite emphasizes the liveness of the event. Jobsite uses the spatial and temporal locality of theater in order to transform *Night* into local horror.

Conversely, however, the performers also treat the material as camp. Sally Bosco, a reviewer for *Arts Net, Tampa Bay*, in her 2009 review, stated:

> The play is entirely faithful to the original 1968 film, almost line-for-line it would seem. The original was absolutely not funny, yet this cast plays it for comedic effect when there is none inherent in the script. The audience desperately wanted it to be funny, so the cast played up every little glance and nuance possible, while still remaining faithful to the original film script.

This analysis raises several interesting questions. It praises the production for being "faithful," but "faithful" is a problematic term at best. Faithful to what? Bosco seems to mean that it is an accurate repetition of the words and situations of the film; but if the actors are playing it for comedy, can the production actually be said to be "faithful"? Instead, it is an accurate recreation of the lines and narratives, but done for the purposes of entertainment — faithful to the text but unfaithful to the spirit of the original.

Bosco focuses on the production as camp or comedy, and notes that it becomes such due to both the artists and the audience. The audience "desperately wanted it to be funny" (one wonders how she knows what an entire audience wanted), so the actors "played up" the comedy while somehow "remaining faithful." In this case, a perceived lack of horror and fear on the audience's part was either reinforced or created by a lack of genuine horror on the stage. *St. Petersburg Times* critic Marty Clear referred to the production as "lighthearted," and observed, "Things that once were scary now make an audience laugh" (Clear). I would argue that while other companies have tried to create a live *Night* that maintains some sense of the horror, Jobsite's production is emblematic of a contemporary theater company's concern that the material is no longer capable of eliciting horror, and that the original is both so well known and incapable of being accurately recreated on stage that a straightforward production will be seen as camp anyway, so the camp aspect is embraced as the path of least resistance.

Onstage remakes of *Night of the Living Dead* do not necessarily display any sociocultural shift in fear. Rather than focus on horrors found outside the cinema, the focus of a stage production is the original film itself. Any horror to be found is a general one: the zombies are out to get you, and they are here now. *Night* onstage is a Halloween horror house that constructs the zombie as ghost, vampire or general Halloween monster. Let us remember, the film is not set in October. It is, rather, set on a Sunday when daylight savings changes (April!). As *Children* and *Night 3D* turned *Night* into a slasher film, stage productions of *Night* transform it into a Halloween haunted house. In that sense, the sociocultural shift is the removal of any political or cultural fears from the production in order to focus on the film itself. As a result, not only is much of the sociophobia gone, much of any horror is gone, and the productions tend to move toward camp. When the outside fear is removed and *Night* becomes about *Night*, it also becomes far less frightening and far more funny.

In fairness, the zombie is a monster that tends toward either horror or camp. The remake of *Dawn of the Dead*, itself quite horrific, was immediately followed by the film *Shaun of the Dead*, itself camp and humorous. The motif of humor and horror, when it comes to zombies of the stage, can also be seen in other, recent theatrical productions that use zombies. *Zombie Prom*, by John Dempsey and Dana P. Rowe, was first performed in New York in 1996. Set in the fifties, at "Enrico Fermi High School," this musical narrates the story of bad boy Jonny Warner, a high school rebel who dies and is reanimated in time for the prom. Playing on nostalgia for the fifties, and using the tropes of the high school musical, this is *Night of the Living Dead* as *Grease*: no horror, pure camp. On the other extreme, we have Scott Barsotti's *The Revenants*; like the end of *Night*, it is also set in a cellar.[10] In Barsoti's play, first performed in 2006 by the Present Company at the New York International Fringe Festival, and subsequently performed in Chicago and Pittsburgh, two couples hide in a basement during a zombie outbreak. While the zombie material is played seriously and for horror, behind it is the horror of the relationships of these couples slowly dying. "Zombie" becomes a metaphor for a living dead relationship; as Barsoti's title suggests, these relationships are not alive, but ghosts.

The larger lesson to take away from all of these zombies on stage, from the adaptations of *Night* to *Zombie Prom* and *The Revenants*, is that when the production embraces something outside of itself, when it focuses on a sociophobic (such as the death of relationships and infidelity in an era where more than half of marriages end in divorce), the zombies can maintain their horror and create a genuine sense of fear in the audience. When the focus is on the tropes of the zombie film itself, the end result tends toward humor instead of horror. Serious, horrific zombie theater is possible, but only if the things of which we are meant to be afraid of are things that genuinely scare us.

Zombie Remix: Tonight of the Living Dead

The zombie renaissance is not limited to film, literature, theater, graphic novels and television. Zombie music, or, more accurately, music about zombies, has also emerged. Pop songs such as "Walk Like a Zombie" by the HorrorPops, "Zombie Boy" by the Magnetic Fields, and "RE: Your Brains" by Jonathan Coulton, not to even begin to catalogue the hundreds of songs about the living dead by a variety of speed metal, death metal and punk bands, use the tropes and elements of zombie narratives. As noted above, the title "Night of the Living Dead" has been specifically used by the Misfits and Jackyl, among others, for musical projects.

In November 2008 the band 400 Lonely Things released "Tonight of the Living Dead," a concept album based on the original soundtrack for *Night of the Living Dead*. Jonathan McCall and Craig Varian formed the "band" in 1988 in college. In the twenty-two years since, they have released six albums, mostly a blend of electronic and acoustic sounds and samples. The band themselves state:

> With their tendency for darkish music told mostly through samples, remixing *Night of the Living Dead* is a project ideally suited to 400 Lonely Things.... *Tonight*

of the Living Dead pays tribute to a lesser-known legacy of this film: the groundbreaking precedent of plunderphonics and remixing established in the composition of the original 1968soundtrack.[11]

"Plunderphonics," a term coined by John Oswald in his 1985 essay "Plunderphonics, or Audio Piracy as a Compositional Prerogative," refers to a kind of sound collage created by borrowing recognizable pieces of music and/or sounds and then transforming them into a new creation still recognizably related to the original. According to the band, the original soundtrack of *Night* was already a borrowed score:

> Crew and cast member Karl Hardman ... used recordings by other composers from stock film music libraries — many of which had already appeared in other movies and television shows — and then "augmented them electronically" to form their own original score for *Night of the Living Dead*. 400 Lonely Things has extended this notion of augmentation by using mutated samples from the film itself (many with their excellent foley work intact) as the only ingredients, and weaving these treatments into a subtle and creepy, dialog-free, instrumental companion [400 Lonely Things website].

In other words, 400 Lonely Things offers a remix of a remix of stock film music. It does so, however, to remake *Night* acoustically. Their sampled and remixed tribute soundtrack evokes the film and comments on it.

The band states that the goal of the project was to pay tribute to the film as an original example of "plunderphonics," and to offer an audio commentary on the film. The film "is concerned with the more understated and haunting moments of this movie, focusing on the fragility of 'Barbara' and drawing out the sense of bewildering relentlessness and hypnotic inevitability of waiting in an old farm-house for the world to end" (400 Lonely Things website).

The music stands on its own, but for those who know the film, it is a fascinating remix. It also does two things related to the stage versions of *Night*. First, it adapts part of the "text" (in this case, the music) of *Night* into a new medium. Second, it is thus another example of participatory creativity on the part of fans of *Night*, transforming it while paying tribute to it. The audience primarily consists of fans of the original *Night* who are able to appreciate the audio "remake."

"Tonight of the Living Dead" features eight songs which consist of music from the original, with additional sounds, noises and instrumentation, remixed and arranged to retell the story of *Night* musically. Unlike the stage musical versions, no words, spoken or sung, are employed to tell the story. The song titles, however, do echo relevant moments from the film. "It Begins," the first track, uses the opening credit music, played during the drive to the cemetery. "The Old House" and "The Music Box" refer to images and specific objects from the film, and employ the music when each is encountered. The album finishes with "Another Fire Always Smiles," which both echoes the line "Another one for the fire," said when Ben is killed, and reconstructs the ending as a triumph of fire. It is a playful way to understand the ending of the original *Night*.

In both of these cases — stage performance and audio remix — the new creation, based on *Night*, is an intertextual creation aimed primarily at a "knowing" (as opposed to "unknowing") audience. It is, in fact, a model that requires active participation from the individual(s) who encounter the new creation. This model involves a four-way dialogue between original work, audience, artist and new work. The adaptation from medium to medium is, in many ways, the ultimate "reimagining," as it requires one not only to remake the film but to remake the film to a different art, requiring the knowledge and understanding of how that medium functions differently from the cinema.

Notes

1. One might note that neither *Dawn* nor *Day* nor any of the other films in this book have been presented onstage. The reason for this is simple. The same lack of copyright on the film that allowed for anyone to release it on video or DVD, and that allowed anyone to remake it, also means the film can be adapted to any medium without permission or paying royalties. Thus, anyone who wants to is free to present an onstage version.

2. See the Maverick Theater's website for more information: http://www.mavericktheater.com/index.htm.

3. Quoted in the "*Night of the Living Dead* Collector's Booklet" included with the *30th Anniversary Edition* DVD of *Night of the Living Dead*, n.p.

4. Information on the Coterie production is taken mainly from the Coterie Theatre website: http://www.coterietheatre.org/home.aspx (accessed 10 August 2010).

5. As I write this, the Del Rey Players, the student drama organization at my own institution, Loyola Marymount University, is planning a student production of *Night of the Living Dead*.

6. Information on Squonk Opera may be found at their website: www.squonkopera.org. Information about this specific production may be found at www.squonkopera.org/archives/notld.html.

7. While interesting, this effect is problematized by both the original film and the play. The new reporter in the film states that the Venus probe never made it back, and that NASA intentionally destroyed it before it reached Earth after discovering it was carrying "mysterious, high-level radiation," a set of lines repeated in Ohm's script (32).

8. All quotations from Leon Shanglebee come from the "Translator's Note" in the Gangbusters program for the 2006 production of *Night of the Living Dead*.

9. Quotations taken from the Riverfront Playhouse Online Press Release, http://www.enjoyaurora.com/prnight.html posted August 21, 2007 (accessed 15 July 2010).

10. For more information, see Barsotti's website on *The Revenants*: http://scottbarsotti.wordpress.com/plays/full-length/the-revenants/ (accessed 15 July 2010).

11. This and subsequent quotations about the work come from the entry on "Tonight of the Living Dead" at the 400 Lonely Things Website: http://400lonelythings.com/ (accessed 17 July 2010).

II
Dawn

6

"We're blowing it ourselves": *Dawn of the Dead* (1978)

Whereas "Night of" implies the events of a single night, as can be witnessed by dozens of films that begin with the words, as well as Tennessee Williams' award-winning film and play *Night of the Iguana* or *Night of the Hunter* (or historic events such as the Night of Long Knives or Night of Broken Glass), "Dawn of" has a different meaning. It is a metaphor for the beginning of something. *"Dawn of the Dead"* suggests the beginning of a period when the dead will now be ascendant, as in "Dawn of Man," "Dawn of Time" and "Dawn of the Dinosaurs," to name but three common ones. *Night* refers to a period of chronological time; *Dawn* refers to a much larger epoch, implying something about a transformation of the world. *Night* is an endurance contest; *Dawn* is the beginning of something new.

Night is fairly bleak, apart from some black humor. Beginning with *Dawn*, however, Romero's zombie films become infused with a carnivalesque humor that runs to slapstick in *Dawn* but maintains an absurd presence through the films. Gahan Wilson refers to it as "bawdy" and "raucous" in *Document of the Dead*: "He understood that horror and humor are the identical thing.... You're looking at this grotesque event in identical ways." Romero depicts an end of the world that is despairing — the children zombies in the airport, the death of Roger, the horrific slaughter in the tenement building — but also ridiculous (the biker gang is reduced to hitting zombies in the face with pies). Tom Allen called it a "comic apocalypse" in his review in *The Village Voice* (qtd. in Gagne 100). This is the way the world ends — not with a bang or a whimper, but with an animated corpse with a face full of banana cream. Although some criticized the film for the slapstick, it adequately matches the ludicrousness of its period, in which the horrors of late seventies postmodernity are laughably terrifying and terrifyingly laughable.

Paul R. Gagne reports that Romero wanted *Dawn* to reflect the conflicts of the seventies the way *Night* reflected those of the sixties (87). I argue in this chapter that he successfully fulfilled this wish. After a survey of the ways in which *Dawn* has been interpreted, mostly centering on critiques of late cultural capitalism in America and the metaphor of the mall, I then briefly consider *Dawn* as a fluid text in John Bryant's sense. I then look at the significance of the film's signature phrase: "When there is no more room in hell, the dead will walk the earth." Lastly, I conclude with a consideration of the film as the depiction of "the apocalypse of reason."

Readings of Dawn: Shop 'Til You Drop

A. Loudermilk argues that *Dawn* is itself "a remake rather than a sequel as it defies *Night of the Living Dead*'s concluding 'return to normal' and more or less relocates for retelling this zombie brand of apocalypse from *Night*'s rural farmhouse in 1968 to a Cleveland shopping center in 1979" (84). Ignoring the factual error of the mall's municipality (and the fact that most Pittsburghers would call for Loudermilk's head for confusing "the mistake on the lake" for "Steel City"), we might concede the point that *Dawn* is not a true sequel to *Night*, but rather, in the current terminology, a "reimagining" set in the same milieu.

It is a truism that the general consensus is that *Dawn* is a critique of consumer culture. *Dawn* is also perceived as being much more overt in its sociocultural commentary than *Night*. Loudermilk also argues that *Night* may have added the element of cannibalism to zombies, but *Dawn* is responsible for the "popular perception of that cannibalism as ironic, as allegory, as a sort of cautionary tale for consumer America" (85). The location, obviously, forms the heart of the critique of *Dawn*. By setting his zombie film in a mall, Romero employed a location upon which viewers could project a number of meanings.

Kyle William Bishop, for example, states, "The metaphor is simple: Americans in the 1970s have become a kind of zombie already, slaves to master of consumption, and mindlessly migrating to the malls for the almost instinctive consumption of goods" ("Idle Proletariat," 234–5). The zombie, according to Bishop, is "a gross exaggeration of the late-capitalist bourgeoisie — blind consumption without any productive contribution" ("Idle Proletariat," 237). The zombies are reduced in this film to costumed types: Hare Krishna, working class stiff, nurse, salesman, etc. The costume makes the zombie and reduces them to a social type, almost all of whom are working class or lower middle class, based upon apparel.

Fran (Gaylen Ross) asks Stephen (David Emge), "What are they doing? Why do they come here?" He responds with a key line from the film: "Some kind of instinct. Memory, of what they used to do. This was an important place in their lives." When these dead reanimate, they do not go to their house or their place of employment, they go to the mall, because it was important to them. We have made shopping centers and places of commerce central locations in our existences. A. Loudermilk, writing in a publication called *The Journal of Consumer Culture*, offers the most expansive critique of *Dawn* as a film about consumers, not merely the zombies but also the four survivors who build a wish-fulfilling private kingdom in the mall. "Their consumption parallels the zombies *while rejecting the middle class*," writes Loudermilk (94; emphasis in original). "What Romero criticizes in *Dawn of the Dead* is the false security of consumer society, not necessarily consumer culture itself" (Loudermilk 97). After killing all the zombies, covering the doors and making the mall "safe," the four characters settle into a life of boredom and meaningless, repetitive activities. The actions that give meaning to the average middle-class life become meaningless. Fran rejects Stephen's presentation of an engagement ring because it "wouldn't be real." They play poker with real money, but there is no thrill in it. The bills now have the same value as *Monopoly* money or blank paper. After the mall is secure, the next time the survivors seem alive is when the bikers break in. The security the mall provides has been an illusion.

The bikers themselves provide a contrast to the three still in the mall. When Stephen, Peter (Ken Foree), Roger (Scott H. Reiniger) and Fran engage their fantasies and indulge themselves in fur coats and the run of the mall (with expense no longer an object), they parody middle-class fantasies of wealth and privilege. But, as noted above, they know it "isn't real." The bikers, however, have a different understanding of the mall. As Loudermilk observes, "Their consumerism vandalizes; it is not status-driven but an anti-status power kick" (94). It is this "anti-status power kick" that will find its full reflection in *Return of the Living Dead*'s punk characters, who are neither interested in the return to normalcy nor the possibilities of post-apocalyptic fantasies. The bikers have also found fulfillment in the apocalypse, as it allows them to destroy and take without consequence.

Stephen dies when he moves to protect what he sees as his by right. He refers to the mall and its contents as "ours," not recognizing that the bikers are doing the same exact thing he and the others have done: taking what is there for their own use. He chooses to fight to protect it and dies because it is not actually his. Fran and Peter, unwilling to fight to protect a fantasy, live. The dead Stephen then leads the other zombies to their secret room in the roof, forcing Fran and Peter to flee. Paul R. Gagne writes, "Throughout the film, a predominant aspect of the monster/victim theme is human unwillingness or inability to let go of the surface values and symbols of a disintegrating lifestyle" (87). Stephen dies and then endangers the others because he wants to maintain possession and ownership over something ultimately not his, but also something that, even if raided by the bikers, still would give him the necessities of survival. He does not fight for food; he fights for fur coats, basketball hoops, jewelry and ice-skating rinks, none of which are necessary for survival. He holds on to what he does not need.

A perfect example of this occurs early in the film as they first establish themselves in the mall. When cleaning the mall of dead bodies, the characters place the corpses in the mall's walk-in freezer, an odd choice, considering. We save and keep even that which we cannot use, that which can only in the end hurt us, and which perhaps should be disposed of. The keeping and storing of the dead bodies is not out of any ritual or religious sense — no prayers are said over them, and no burial in the mall (as Roger receives later). They are simply unceremoniously dumped, but inside the mall. In the remake, the characters carry the bodies to the roof and throw them outside, which makes a certain sense, as it removes decaying corpses (no doubt a health threat) from the immediate environment and away from a valuable food-storage area. In the original, the bodies are kept in a freezer. This action reflects the larger theme of the work: the acquisition, consumption and defense of "stuff." Even the bodies of slain zombies are kept, "just in case."

Although the focus of critics, and central to the film's themes, the mall is not the entirety of the film. The characters do not even reach the mall until twenty-seven minutes into the movie (in the original U.S. theatrical release). The film begins with three other key elements that have received less attention: the chaos at a television station, the S.W.A.T. assault on the inner city apartment building, and the escape of the four protagonists from Philadelphia by helicopter across Pennsylvania.

The film begins with Fran dreaming fitfully at the television station, awakened suddenly by the chaos around her. We learn from another woman that people are beginning to leave the station, introducing a theme that will run throughout the film: When is it acceptable to abandon one's post? Soon, Stephen wants to steal the helicopter; Fran wants to stay and help. "Our *responsibility* is finished," the cameraman who overhears them tells her, giving tacit permission to leave (emphasis mine). Similarly, when Roger and Peter meet, Roger remarks, "A lot of people running now. I could run. I could run right tonight.... You think it's right to run?" When they meet Stephen and Fran at the helicopter, they also encounter a number of cops stealing a boat and supplies, preparing to abandon society and go to an island, "any island." Unlike *Night*, where local authorities rally to stop the living dead, in *Dawn* the threat is so great that people abandon their responsibilities and move only to save themselves and those close to them. As Peter concludes, "We are thieves and we're bad guys. That's exactly who we are."

Romero leaves this theme behind for the moment (though he will return to it frequently throughout the film) in favor of another target: the media. *Dawn*, even more than *Night*, critiques the media for being irresponsible and uninformative. The film begins in a chaotic television studio, allowing us to see what happens behind the scenes and indicating how the media, in fact, mediates information. Dr. James Foster (David Crawford) is being interviewed by the television host, Sidney Berman (David Early).

The first thing we hear from the live broadcast is Foster insisting, "We don't know that! We've got to operate on what we do know." Romero then focuses on the exchange between the two:

FOSTER: The dead are returning to life and attacking the living.
BERMAN: I'm not so sure what to believe, doctor. All we get is what you people tell us, and it's hard enough to believe.
FOSTER: It's fact! It's fact!
BERMAN: It's hard enough to believe without you coming in here and telling me...
FOSTER: You're not running a talk show here, Mr. Berman, you can forget pitching to an audience with your bullshit.

The studio crew react negatively to Foster's use of an obscenity, but the real obscenity is what is occurring on the program. The audience knows that Foster is right: the dead are returning to life and attacking the living. Berman, however, rather than relaying this information and exploring it and how this knowledge might help the audience, attacks and criticizes his guest. On television, fact is presented as opinion and opinion is presented as fact.

Romero presciently presents the same critique in this film that Neil Postman would offer in *Amusing Ourselves to Death: Public Discourse in the Age of Show Business*, published in the same year *Day* was released. Postman asserts that television is a medium of entertainment incapable of delivering information and nuanced analysis. Television news, like everything on television, de-emphasizes facts and details and emphasizes distraction, diversion and amusement (106). Television news, offered alongside sitcoms, talk shows and infomercials, reduces the news to yet another product or form of entertainment (113). In the newsroom in *Dawn*, the information is less important than keeping the viewers entertained and watching. Foster states, "The public needs facts." He is right, Berman is wrong; but what is being offered at the height of the living dead crisis is infotainment at best.

Romero introduces Fran as the voice of responsible journalism. When told, "We've had old information on the air for twelve hours," Fran kills the list of rescue stations and demands a list of updated stations be re-entered before they run them again. The station manager immediately runs in and wants the list of rescue stations on the air all the time: "Without those rescue centers on the screen every minute, people won't watch us. They'll tune out!" Fran responds, "Are you willing to murder people by sending them out to stations that have closed down?" The manager does not answer her question. He merely repeats, "I want those stations up on the screen every minute we're on the air." In the face of his irrationality, the technical team in the booth walks out, and he then demands that the security guard bring them back. Failing that, he attempts to run the booth by himself. While the sequence is amusing, Romero's critique of the media is clear: the information provided is not necessarily relevant or useful, but serves the needs of the business providing them — the television station. Even as the world ends, the manager is concerned with ratings and number of viewers. The media, Romero cautions, does not work in the public's best interests but in their own.

Next the film shows a S.W.A.T. team surrounding a minority-occupied building in Philly. Wooley (Jim Baffico), an overtly racist cop who wants to "blow all their little Puerto Rican and nigger asses right off," is highly aggressive and prejudiced. In *Dawn*, as in *Day*, racist comments are indicative of people who are part of the problem. Rather than fighting the living dead, who are the real threat, they wish to continue to fight old battles based on racist beliefs or social grudges. The fact that it is a policeman voicing these sentiments demonstrates the institutionalized corruption and prejudice. The very men charged with enforcing justice and protecting the population are literally incapable of doing either. Like the media, law enforcement does not serve the public interest but their own.

In contrast with the racist cop is Roger, who reassures the new guy and speaks calmly to him about the situation. Within four lines Romero has established two different authoritative models of behavior: one resentful, racist and dangerous; one calm, protective and reassuring. When confronted by Martinez, the man they are there to arrest, Roger attempts to take him in without violence. When he runs, Roger warns him about the assault team right behind him, who shoot Martinez.

The S.W.A.T. team begins going through the building, clearing it. Wooley kicks open doors and shoots indiscriminately, killing innocent people. He blows an old man's head off for no reason, flush in bloodlust against hated minorities. Roger tries to stop him and gets beaten for his efforts. A S.W.A.T. officer wearing a gas mask, later revealed to be Peter, shoots Wooley, taking him out. The living dead, however, have begun to attack. Roger attempts to help his fellow officers, but the assault continues. A dead man is embraced by his wife and bites her shoulder and arm. The young S.W.A.T. officer Roger helped places a gun to his head and kills himself. Society and order collapse in front of our very eyes. The institutions designed to protect society do not. They collapse first, driven by motives other than what is best for the people.

The third element often glossed over in studies of *Dawn* is the helicopter flight from Philadelphia to Pittsburgh. After passing Harrisburg, the state capital, while over rural Pennsylvania near Johnstown, the four look out and see a line of zombies being shot at by a line of hunters in a shot highly suggestive of the ending of *Night*. "Those rednecks are probably enjoying the whole thing," Stephen mocks. The film, however, confirms his elitist position. The rednecks are enjoying the whole thing. Unlike the city, which was in a panic, and from which individuals, including our protagonists, were trying to flee, the rural areas are organized and dealing quite well with the living dead.

As if to confirm this, Romero switches from the dark, ominous, driving synthesizer soundtrack which has underscored every scene in Philadelphia to an amusing country song—"'Cause I'm a Man," by the Pretty Things — which underscores a montage of the hunters having a social event. They joke, pour coffee, swap stories of hunting, pose for photos, and laugh. The National Guard and police, who were overwhelmed in the city, interact laughingly in the country with the hunters. When a few approaching zombies are noticed, two hunters casually set down their coffee and shoot them. The hunters practice target shooting, offering such statements as, "Shit, I missed him. There. Got 'im," as they shoot zombies in the distance. Gone is the sense of panic or fear experienced in the city.

As the helicopter lands to refuel, the ominous soundtrack returns. Out of their element, the city folk from the helicopter are in danger in the country. Peter is attacked by zombified children; Stephen is attacked by a man in a suit while Fran just watches, paralyzed, as a very slow-moving zombie approaches her; and Roger is saved from a zombie attack only by the helicopter blades. The contrast between the two sequences is vital. For those who live in the country, it is relatively easy to rally and fight back; the urban dwellers, even in a less dangerous environment, face much greater peril.

The greatest threat to Peter, however, is not from the dead children but from Stephen shooting at a zombie in the doorway, nearly hitting Roger. Roger aims his gun at Stephen, telling him, "You never aim a gun at anyone. Scary, isn't it?" And it is. Once again, Romero echoes one of his major themes: humans are in far more danger from other humans than from the living dead. These elements, before the mall is even reached, also form part of the much larger tapestry of social commentary in *Dawn*. It is a film that reflects many of the tensions and sociophobics of the late seventies.

Interestingly, some, like David Flint, reject the subtext: "It is this 'social commentary,'" he writes, "that is the biggest problem in the film" (85). When "The Gonk" begins playing, and zombies are hit in the faces with pies, the audience is no longer horrified or scared, claims Flint. It is for this reason that

Shane Borrowman, in an essay entitled "Remaking Romero," states his preference for the "European Cut" of *Dawn*:

> More significantly, the "European Version" employs a sober soundtrack that adds to the film's mounting tension and dumps both the campy, comic music of the U.S. cut and the majority of the pointless pie fight which drags down the terrifying resolution [63].

As this book indicates, I am interested in how the films use the horror to create cultural critique, and I disagree with Borrowman that the playfulness of *Dawn* undercuts its horror. Much of the horror of *Dawn* comes from the absurdity of the situation. While the gore and the terror of the zombies is indeed scary, the true terror of the film comes from the society it depicts.

Borrowman does bring up another significant point, though. *Dawn* was not only a sequel to *Night*, it was its own remake in a sense. There were multiple versions of *Dawn* from the very beginning. Each of these versions functions in its own way, and in some cases, the differences between them change the sociophobics or the nature of the horror.

A Fluid Text

As noted, Loudermilk sees *Dawn* as a remake, not a sequel, of *Night*. The only thing constant between the two is the world and the situation. None of the characters, locations or stories carry over from one to the other. The original *Dawn* is also a "fluid text," in John Bryant's sense. In this day and age of DVD, multiple versions, director's cuts, alternative endings make all films fluid. *Dawn*, however, had multiple versions from the start.

Romero directed and edited a version for American theatrical release without a rating from the MPAA. At 127 minutes, it was distributed by the United Film Distribution Company to theaters in the United States in 1979 and has been the primary version available in America. As part of a production deal, Dario Argento was allowed to recut *Dawn*, add additional music from Goblin (whose music alternates in the original with library tracks, just like *Night*), and extend certain scenes while cutting others. Argento's version runs 118 minutes and was created for the European film markets, as per Argento's agreement with Romero. Thus, *Dawn* was already recreated in Italy in a different version than Romero's American edit.

Dawn was released in Italy as *Zombi*, with a completely different soundtrack by the band Goblin, and sparked a new series, different from Romero's "dead" films. Lucio Fulci's film that was released in the United States as *Zombie* was released in Italy as *Zombi 2* and marketed by producer Fabrizio DeAngelis as a direct sequel to *Dawn*. Special effects director Giannetto DeRossi stated that "he [DeAngelis] wanted to do a remake of Romero's *Dawn of the Dead* and asked me to copy Tom Savini's zombie makeup" (qtd. in Palmerino and Mistretta 119). In other words, whereas *Day* was the sequel to *Dawn* in the United States, *Zombi 2* was presented as the next film in the series in Italy and Europe. Even more significant for the purposes of this study, Chris Alexander points out that the use of "The Gonk" makes the zombies ironic (14). When Dario Argento replaced the original soundtrack with a new one by Goblin, the musical irony was lost, and the film sacrificed social commentary in favor of a deeper horror. Whereas the American version clearly offers a critique of the sociocultural landscape of the United States, the European version focuses directly on horror and mutes the critique.

Interestingly, neither version was the "original." *Dawn* premiered at the 1978 Cannes Film Festival several months before the U.S. theatrical version was released in America. Romero's first cut was twelve minutes longer than the final version and is identified by Romero as his "preferred" version.[1] The "extended version," as it is called, extends some scenes which radically change the film. The scene at the docks, in which the four protagonists banter with a goofy cop about escaping in different directions actually begins as a dangerous showdown with S.W.A.T. officers. It is a much darker scene showing society falling apart even faster. The U.S. version offers a playful scene in keeping with the "comic apocalypse," but the original version is disturbing in its portrait of the police and how, when society breaks down, individuals will use all means to escape, including harming others.

Ultimately what all this means is that long before the 2004 remake there were already multiple versions of the original *Dawn*. In fact, the term "original *Dawn*" is a bit of an oxymoron, as there were already three in existence by 1979. The changes in tone and music, the edits and additions, the cuts and the rearrangement of scenes resulted in three rather different *Dawn*s — the American version, which was a critique of America; the extended version, which was a less-playful, darker critique of America; and the European version, which also removed the sociocultural critique of the United States in favor of a generic zombie horror.

When There Is No More Room in Hell...

The reason for the dead returning is never concretely outlined in Romero's films. He never gives a definite, specific cause, only hints and suggestions. In *Night* the characters learn that strange radiation from a Venus probe may be the reason. *Dawn*, however, offers another insubstantial justification: "spiritual bankruptcy" (in Loudermilk's terminology, 104). The world Romero depicts in *Dawn* is one of crass material values, with no thought given to higher realities. Beyond the usual shortsightedness of humans killing other humans, there is also little thought to any sense of ethics or larger purpose than mere survival. Concern for fellow human beings is in short supply, as evinced by the station manager and Officer Wooley.

Not only are the supporting characters shown in a negative light, there are substantial lapses in ethics and human concern in the protagonists. Peter shoots Wooley in cold blood to stop him from shooting people in cold blood. Peter also offers to Stephen to abort Fran's baby without even consulting her. All four abandon their posts when it is necessary to do so, but only Fran and Roger have any qualms about it. As they fly over the countryside, Stephen cannot help muttering his contempt for the rednecks below. Stephen's own insufficiencies often result in him placing his life or the lives of others in danger. He nearly shoots Peter; he must be rescued by Peter and Roger when they first reach the mall, and his suicidal attack on the biker gang, followed by his death and resurrection, lead the dead directly to the hidden apartment. In short, even the four main characters are capable of selfish, petty, violent, unethical behavior on a frighteningly regular basis.

Peter offers the film's only explanation as to why the dead have been returning:

> Something my granddad used to tell us. You know Macumba? Voodoo. My granddad was a priest in Trinidad. He used to tell us, "When there's no more room in hell, the dead will walk the earth."

This final phrase has become the film's most recognizable line. It suggests that hell has become full. In other words, humanity has grown so morally unredeemable, so sin-filled and incapable of being saved, that the vast majority of those who die end up being sent to hell. This tidal wave of unredeemable souls so overwhelms hell that they return to their dead bodies, now free to kill and devour as punishment for their and our sins. Another way to interpret the line is that hell has become so overwhelmed it has become necessary to literally create hell on earth to handle the overflow, so that earth itself has become a subdivision of hell. The implication is that we as a species have become unredeemable. The world has fallen into such a state that we can no longer be saved in any sense of the word. It also implies that we are already in hell.

"When there is no more room in hell" is actually the second statement in the film of a religious critique of the crisis and American society. During the tenement raid, Roger and Peter meet in the basement, where they encounter an old priest, who tells them:

> Many have died last week on these streets. In the basement of this building you will find them. I have given them the last rites. Now, you do what you will. You

are stronger than us, but soon I think they be stronger than you. When the dead walk, señores, we must stop the killing or lose the war.

The very next image is of a large number of zombies pushing through a wall and overwhelming the police and the National Guard, proving the priest right. As a heartbeat is heard on the soundtrack, Peter and Roger, deeply disturbed, find the dead the priest told them about, fighting over body parts, wriggling in shrouds, eating human flesh and attempting to attack them. The two police begin shooting the dead in the head, this time presented not as a war but as mercy killings. Written clearly on both of their faces is the shock and sadness the task generates in them. These are men who shoot for a living but who take no joy in it.

The priest's critique is both prophetic and at the heart of the issue for Romero: When the dead come back to life to attack the living, "we must stop the killing or lose the war." In the heart of the epidemic of the dead rising, police such as Wooley add to the ranks of the real enemy by shooting living human beings. Individuals such as the station manager, who knowingly feeds false information to the public, add to the problem by creating more zombies. Our value system, argues Romero through the old priest, is completely wrong and possibly inversed. When the crisis happens our instinct is to do things that make it worse. Then we go shopping.

When they first view the cellar room full of dead bodies (itself a reversal of *Night*, where the living hide from the dead in a cellar), Roger asks, "Why did these people keep them here?" Peter answers, "Because they still believe there is respect in dying." At the height of the crisis, the people in the building (most, if not all, ethnic minorities) wanted to treat their relatives and loved ones with dignity and respect. The priest gives them the last rites and then tells the police to "do what you will," meaning shoot them in the head to stop them from attacking the living. These dead, however, were contained, wrapped mostly in shrouds and of no danger to anyone. They did not attempt to break out of the room; they did not attack anyone until the police entered the room. Unlike the shooting of the living dead on the floors above, Roger and Peter regard this task with distaste, as it is more of a violation than an act of self-defense.

The horror of *Dawn* is not only that the dead are rising and attacking the living, but also that this crisis brings out the worst in humanity and allows us to give over to our darkest impulses, whether destructive, racist, or the tendency to ignore the rights and dignity of others. Even the best of us give in to these impulses. Fran, Stephen, Peter and Roger abandon their posts and flee, stealing supplies and a helicopter. They arrive at the mall, take it over and have no sympathy for the walking dead there. Whereas the dead in the tenement basement are sad and deserving of sympathy and respect, the dead at the mall are comic target practice, not only for the protagonists but also for Romero and the audience. During a montage of zombies in the mall when the survivors first arrive, we see zombies sliding around the ice rink and trapped inside a hockey goal. They wander around, smashing up against the glass, dressed comically (or in one case, a shirtless fat man is *un*dressed comically). Mall zombies do not have dignity. In an interesting inversion of what is too often seen on the news, the dead middle class of the mall are comic fodder, while working class and poor minorities are treated with dignity and respect.

As they eliminate the dead of the mall, Peter calls them "zombies," one of the only times someone in a Romero film does so.[2] No such sympathy is shown toward the mall zombies as was shown those in the tenement. As noted above, the zombies' corpses are tossed into a freezer and simply left there. The remaining zombies are stuck outside, no longer a concern until let back into the mall by the bikers.

Interestingly, Romero would not let Fran kill the nun zombie as originally planned. Instead, the nun, whose habit was caught in a mall door, was simply released and allowed to wander. Gaylen Ross notes, "It's like an animal. It's not an inherently evil thing. He had a very interesting take on what was OK and what was not, and very Catholic."[3] What is most unique about *Dawn*, over and above *Night* and *Day*, is that the dead are presented as animals. Some are vicious, some are shy, some are dangerous, and some are not. It is interesting that Romero decided not to kill a nun zombie. The fact that the most spiritual characters of the film, Peter and the old priest, also survive may speak to the spiritual bankruptcy which Romero critiques in this film.

If the dead walk when there is no more room in hell, we might conclude by considering the middle third of the film. The dead are no longer a threat. While Roger has been bitten and is slowly dying from his wound, requiring Peter to eventually shoot him when he rises (after promising to try not to), there are no other zombies in the mall. Once the mall is clear, the film is no longer about the dead. It is, however, still about hell. In Jean-Paul Sartre's play *No Exit*, three deceased characters are placed in a room with no windows, doors or mirrors, which they cannot leave for eternity — much like Peter, Fran and Stephen. The mall, zombie-free, becomes a new kind of hell, because, as Sartre reminds us, "*l'enfer, c'est les autres*" ("Hell is other people"). Like the characters in Sartre's play, Romero's characters cannot leave, have no way of looking out at the outside world beyond the mall, and grow to despise each other and their lives. They are not in constant danger from the living dead, but nor are they truly living. At the end of the sequence right before the bikers arrive, Romero shows a medium shot of Fran and Stephen in bed together, staring off into space, not looking at each other at all. There is no warmth between them, no connection, no love. They are in the hell of other people. Ironically, it is the arrival of the biker gang and the reentry into the mall of the living dead that gives them all purpose again. Zombies might make for hell on earth, but boredom and only two other individuals to interact with in close quarters for the rest of one's life is also hell.

"The Apocalypse of Reason"

Jaime Russell observes, "The apocalypse of reason dominates" *Dawn*, which is not only a beautiful turn of phrase but an accurate description of the events depicted (93). Relying solely on the moments I have focused on so far, we can read *Dawn* as a depiction of the destruction of human reason in dealing with crises and other humans. *Dawn* proves over and over again that self-interest and stupidity motivate individuals far more than altruism and intelligence. Wooly, given the opportunity, goes crazy and begins killing the living as well as the dead until one of his fellow officers is forced to shoot him. His actions were not reasonable; they were driven by fear and hate and a desire for revenge against perceived injustices. Right before he begins shooting, he complains that the tenement building is "a lot nicer than what I got." He motivates his violence by convincing himself that the residents of the building have been given something that they do not deserve, something that he deserves and does not have.

The station manager's actions are not reasonable. He is motivated not by a genuine need to serve the public but rather to ensure that people keep watching his station during a crisis of biblical proportions. At a time when the dead rise and attack the living, his chief concern is with ratings. As his employees begin to leave to be with their families or save themselves, he demands that the security guard stop them and force them to work. None of these demands are rational.

Stephen, who has had to be rescued several times himself, who has almost shot Peter, who has consistently revealed himself to have poor judgment, wants to wage a defense against a superior force, much better armed, and not afraid to fight and kill him for fun. Peter, whose tactical judgment has proven above reproach, warns him the biker gang is "an army" who has survived on the road a long time. Peter's advice is to hide and deal with the aftermath after the bikers leave the mall. Instead, Stephen begins fighting with the bikers, resulting in his death. By reacting emotionally to their intrusion into the mall, his actions are not reasonable nor rational.

The bikers, as well, are not merely vandals on an "anti-status kick," as Loudermilk terms it. They are also the embodiment of the apocalypse of reason. With the collapse of law enforcement they have become a roving gang, destroying for the pleasure of it, with no fear of consequence. They are an organized and tough fighting force. Yet, individually, they display poor judgment and unreasonable behavior. After letting zombies into the mall, they ignore the danger they themselves have created. They give in to every impulse, even if against the normal sense of self-preservation. At best, this results in a pie in the face of a zombie. At worst, one biker sits down in the middle of a battle to use the blood pressure testing machine. The zombies tear his arm off, leaving it in the machine while they tear him apart and devour him. Most of the items grabbed by the biker gang will neither help them survive nor make their existence any easier. They grab the nearest thing, or something that catches their eye, or something funny. In the end, many deaths are caused by the biker's poor impulse control and lack of rationality.

Lastly, Peter himself, during the final showdown at the mall, sends Fran out to the helicopter and plans to shoot himself in the head. His behavior is not rational and is the product of despair. It will also result in Fran being left alone with her unborn child. Peter comes close to choosing a selfish act, but at the last moment decides to fight back and escape with Fran to an uncertain future. It is as if Romero, after showing hundreds of examples of the failure of humans to act rationally and reasonably, has Peter make the choice to be rational and not selfish. There is also a particular aptness to both his manner of suicide and his rejection of it. By shooting himself in the head he would be destroying the very center of his rationality. By rejecting this option, he embraces the rational and refuses to give in to the apocalypse of reason. Russell points up the theme of "removing the head," first mentioned by Dr. Foster in the opening sequence: "the world is increasingly 'headless'" (93). This idea recurs throughout the film. Romero offers numerous shots of heads being shot, hit with machetes, crushed under things, etc. Anyone in any leadership position is revealed to be incompetent, dangerous or motivated by self-interest.

As the helicopter rises into the air at the end of the film, we have seen multiple societies fall apart, hundreds of deaths and incredible destruction. Every step of the way those deaths and the destruction have been exacerbated by, if not directly caused by, human stupidity, selfishness, and irrationality. The dead are not the threat. Living humans are. The only conclusion one can reach from *Dawn* is that Fran is right: in the end, we're blowing it ourselves.

Notes

1. Romero states this on the commentary track, and it is noted in the accompanying booklet to the "ultimate edition" DVD collection of *Dawn*, which includes the extended original cut.

2. The only other reference of which I am familiar is Kaufman's use of the word in *Land of the Dead*.

3. Quoted in *The Dead Will Walk*, a documentary for the 25th anniversary version of *Dawn of the Dead*. Unlike the previous documentary on *Dawn*, *Document of the Dead*, which actually spent as much time on other Romero films, especially his (then) upcoming *Two Evil Eyes*, *The Dead Will Walk* features interviews with the actors and production team at length, and really goes into a good deal of detail on the process and experience of making just *Dawn*.

7
"Number One: Trust": *Dawn of the Dead* (2004)

"Giving Up Any Sense of the Political Commentary in the Original"

I must confess, the first time I saw the remake of *Dawn of the Dead* I was underwhelmed. It was an interesting film, but I was not certain it had the power or the insight into American society of the original. It also seemed to owe a debt to *28 Days Later*. However, I have found that I discover more and more in this film each time I watch it — the mark of an excellent movie — and I have truly come to admire the many levels it offers, the ideas behind it and the way it transforms Romero's vision while remaining faithful to it in its own way. I also think this film's social content and commentary is undervalued by the critics.[1] It is, admittedly, a very reactionary film, but a conflicted one. This paradox is rooted in the nature of the horror film after 9/11, which I shall subsequently explore in far greater detail.

Although this is obviously a remake of Romero's film, the creators of the 2004 version prefer the term "reimagining." Constantine Verevis observes that in the promotional material for the film, director Zach Snyder stated, "A re-filming of the original version was so not needed. *Reinterpretation is what we wanted to do. Re-envision it*" (italics in original, 134). The denials by Snyder were categorical: "There was not, is not, a valid reason to 'remake' *Dawn of the Dead*. That's not what we set out to do, not what any of us wanted" (qtd. in Verevis 134). Instead, Snyder, screenwriter James Gunn and the other artists involved took Romero's basic premise (a small group of survivors trapped inside a shopping mall after the dead rise) and used it to craft a narrative of life in contemporary suburbia in America, just as the original did. Unlike the 1990 remake of *Night*, there was no attempt to follow the original closely.

Verevis notes that the reviewers "bemoan the fact that Snyder uses the shopping mall as a location, but not additionally (as Romero had) as an occasion to critique consumer culture by drawing parallels between mall shoppers and zombies" (147). Kendell R. Phillips believes the Snyder-helmed remake "gives up any sense of the political commentary in Romero's 1978 classic" (195). I argue here that there was no need to create a critique of American consumer culture in the remake. Romero did that in the original. And the war is over. The Mall won! If there seems to be less overt sociopolitical commentary in this remake of *Dawn*, that illusion is part of the larger critique by the film of the failure of contemporary culture to address not only the issues in the original *Dawn* but all of the issues that have developed since. The original *Dawn* did not make anyone less of a consumer. The reviewers who reject the remake for not making the same sociocultural commentary as the original may as well fault the original for its failure to manifest any real change in the world. Instead, the new *Dawn* is a depiction of American fears and concerns in a post–9/11 world that also explores the inability of people to create and develop lasting, trusting relationships on any level. If the original *Dawn* was a critique of Americans as consumers, the remake of *Dawn* is a critique of Americans as unable to commit.

Glenn Kay, who praises Romero's work consistently in *Zombie Movies: The Ultimate Guide*, critiques the *Dawn* remake as a far lesser film: "as it progresses the plot holes and inconsistencies become increasingly absurd," and the characters are "underdeveloped" (237). He deplores the absence of "meaningful subtext" in a film derived from a film with presumably a great deal of meaningful subtext (237). "*Dawn* [does] not rise to the level of a terrifyingly socially conscious horror film," he concludes (238). I would argue that while it is not an *overt* socially conscious horror film in the way that the original *Dawn* or *Land* are, Zack Snyder's film and James Gunn's screenplay capture the concerns of post–9/11 America just as effectively as the original captures the concerns of seventies consumer culture.

Dawn 2004 is a radically different film, not least because of a much larger number of survivors in the mall. The larger number of people means the remake can also focus much more on social class than the original. The four mall-dwellers of the original are all professionals: two SWAT officers, a helicopter pilot and a television producer. They are all middle class and of roughly the same age. The remake features characters representing a variety of professions, mostly working class: CJ (Michael Kelly), Bart (Michael Barry) and Terry (Kevin Zegers) are young security guards at a mall; Ken (Ving Rhames) is a beat cop (not S.W.A.T.; he wears the uniform of a patrol officer); Ana (Sarah Polley) is a nurse; Michael (Jake Webber) works retail; Norma (Jayne Eastwood) is a truck driver; and Glen (R.D. Reid) plays organ in a church. These are working class and lower middle class individuals.

We only meet one upper middle class/white collar individual: Steve (Ty Burrell). Steve owns a boat, wears a tie and suit, and is a wealthy, selfish jerk. He contributes nothing to the group, fails in the one job assigned to him (opening the door when the rescue team sent to Andy's Gun Shop returns), and is generally unreliable. We know from both the boredom montage in the film (images presented to Richard Cheese's cover of "Down with the Sickness") and the images found on the camera on his boat that Steve enjoys taping himself having sex with women. For him, sex is not an act of lovemaking, it is an act of personal gratification. He likes to watch himself having sex more than he cares to be intimate with another human being. We should also note that Steve's is the only name that is a holdover from the original: Fran, Roger and Peter do not exist at all in the remake. Stephen becomes "Steve." The shallow, self-interested man is referred to by a nickname. Like with his namesake, his shallowness results in the deaths of others.

The new *Dawn* has much in common with the old *Dawn*, even as it radically differs from it. The remake does not have the same social critique of consumerism found in the original, but it is very class-conscious. It is also concerned, as was the original, with the mall and the zombies as metaphors for bankrupt American values; but it also focuses on the sociophobics of 2004, when it was made. As with the original, the "unrated director's cut" available on DVD is longer and contains additional scenes, both gory and character-driven, that were cut from the version released to cinemas in 2004. Thus, the remake of *Dawn* is also a "fluid" text, like the original. It already exists in different versions.

In this chapter I will consider the opening sequence and how it establishes the major motifs and themes of the film, most notably the inability of contemporary Americans to create meaningful relationships. I then read *Dawn* as a post–9/11 horror film, using the imagery and language of post–9/11 America to establish a political critique. I explore what the remake "means" in opposition to the original by comparing two aspects of the films: Ken Foree's line (in both) "When there is no more room in hell, the dead will walk the earth," and the speed and demeanor of the living dead. Lastly, I return to the idea of relationships as engaged by the rest of the film. In the original *Dawn*, two people escape the mall at the end in a helicopter, and we do not know what happened to them.

The remake's ending gives us a group of four and a dog that make it to a boat, and then their fate is revealed during the end credits. From beginning to end, the remake is a radically different film than the original, one that builds upon the ideas and structures of the original but with very different themes.

"Have a Nice Day" & "Reality Television": Relationships I

The ten-and-a-half-minute opening pre-credit sequence not only sets all of the major themes and images of the film, it also structures how it will re-imagine Romero's original. An entire book could be written on this opening sequence alone. The opening image of the film moves from the production company logos to an extended visual transformation. The "Strike" logo burns up, and a series of flames and fires morphs into the x-ray of a human skull held by Dr. Dandewar (Sanjay Talwar), who is also on the phone planning tomorrow's golf game. His focus is on his conversation, not on the medical emergency in front of him. Once he has arranged for his tee time, he hangs up and asks nurse Ana why Dr. Cho has ordered a head x-ray for a man bitten on the hand. She tells him the patient has unusual symptoms, but also implies she has been working since six in the morning. The doctor ignores her implication that he should speak to a night nurse and instead instructs her to page him when she finds the patient.

The original began in the chaos of a newsroom as the zombie crisis began to peak. The remake begins in the chaos of a hospital before the zombie crisis even begins. This is a health system on the verge of being overwhelmed and collapsing even without a zombie outbreak. The doctor's indifference indicates a lack of care, not only for the patient but for the other medical support staff, such as Ana. Neither the doctor nor the nurse know where the patient actually is and must track him down in the hospital. Modern medicine has become both impersonal and driven by profit, not care.

Similarly, the audience's sympathies are clearly directed toward Ana. She has just worked a twelve-hour shift. Her focus is on the care of the patients. The doctor is more concerned with his golf game. She is not only working class, she is a hard worker. He lives a life of privilege into which the practice of medicine seems an intrusion. Her job is her life. She must trade days off with her colleagues in order to have two days off in a row. The film's sympathies are clearly with the nurse, not the doctor. Later, in the mall, all but one of the surviving characters in the group is working class: nurse, cop, truck driver, security guard, retail sales clerk, etc. Only Steve is upper middle class or privileged, and he is loathed by the other characters and the audience alike.

When the patient, Edward Solomon (whom we never see), is located, he is in the intensive care unit, about to get a "toxicology workup" in the morning. "From a bite?" asks Ana, but the computer does not say. She shrugs and leaves the hospital after instructing Cora, the night nurse (Kim Roberts), to page Dr. Dandewar. For her, the concern and crisis is over. However, this small beginning foreshadows the outbreak to come and also indicates that even Ana is complicit in a health system that is not overly concerned with the health of the individual. It is impersonal and on the verge of collapse.

Further foreshadowing occurs outside the hospital as Ana leaves. Legs are sticking out the back of an ambulance. The camera switches to inside the ambulance, looking out at Ana as she looks in. A man slowly sits up as the ambulance radio suddenly bursts to life with a call. While the shot implies the eerie rising of someone from the dead, in fact the man in the ambulance is an E.M.T. who was simply resting. He greets Ana and then, with his partner, closes up the ambulance, noting, "It's starting early." This foreshadowing carries a double meaning for the audience, who knows that the zombies are coming.

This brief set-up introduces some of the themes that will run through the film. The first theme is the failure of institutions that we believe in and rely on. As in the original, in which the station manager and Wooley show that the media and law enforcement are incapable of protecting the public's best interest, in the remake the health care system is cold and impersonal and fails those who need it most. The second theme to be introduced is the inability to connect, and our individual and collective failure to maintain lasting relationships in the contemporary, postmodern west. This theme will dominate much of *Dawn* 2004.

The next shot is of Ana in her car. The radio features a news report. A woman's voice begins, "Unconfirmed reports..." and Ana switches the station to another news broadcast in which a man's voice states, "Confirmed it is not an isolated...." She then hits a third button on the radio, and music begins to play. She ignores the news reports, both of which also foreshadow what is occurring outside her bubble. She does not care what is happening in the world. After a long day at the hospital, she simply wants to get home. The song on the radio is Stereophonic's "Have a Nice Day," which also forms an ironic commentary on the action. Ana drives home during the beginning hours of the zombie outbreak listening to someone blandly telling her repeatedly, "So have a nice day."

While the song plays, the film features an aerial shot of Ana's car. "Have a nice day" continues to echo, but what is remarkable in the shot is that we see literally dozens of houses on the street from above, cars in driveways, pools in some backyards, but no people. No actual signs of life. Ana's car is the only thing moving. The neighborhood itself looks to be a fairly contemporary development—cookie-cutter houses that are remarkably similar but with fences between them. The shot demonstrates that Ana's world is already one of isolation. In her own home she is cut off completely, even from those who live nearby. The street looks abandoned from above. There is no need for a zombie apocalypse to strike the town, it already looks abandoned and empty of life.

Snyder returns us to a surface-level shot as the only neighbor of Ana's we will meet before the crisis truly begins rollerskates up to her. Vivian (Hannah Lochner), a young girl, shows off her ability to skate backwards. Ana tells her they might "do a few backwards laps tomorrow," but the promise is clearly half-hearted at best. Ana also tells Vivian to "say hey to your mom for me." The only neighbor whom the audience is shown is a little girl. In just the first three minutes of the film we are shown a world in which personal relationships are all surface or nonexistent, and professional relationships hold little respect for either party.

Ana enters her own home, where Luis, her husband (Justin Louis), watches television in the bedroom. None of the articles or reviews concerning the film state that Luis is her husband, most referring to him as a "partner." What is interesting is that their relationship is never overtly stated in the film. As they lie on the bed, their wedding rings are visible. They are clearly married, but they do not look at each other on the bed. She leans on him and they talk about their days and their plans without making eye contact. Instead, both fixate on the television.

He informs her, "The mailman got sent home," and we hear the first genuine compassion in her voice: "Oh my God. He had such a sweet voice. I can't believe that." She feels more connection with a contestant on a reality show than she does with the people at the hospital or in her neighborhood. The characters on a television program are more real than the real people in her life. It is a telling and brilliant moment in the film that sets up some of the major themes that will be repeated throughout the movie.

Reality television is, of course, not real. More often than not it is contrived and manufactured and then further edited to tell whatever narrative the producers desire to create. It is also more often than not a competition in which all of the participants are also types. Ana does not know the name of the one she likes, just that he is "the mailman" who is "chubby" and "has a sweet voice." Names are indicators of personhood; descriptors of occupation, body type or personal attributes reduce a person to a type. This reductive state will also occur within the film itself at the mall, wherein a number of different "types" will congregate: the cop, the nurse, the thug, the sweet girl, the nice guy, etc. And, as in reality television, one by one the "contestants" will be eliminated and forced to leave, metaphorically speaking. The denizens of the mall will be like reality show contestants, and that means they are in direct competition to survive as well. It is not coincidental that one of the first and most popular reality television programs was called *Survivor*. *Dawn of the Dead* is *Survivor: Midwestern Mall*.

Luis then states that he thought Ana might have joined her friends for a "girl's night out." She jokes back, "What, miss date night?" The concept of a "date night" is a recent cultural phenomenon in the United States. It is rooted in the idea that after marriage (or for those in a long-term relationship), the couple must schedule romantic connection time away from work, children and other activities. It is seen as a way to avoid falling into a romantic routine. In other words, "date night" is a culturally created phenomenon designed to keep a romantic relationship active and healthy after being together for a long period. Most therapists recommend a variety of activities "away from the kids and television" on a regularly scheduled "date night."[2] Ana and Luis' "date night" then consists of making love in their shower while the television plays in the background.

As in the original, and following Postman's critique in *Amusing Ourselves to Death*, this is not television as informational media but television as distraction and entertainment. They watch reality TV but ignore the news and emergency broadcasts. Though the television is still on as Ana and Luis make love in the shower, it is mere background noise. Nothing of genuine value comes out of the television. Yet they do not turn it off for their one intimate moment, perhaps for the whole week (this is, after all "date night"). The television is central to their lives, but not as a source of information. They are disconnected from reality, but also quite possibly from each other, as their television viewing earlier, and their making love with it on, demonstrates.

From "date night" Snyder cuts to a shot of a clock at 6:37 A.M., followed by a tracking shot from a photo of Luis and Ana on their nightstand to the open bedroom door. This not only establishes time and place, it also marks the event that will end their relationship. The bedroom door opens, and behind it is an out-of-focus figure. As seen from above, Luis wakes up with a start and notices someone in the doorway. Interestingly, he does not panic or become startled. He simply says, "Vivian's here." The camera then reveals Vivian standing in the doorway with blood on her nightgown, her face shrouded in shadow. She steps forward to reveal that her face has been torn open around her mouth and her body is covered in blood. Luis runs to help her, calling out, "Call an ambulance," which wakes Ana, but Vivian immediately bites his neck. Vivian, we might also note, means "lively" in Latin, which makes it ironic that she is the first zombie we see. And, as we will discover, these are not the slow-moving, shambling zombies of the original. They are, indeed, lively animated corpses.

Ana pulls Vivian off Luis and throws her down the hallway. Vivian immediately jumps up and begins running back down the hallway as Luis falls on the bed. Ana locks the door and attempts first aid, then calls 911, but all circuits are busy. As she tries to reach help, Luis dies but immediately reanimates. Ana is uncertain of what is happening. He turns, screams and attacks her. She grabs her keys and flees into the bathroom, where she falls into the tub. She then escapes through the bathroom window, but not before having to kick him in the face in order to escape.

The very spot where the night before they made love as part of their date night is where first she flees, and then does violence to him before he can do violence to her. Luis, upon being reanimated, attacks Ana, attempting to kill her. She flees to the car as he continues to attack her. As he chases her, he sees another woman and literally begins to pursue the other woman as his wife drives away from him. Their relationship has obviously fallen apart with his death, but the image of him being distracted by another woman and pursuing her is also indicative of marital relations in twenty-first century America, where more than half of all marriages end in divorce. After attacking his wife, Luis chases other women. It is a literalization of a metaphor and the operative sociophobic in the *Dawn* remake: how can one build and maintain trustworthy relationships in our current culture?

As she flees her house, Ana opens her car door and notices her neighbor and calls to him for help. This man is the second person we have met since Vivian, and although he recognizes her, the man points a gun at Ana and tells her to "get back." She says, "Jesus, just tell me what's going on," and he goes into a shooter's stance, holding the gun with both hands and instructing her again to get back. Snyder depicts neighbor against neighbor. Although these individuals live next door to each other, they do not really know one another. Nobody helps anyone else. The man with the gun will not even tell Ana what he thinks is going on; he only threatens her with a firearm.

She realizes he will not help; but in the next shot he is hit by an ambulance, tossed in the air and clearly killed. We then see, from Ana's point of view, a much larger picture of the neighborhood. Smoke is coming out of some houses, flames out of others. In the distance, two individuals chase a third, and an explosion is heard from another part of the street. At this point, Luis emerges from the house and begins to pursue Ana. He pounds on her windshield and chases her until, as previously noted, he is distracted by another woman.

Ana punches on the radio, finally looking for news or answers, and we learn that the film is set in the Milwaukee area. The announcer begins to list emergency evacuation centers in the area. A woman leaps out and begins knocking on the passenger side door of Ana's car, asking, "Help! Can you help? Please, help!" She is panicked, but does not have a weapon or seem threatening. Ana, a nurse, ignores her and drives on. She drives past scenes of carnage, police cars and others fleeing the living dead.

Snyder then switches to another aerial view, a shot of smoke rising from the city and fires. The overall milieu is suggestive of a city under attack and specifically evokes the images of 9/11: burning buildings, plumes of smoke over the American landscape, crowds fleeing, and destruction and mayhem. A helicopter flies through the scene, followed by a car crashing into a tanker truck, and the two vehicles subsequently plowing into a gas station which explodes. As the camera follows Ana's car, she negotiates a strange scene. A naked woman stumbles away from a city bus; in the back of the same bus, another woman, lying on her back, is attacked by two individuals who are clearly biting her. A man dressed in some sort of uniform opens the car door and attempts to pull her out and steal the car. Ana floors it and the man falls away, but the attempt to fight him off has forced her to ignore where she was driving and the car plunges through a guardrail, down an embankment and into a tree.

While she was driving, Ana is accosted by two people looking for access to her vehicle, since she is in a moving car and can flee the scene. A woman knocks on the window and asks for help. A man opens the door and tries to pull Ana out and take the car for himself. Interestingly, both meet the same fate — they are left behind as she speeds up. Even in our protagonist there is no civility, no trust, no attempt to help others. Even though she is a nurse, someone who has dedicated her life to the care of others, as the world falls apart she abandons this post, just as Fran, Stephen, Peter and Roger did in the original. She drives to protect herself, without care for others, whether they are aggressive or asking for help.

Ana passes out as the airbags deploy. The next image is one of Muslims bowing in prayer as the beginning credits, taking the form of streaking red liquid, suggesting blood, begin to run while Johnny Cash's apocalyptic song "When the Man Comes Around" plays. The Muslims bowing is quite clear. There follows a series of rapid, indistinct images: something falling into water, a screaming face with blood on it. The title is then announced, followed by screaming and more rapid images.

We cut briefly into a press conference in which the spokesman responds to all questions with "We don't know." He is asked, "Is this an international health hazard or a military concern?" He answers, "Both." In other words, he has no real answers. Snyder follows with images from riots, some in the West, some clearly in the Middle East; images of cracking glass with indistinct but vaguely threatening beings behind it; images of buildings burning and of newscasters unable to provide any real information. Either the reporters are indistinct or they are uninformed (one states, "The following shelters have been compromised ... uh, we lost a teleprompter," and stops talking altogether).

The original *Dawn* featured a station manager who wanted to keep presenting fake information so people keep watching. The media world has changed in twenty-six years, however. The remake was made in a time of the

24-hour news cycle where it all plays out in front of us, warts and all. This *Dawn* was born in a much more media-savvy world. In 1978 there were three networks, plus PBS and local independent stations. In 2004 we had hundreds of networks, including four major 24-hour news networks, and the internet. Much more information comes our way much more quickly, but much of it is just noise, or opinion not rooted in fact. The twenty-four hour news cycle simply exposes the ignorance of "experts" much faster.

As the credits progress, we see more and more distinctly crowds of zombies. They attack and move forward. With many of the shots, the transition is through a snowy screen. The breakdown of media is literalized in this film as it transitions from the precredit prolog of Ana and Luis to the credits themselves. In that time, the world falls apart and the media is there to capture it. The networks are still on, as C.J. and Bart watch television at the mall, but the images are not reassuring. Local groups may have control over their areas, but we see (for perhaps the first time in a Romero film or remake) evidence of a global pandemic. The world-wide media present in 2004 allows Snyder to show that the United States is not experiencing this plague of the living dead alone, but rather that it is afflicting all humanity. Remarkably, the personal and global narratives of this film are established in a ten-and-a-half-minute pre-credit sequence, followed by a two-and-a-half-minute credit sequence. Everything in the film is captured in the first thirteen minutes.

"America Always Sorts Its Shit Out": A 9/11 Zombie Movie

Dawn is the quintessential post–9/11 horror film. I was living in rural Ohio on September 11, though I had friends in New York and Washington. The events were distant and yet "here," wherever "here" was. It was experienced through the television outside of New York and Washington, D.C. *Dawn* 2004 echoes this experience and recreates it as a horror film.

Like many horror films after 9/11, certain qualities emerge in *Dawn*, influenced by the post–9/11 zeitgeist. Among these elements are a bleak nihilism that results in the deaths of all the characters, which is suggested by the continued footage during the credits. Second, news reports form a central part of the early narrative. We are not, however, in the halls of power, such as the White House or the Pentagon, as we would be in a Cold War film. Instead, we watch from a mall in Minnesota. None of the characters know what is going on. They watch the news but do not trust it. Third, both the opening and closing credits employ shaky, hand-held camerawork, showing the chaos and confusion as people flee from danger in a direct citation of footage from 9/11. Fourth, in the opening sequence as Ana flees, we see plumes of smoke rising up over the city, people covered in blood, dirt and ash, and first responders becoming victims as well, also directly citing 9/11. The end result is that behind *Dawn* lies a conservative outlook tempered by a nihilistic cynicism. When the chips are down, it is "us" versus "them," but we might not win.

The opening credit sequence features a number of news clips and seemingly raw, live, documentary footage. One of the first images is a group of Muslims bowing in prayer, followed by images from disasters, news broadcasts, and indistinct shots, brief and out of focus. The film begins with imagery designed to evoke terrorism and 9/11. The bowing Muslims from the opening give way to images of zombies. The credits end with what looks like a television journalist reporting from a hotel in the Middle East; the camera suddenly turns to show soldiers being attacked by zombies in the hotel room, and the final zombie attacking the camera, also looking Middle-Eastern. The visual link is made — threat is world-wide, but America and the American way of life are particularly at risk. We are under assault from without and within, just as on 9/11. The zombie is a terrorist.

When they first arrive in the mall, after the security guards disarm the newcomers, Snyder pans the camera down the line of characters as they watch television. They see live footage on a half-dozen screens showing cops beating and shooting individuals, fires and explosions, and images which seem to indicate a battle being fought and lost. After observing a sheriff (Tom Savini) on television deal with the crisis, head mall cop C.J. tells the others, "America always sorts its shit out." Gun in hand, seeing the crisis unfold in front of him, C.J. responds with belligerent confidence. He is, of course, completely wrong.

As seen in the credit sequence, the world is falling apart as the zombie hordes grow in every nation, including the United States. Very rapidly we will see that America cannot "sort its shit out" in this case, which is a very real sociophobic in the wake of 9/11. The war on terror is ongoing, perpetual and requires complete success. As Condoleezza Rice remarked to the 9/11 Commission: "And let's remember that those charged with protecting us from attack have to be right one hundred percent of the time. To inflict devastation on a massive scale, the terrorists only have to succeed once." *Dawn* is a film in which the zombie terrorists have succeeded not only once but many times. The fear being exhibited in this movie is over the seeming inability of the United States to "sort its shit out" in the case of the war on terror. It is, by definition, unwinable, as it is a war on a tactic, not on a particular group, nation or individual. Success can only be measured by how much you prevent something from happening. Once the dead begin to walk, the effect cascades, and soon the dead outnumber the living, and the living are in great danger.

So in one sense *Dawn* presents zombies as terrorists. They are an external threat to the living, out to destroy our way of life. In the wake of 9/11, then–President Bush suggested that the most patriotic thing Americans could do was go shopping. *Dawn* literalizes this suggestion. In the wake of a zombie terrorist attack, the only survivors we see literally gather at a mall. No one is coming to save them. The government cannot help, but they are at a mega mall, a giant shopping center where they can shop to fight terrorist zombies. Conversely and perversely, in *Dawn* the zombies are terrorists and the American government fails to protect the ordinary citizens from their attacks. *Dawn* is also a film, therefore, about the failure of government to aid and protect its citizens.

In the original *Dawn* the characters have a helicopter. In this remake, they see a helicopter but do not have one. A military helicopter passes overhead while people remain stranded on a roof with the words "Help us" and "Alive inside" written in paint on the roof. The helicopter does not stray from its path, makes no acknowledgment, and continues on. No help comes from the government, whether local, state or federal. Nick Muntean and Matthew Thomas Payne see in this moment a prophetic view of the Bush administration's response to Hurricane Katrina (252). Interestingly, the *Dawn* protagonists do have access to a boat, but they must get to it.

One of the tropes of the postmodern apocalyptic zombie film is the empty streets of a major city: *28 Days Later* (London), *I Am Legend* (New York City), and *Last of the Living* (Christchurch, New Zealand), for example, all feature scenes of the protagonist(s) walking past known urban landmarks in their respective cities, seeing empty public spaces. The living are gone; spaces that are never free of humanity, even in the middle of the night, are now seen as empty in the middle of the day. *Dawn*, however, shows the space around the mall as not empty but full. *28 Days* doesn't have crowds of zombies — they hunt in small packs. The same holds true with *I Am Legend* and *Last of the Living*. But *Dawn* displays a world full of threats and danger. Whereas the other films portray empty streets and embody the fear of being left alone with the monsters, *Dawn* embodies a small group of average Americans surrounded by threatening monsters that wish to destroy them and will attempt to do so with speed and hostility.

Even the music in the mall is subversively appropriate. A toilet smashes through a window as the small group seeks to break into the mall and escape the zombie onslaught outside. As they enter, a muzak cover of "Don't Worry, Be Happy" plays in the background, Bobby McFerrin's ode to relaxing and rejecting one's concerns. The song is very specifically chosen. The film shows very real reasons to worry and not be happy. It is also mall-appropriate. At the height of a time when Americans should be worried and unhappy, our president encouraged us not to be and to go shopping. *Dawn* demonstrates how ineffective such a policy is.

No More Room in Hell for Angry Zombies?

The zombies in the *Dawn* remake match the current trend of fast, hostile zombies. Whereas the zombies in the original are slow-moving, with blank stares, these zombies are aggressive. As noted in chapter 6, Peter in the original quotes his grandfather, "He used to tell us, 'When there's no more room in hell, the dead will walk the earth.'" In the remake, a televangelist, played by Ken Foree (Peter in the original), repeats the most famous line of the original:

> Hell is overflowing, and Satan is sending his damned to us. Why? God is punishing us. You have sex out of wedlock. You kill your unborn. You have man-on-man relations, same-sex marriages. How do you think your God will judge you? Well, friends, now we know. When there is no more room in hell, the dead will walk the earth.

We might note that the line directly references the original, but that the new context and preceding lines radically change the meaning from the original. First, there is a change of context of the line. Foree says it in both films. He is one of the protagonists of the original. In the remake he is a fleeting image on a TV screen. In the original, the line was an individual person of African descent offering a Macumba explanation for the living dead. It was an indictment of America from a subaltern position. In the remake, the character is a Fundamentalist Christian blaming not the United States but the moral (especially sexual) decay of a certain segment of the population. There are zombies, he seems to be saying, because there are gay people.

One cannot help but hear the words of the Rev. Jerry Falwell on *The 700 Club* immediately after September 11:

> The abortionists have got to bear some burden for this because God will not be mocked. And when we destroy 40 million innocent little babies, we make God mad. I really believe that the pagans, and the abortionists, and the feminists, and the gays and the lesbians who are actively trying to make that an alternative lifestyle, the ACLU, People for the American Way—all of them who have tried to secularize America—I point the finger in their face and say, "You helped this happen."

Rather than considering America's own aggressive imperialism and its own actions in the Middle East as possible provocations, Falwell blamed homosexuals, feminists and the ACLU for 9/11. Foree's line in the remake is meant to directly echo this sentiment.

The post–9/11 zombie is a faster, "emotive" zombie (in Muntean and

Payne's terminology). They are quick, they are aggressive, they are vicious, and they are pissed off in appearance: Vivian; the janitor in the mall who attacks Michael; and the one-armed Asian man in parking lot (to cite but three) are not only aggressive but appear enraged. These are not the hungry dead, they are the angry dead, resulting in what *Entertainment Weekly* critic Owen Gleiberman called "a blitzkrieg-of-fear remake" (47). The dead themselves are furious and enraged. They cannot be outrun, as in the remake of *Night*. One can only destroy them or be destroyed. They are our nation's collective sins catching up to us, and we cannot escape them.

Yet, ironically, William S. Larkin argues that the zombies themselves are inherently tragic:

> We are made aware of the tragic dimension of the undead by another characteristic device of the genre — populating the zombie crowd with recognizable characters and costumes. The zombie crowd is not faceless. The faces may be scabby and decaying, but they are faces we recognize [21].

Those faces can be specific and known ones, such as Johnny in *Night* and Stephen in the original *Dawn*, or they can be recognizable "types," such as the nurse, football player, or even Hare Krishna. Yet, in the remake of *Dawn* this tragic dimension is deconstructed. The familiar faces in the crowd are celebrity doppelgangers: "Burt Reynolds," "Rosie O'Donnell," and "Jay Leno." Everyone else in the crowd is a hideously disfigured monster. No Hare Krishna zombies in the remake. Instead, the humor and the humanity come from watching Andy shoot celebrities in the head. Postman's observations about infotainment are made manifest in this moment in the film: the main entertainment is watching celebrities (or at least their look-alikes) die. Even zombies become entertainment in this film.

"Ingredients to a Successful Relationship" — Relationships II

As Bart and C.J. languish in the mall jail, C.J. passes the time reading a women's magazine. He reads an article aloud to Bart, who is trying to sleep:

> OK, ok, here is a good one: "Top Ten Ingredients to a Successful Relationship." [mumbles] All right, I'm gonna skip to the top three. Number three: "He listens to me." Number two: "He tells me he loves me." And number one: Oh, it's "Trust." Number one's "Trust."

Dawn demonstrates both the value of trust and the danger that occurs in its absence. The character of C.J. undergoes the most profound character arc, arguably changing the most and learning the primary lesson of *Dawn*: you need trust in order for any relationship to work; but even if trust is there, things can still end horribly. *Dawn* also demonstrates the need to consider the needs and safety of others. Lastly, however, it demonstrates our inability to maintain any relationships, even and especially family or romantic ones.

After Ana's crash, Ken points a shotgun at her face and says, "Say something." She says, "Please," the most basic request for help. He then lowers the shotgun but does not help her; instead, he turns and walks away. This action is emblematic of the characters in the beginning. Each has their own goals and desires. Ken wants to reach his brother in Fort Pastor. Andre (Mekhi Phifer) wants a safe place for Luda (Inna Korobkina) to give birth to their child. Others, such as Ana and Michael, are rootless, simply looking to survive. None of the characters trust each other.

Andre shoots at Ken and Ana, despite the fact that Ken is a policeman (or maybe because Ken is a policeman) and they are clearly not dead. C.J. locks the others up the first night in the mall because "I don't want anybody sneaking around and stealing shit." C.J. does not believe in helping others. He wants the original group to leave the mall. His first line of the film is "Find someplace else." Michael begins to reply. C.J. cocks his gun and growls, "Maybe you didn't hear me." When Michael tells him, "There is no place else," C.J. simply responds, "Well, that's tough shit because this is our place and you can't stay here." The others in the elevator clearly do not want to leave the first real shelter they have known in hours: "Those things are out there." C.J. responds, "These are all your problems, not mine."

C.J. believes that now the mall is his and that to allow any others in would be bad. He is not merely following the dictates of his job and protecting the mall. He tells them up front, "This is *our* place." He cannot possibly use all the resources. Others would benefit, and so would he from shared labor, but he wants it all for himself and the other two guards. When Bart and C.J. discover Ben Kosman, the fourth security guard, is a zombie and a "twitcher," C.J. responds, "Fuck the fucker, I told him not to go downstairs," and shoots him in the head without hesitation. When the second group shows up in a truck, he does not want to help them either. A quick coup on the roof relieves him of his weapon and his authority, and the others lock him in the mall jail, as they believe he cannot be trusted.

After the scene described at the start of this section, Glen describes his own understanding of his awakening homosexuality to the literally captive audience of C.J. and Bart, who react negatively: "I'm in hell!" (C.J., it should be noted, has already been revealed as a racist—he calls Ken "Shaq" when they first meet—and sexist, so the homophobia comes as no surprise. As always, in a Romero-related zombie movie, racism is a character marker of a truly abhorrent human being. C.J., however, changes, sacrificing his own life for Ken, Ana, Nicole and Terry.) While the mall cops' discomfort at Glen's confession is meant to be comic, it functions as another example of trust and relationships in the film. Glen's confession confronts C.J. and Bart with their own homophobia and the irony of their situation. Two men, literally going to bed together, undressing next to each other, are being told by another man about how he realized he was gay, and they freak out. What is inherently and ordinarily an act of trust and a lowering of personal barriers so that there can be an honest relationship — the admission of one's sexual orientation — is instead perceived as torture by men whose behavior at the moment is far more "gay" than the act of listening.

C.J., however, ultimately demonstrates the trust he is incapable of at the beginning of the film. He joins the group that goes to the garage to refuel the generator. C.J. is initially denied a gun (Michael hands him a fire ax and says, "Have at it, cowboy"), but the situation seems dire until Michael throws him a shotgun and he works with the others to fight and kill the zombies. After the deaths of Luda, Andre and Norma, the group plans an escape to Steve's boat. C.J. listens, repeats the plan back to them incredulously, pointing out the ridiculousness of "head[ing] for some island that for all we know doesn't even exist?" Ken responds, "Yeah," echoed by some of the other characters. C.J. responds, "OK. I'm in." With these words he finally joins the group as a full trusting and trusted member. His image dominates the montage that immediately follows, and he appears to be the most enthusiastic worker on the converted shuttle buses. His death as the group reaches the marina is the most heroic in the film. He gives his life so that the others have a chance to survive.

C.J. learns to trust and be trusted by the group. The group itself becomes a substitute family for all its members, because real families do not stand a chance in *Dawn*. As they bunk down for the night, Terry tells Bart, "Dude, everybody's dead. Okay, your mom's dead. Your brother's dead. That fat chick at Dairy Queen — dead." Bart responds, "Yeah. That sucks, too." It's not just that everyone is dead, which is bad enough, it is Bart's understated response to this proclamation. Everyone he knows is dead, and his response is "That sucks, too." He neither mourns the loss of his family nor even seems too upset about it.

This is because families are not possible in this *Dawn*. We do not have the all-male debate about aborting the (sole) female's baby. We barely have relationships, and we certainly do not have families: Ana loses her husband Luis. Ken spends much of the first third of the film planning to find and rescue his brother from Fort Pastor. He is talked out of it and never mentions him again. Nicole (Lindy Booth) loses a father (Matt Frewer), who, because of a bite, is dying when he is first seen. She starts a relationship with Terry, but the only one she seems to truly love and care about is the dog "Chips."

She is closer to an animal than she is to any person in the mall, even her new boyfriend. When she thinks Chips is missing, and the little dog comes running, she grabs him and says, "Don't you ever leave me again. Never ever." When zombies get inside Andy's shop after Chips enters through the doggy door, she steals a van and goes to rescue the dog, something she would not have done for any of the human characters.

Andre watches Luda die while giving birth to their zombie baby, whom the group subsequently executes after Andre and Norma kill each other. Michael confesses the job he was best at was "father"; the job he was worst at was "husband." He has clearly done both multiple times. It is striking, however, that none of his children or wives are in the mall with him. Only one member of a family is allowed to survive in the mall for any period of time, and any relationship is ultimately doomed to fail. Ana and Michael begin a romance, which ends when he is bitten at the dock. The film ends (for the first time) with him watching her sail off on the boat while he stands on the dock with the hordes of zombies raging behind him. As the film cuts to black, we hear the gunshot that signals his suicide.

Perhaps the greatest irony of the film is that there is one relationship that seems to become quite solid. Andy is alone in the gun shop, yet he and Ken form as close a friendship as one can from 300 yards away. Ken is more concerned for Andy than he is for most of the people in the mall. In the end, it appears that Snyder seems to suggest that long distance relationships seem more real to us than the flesh and blood people we live with. Ken and Andy's friendship is mediated by binoculars and white boards. This means of communication is literally a primitive instant messaging or texting. We place great value on our mediated relationships, less so on our face-to-face ones. When the group plans their escape, Ken states, unchallenged, "We have to pick up Andy. He's part of the group." Andy is not, technically, part of the mall group. But to Ken he is a best friend. As the film shows the impossibility of enduring, close relationships, it also celebrates our ability to communicate across distances without ever actually connecting to other people.

The End

As with the original, this *Dawn* ends with an escape. Unlike the original, in which the mall denizens leave because they must (after the bikers and zombies invade), these survivors plan and execute their escape strategy, which must go sooner than expected because of the failed rescue attempt on Andy. Ana, Ken, Terry and Nicole survive to reach Steve's boat and motor off into Lake Michigan. The credits then begin to roll. Unlike in the original, however, the narrative continues into the credits. Terry has apparently found Steve's old camera on the boat. In between shots of Steve and a topless woman, we see snippets of film that show the group progressing across the lake. They encounter another boat, abandoned, that has a living severed head in a Styrofoam cooler. They run out of gas and must attempt to navigate and paddle the boat toward an island in the distance. As they land the boat on the island, noises are heard. Ken is heard yelling, and there are screams. A large horde of zombies come out of the foliage on the island toward the camera, which is dropped by Terry; a zombie, shot in the head, falls into frame in front of the camera as the screams continue.

This ending sequence, although somewhat ambiguous and open-ended, genuinely seems to imply that none of the characters survive. While the original allows for the possibility of hope, the remake offers a much more nihilistic ending.[3] As noted previously, Romero's characters often escape to islands, or hope to escape to an island (as the cop in the original *Dawn* states, "We're going downriver to try and make the island." When asked, "Which island," he replies, "Any island"). In Romero's films, islands represent locations safe from both zombies and societies.[4] In the *Dawn* remake, the island is not a refuge but yet another place where the fast dead can and will kill the living.

The ending is emblematic of post–9/11 horror. It is bleak, nihilistic and offers little to no hope of survival. As in such post–9/11 films as *Cloverfield*, *The Strangers*, *The Collector* and *REC*, there are no survivors. Everyone dies, and it is caught on camera. This *Dawn* is bleak and unremitting and without hope. It therefore also beautifully expresses the sociophobics of its time.

Notes

1. In the interests of full disclosure, the remake of *Dawn of the Dead* was ultimately the impetus behind this book. While fanboys argued about the merits of fast or slow zombies, academic authors and critics dismissed the film as lacking the social commentary of the original. As one can see from this chapter, I disagree.

2. Information on "date night" taken from Jay Slupesky's "A Marriage Therapist's Blog." Posted 12 February 2010. <http://eastbaycouples.com/blog/tag/suggestions/>. Accessed 14 July 2010.

3. Although in the commentary track on the DVD the filmmakers insist they want the ending to be read as open-ended, the situation presented is dire. The characters have no food, no water, no gasoline, no way to power the boat, and an overwhelming, fast zombie horde is running toward them. All that is heard on the soundtrack is screams. While it is possible one or more of the four might escape, it does not seem likely. And if they do escape, where can they go? The ending is much more bleak than open-ended. Not to mention that all this occurs while a song entitled "People Who Died," by the Jim Carroll Band, plays on the soundtrack, endlessly repeating "Those are people who died." The musical implication is that everyone in the film is one of the "people who died."

4. Romero himself will critique this motif in *Survival of the Dead*, in which Plum Island is even worse than the mainland, both in terms of the presence of zombies and an oppressive society. See chapter 10.

Interlude: "Did you know that movie was based on a true case?" *Return of the Living Dead* (1985)

Brains!

Seth Grahame-Smith's delightful rewrite of Jane Austen in *Pride and Prejudice and Zombies* opens with the line, "It is a truth universally acknowledged that a zombie in possession of brains must be in want of more brains" (7). Except that is not quite true. Such a universal truth is only acknowledged after 1985. The dead in *Night*, *Dawn* and *Day* do not crave brains—or, more accurately, do not crave just brains. They eat the whole body of the victim. The now universally acknowledged belief that zombies crave brains comes from *Return of the Living Dead*. Although presented in popular culture as a given from the Romero school of zombies, brain-eating is a late development in zombie lore, comparatively speaking.

Based on a novel of the same name by John A. Russo, rewritten and directed by Dan O'Bannon, *Return of the Living Dead* was the first film since *Night* to use the words "living dead" (as opposed to "dead") in the title. After *Night*, Russo held the rights to the words "living dead. The film is substantially different than his novel, however, as O'Bannon wanted to drastically differentiate his film from Romero's. And O'Bannon's legacy is the zombie's love of brains, which appears nowhere in Romero's canon.

The "Tarman" is the first to speak the magic word. When Tina goes looking for Freddy at the medical supply warehouse, Tarman identifies her as "Brains! ... Live Brains!" When the other punks arrive to rescue her, his response is, "More brains!" The Tarman's enthusiasm is amusing, but we might also note that he identifies living humans solely by this one element. What distinguishes the living from the dead is the living brain. After all, these dead move, talk, think, are capable of plotting and planning. The dead in *Return* recognize that the key difference between them and the living is "brains."

Subsequently in the film, an explanation for this need to eat brains is given. An emaciated skeletal female corpse grabs and bites Scuz. She is cut in half, and her head and torso dragged into the funeral home and tied down to the embalming table; yet, as in *Day*, she continues to attempt to eat the living, despite the absence of digestive organs. Ernie (Don Calfa) proceeds to question her:

ERNIE: Why do you eat people?
FEMALE ZOMBIE: Not people. Brains.
ERNIE: Brains only?
FEMALE ZOMBIE: Yes.
ERNIE: Why?
FEMALE ZOMBIE: The pain!
ERNIE: What about the pain?
FEMALE ZOMBIE: The pain of being dead!
ERNIE: It hurts ... to be dead.
FEMALE ZOMBIE: I can feel myself rot.
ERNIE: Eating brains.... How does that make you feel?
FEMALE ZOMBIE: It makes the pain go away!

This exchange constitutes the explanation of the need for the dead to eat brains, as well as a radically different understanding of the nature of zombies. They need to eat brains because being dead is painful. After death, the reanimated dead can "feel themselves rot." Decomposition is painful, and as it begins immediately upon the cessation of life, when a person dies they reanimate in pain and instinctively know to seek human brains, as that will alleviate the pain. Romero's zombies are not in pain. They seem to feel no pain, in fact. They are simply driven to consume the living; but a scientific explanation for this will not be given until *Day*. *Return* posits an excruciating existence upon death, both physically agonizing and driving one to consume the brains of one's friends and loved ones.

Frank (James Karen) and Freddy (Thom Matthews) find rigor mortis painful. After he dies and reanimates, Freddy pursues Tina (Beverly Randolph) around the chapel, telling her, "I can finally see the one thing and one thing only that can relieve this horrible suffering ... live brains." He transforms from loving boyfriend to monster out to kill her and eat her brains. Frank, on the other hand, climbs into the crematorium, immolating himself rather than become a brain-eating zombie.

We might read this in terms of American anti-intellectualism, particularly in 1985. The eating of brains is a metaphor for the rejection of rational thought. The dead are just like us, but they cannot be killed and are driven by the need to consume the seat of human intellect. The living dead become especially dangerous in mobs — large groups can overwhelm and destroy the living. The need for brains might also be contrasted with *Dawn* as a metaphor for consumption. The living dead consume only one thing — brains. But they need it in great amounts, think of nothing else, and are extreme in their pursuit of it, even to the point of personal injury. Our first informant, after all, is the female zombie that allows herself to be cut in half in order to continue to try to get brains. This excess becomes a metaphor for a culture of mass consumption not driven by anything rational. These living dead are dangerous consumers who continually and seriously damage themselves, others and their environment in their ruthless pursuit of consumption.

Thus, one of the sociophobias of this fear is a concern over anti-intellectualism in American culture, which is echoed in the punks and the military in this film. All of the groups reject considered thought in favor of an all-consuming nihilism, more of which shall be discussed below. Another sociophobia addressed in this analysis is the fear of mindless, ruthless consumption that begins to destroy the consumers. If American consumer culture was worthy of critique in 1978 through *Dawn*, by 1985 the consumption, excess and disregard for the costs had reached dangerous levels.

Return also anticipates many of the changes in the postmodern zombie films and remade Romero films. These zombies are not Romero's slow, shuffling dead. They run, jump, tackle, dive through windows and chase the living in organized packs and through clever ruses. They scream and moan and they talk: "Brains," "More brains," and the famous, "Send more paramedics" and "Send more cops," thus anticipating the intelligent zombie. *Land*'s Big Daddy and *Day*'s Bub may not talk, but they communicate, sharing thoughts through gesture and vocalization. Big Daddy leads a pack of zombies and organizes them to trap and kill their human enemies.

Return's zombies are Trioxin zombies, named after the chemical compound which animates them. The film sets up its own rules: the zombies, as noted above, need to eat brains, they are intelligent, they talk, and the old ways of stopping zombies no longer work. Trioxin zombies do not stop if shot in the head, are burned or in any way suffer head trauma. They are practically indestructible. As Burt (Clu Gulager) realizes, "You can chop them up into pieces, the pieces would still come after you. All you can do is just burn them. You got to totally reduce them to ashes so there's nothing left to come after you." Except as the film demonstrates, that does not work. It only creates more zombies.

I argue here that the absurdity and nihilism of *Return* offers a snapshot of mid-eighties America. Whereas *Day* offers a serious critique of the military establishment and its appropriation of some of the scientific community, as discussed in chapter 8, *Return* offers a humorous middle finger to the Cold

War, the military, and such doctrines as "Mutually Assured Destruction," a policy of deterrence built on the belief that neither the Soviet Union nor the United States would use nuclear weapons, as it would cause the other side to use the same weapons, resulting in the annihilation of both nations. In other words, paradoxically, both nations had to have as many nuclear weapons as possible in order to ensure that they would not be used. O'Bannon's film highlights the absurdity of such national security policies.

Zombies and Humorous Nihilism: An Eighties Manifesto

Like *Night*, *Return* is set in the heartland: Louisville, Kentucky. Like *Night*, it tells the story of the events of a single evening that occur in one location to a group of individuals trapped in that area. In the DVD director's commentary, Dan O'Bannon cited the influence of *Mad* magazine, noting especially *Mad*'s habit of filling individual pictures with other jokes unrelated to the main story. O'Bannon also fills the screen with satirical bits and references. For example, when characters are having a conversation in front of an eye chart hanging in Burt's office, the careful observer will note that the eye chart, over the space of a dozen lines, spells out "Burt is a slave driver." This is but one example of the playful approach O'Bannon and his collaborators took.

What makes *Return* disturbing, however, it that is also contains very serious references as well: the crematorium doors in Ernie's funeral home were designed to look like the crematoria of Auschwitz. This blend of humor and horror results in a kind of humorous nihilism—a belief in nothing and an ironic distance from everything that happens. *Return* was much more successful at the box office than *Day*, which leads one to wonder if the times were not better suited to humorous nihilism than gritty military critique.

The central aspect of the film's humorous nihilism is its embracing of punk. The main characters are punks who evince a belief in nothing, not even punk. The (ostensibly) self-chosen names of the characters evince the nihilism: Trash (Linnea Quigley), Suicide (Mark Venturini), and Scuz (Brian Peck). The characters reject the names given to them by their parents and assume new identities based on punk's valuing of the low over things middle class. Punk began in the 1970s with a rejection of mainstream values, a lack of concern for the present and an embracing of nihilism. As the Sex Pistols sang in "God Save the Queen": "No future, no future." *Return* literalized that belief in a lack of future.

By the '80s, punk in some ways had sold out. Punk was commercial. There was also a strong horror vibe to punk. The Misfits pioneered "Horror Punk." Founded in 1977 in Lodi, New Jersey, by Glenn Danzig, the band disbanded in 1983, two years before *Return*; but in their six years of existence in that form, the band blended horror motifs with punk music. The Misfits' iconic skull logo still remains popular today. It should be noted that the fourth single by the Misfits was 1979's "Night of the Living Dead," inspired by the film of the same name. The soundtrack for *Return* was full of death rock and horror punk, featuring songs by the Cramps, the Flesh Eaters, the Damned, and 45 Grave, among others.

Return thus celebrated punk and embraced its ideology, while at the same time subverting its non-idealistic ideals. Of the group of eight punks in the film (Suicide, Trash, Scuz, Spider, Chuck, Casey, Tina and Freddy), only Suicide takes punk ideals seriously. He grows angry at the others when they call him "spooky," lamenting and lashing out at Trash:

> Nobody understands me, you know that? I fucking bust my ass for you guys and what do I get? "You're spooky." Fuck you, man. Fuck you all.... I mean, I got something to say, you know? What do you think this is all about? You think this is a fucking costume? This is a way of life!

He keeps calling her "man." They all want to party; only Suicide seems committed to what punk is. Only Suicide walks the talk. The other punks want a place to party, and they invite Suicide because he has a car. Yet, Suicide actually believes in punk, which is, of course, ironic, because behind punk is a lack of belief in anything.

All of the young characters are disaffected youth. They dress the way they do, like the music they do, and act the way they do to in order to react against society. They reject mainstream, middle-class (read: parental) values. And yet their rebellion is not in the name of doing anything better or different. They do not seek to change the world, only find a place to party. In that sense, the film also uses punk to critique punk. The punks suddenly want to live when confronted with actual death.

The film begins and ends with death. It is set in a medical supply house that contains real skeletons and cadavers and body parts. The punks themselves playfully discuss death.

> SCUZ: Oh we can't, the cops said they'd shoot us if we go back to the park.
> SPIDER: Yeah, and I ain't in no mood to die tonight.
> TRASH: I like death.
> CHUCK: I like death with sex. Casey, do you like sex with death?
> CASEY: Yeah, so fuck off and die.

This dialogue is ironic, as the banter is light; and, in fact, Spider will die tonight, as will they all. Trash and Chuck will be proven liars as, when given the option, they do not like death.

They decide to hang out in Resurrection Cemetery while they wait for

Freddy to get off work and tell them where they can find a party. While they wait, they begin to party themselves while also wreaking havoc in the cemetery. Despite their professed love of death, none of them actually know anything about death. Scuz has never been to a funeral because he "never knew nobody that died." By the end of the film, everyone he knows has died, either at the hands of the zombies or by the nuclear bomb dropped on Lexington.

Trash fantasizes "about being killed" and thinks about "all the different ways of dying ... violently ... or what would be the most horrible way to die." For her, "the worst way would be for a bunch of old men to get around me and start biting me and eating me alive," which is, of course, exactly what happens to her. As she grinds against Suicide, he pushes her aside, saying, "What's wrong with you, man? Show some fucking respect for the dead, will you?" which again makes him both the most punk and least punk of the punks. Punk has respect for nothing, but Suicide demands respect for the dead. Simultaneously, however, he also rejects Trash's and the others' mindless partying. *Return* shows a group of kids rebelling against society, but rather than simply taking their side against adults and society, as so many teen films might, it also shows that their punk pose is just that: a pose. They speak of loving death, but they neither know it nor actually crave it. The film actually gives them the nihilism they play at.

In addition to using punk to critique punk, the film also has two other significant targets: the military and business. Interestingly, the film does not directly attack the military-industrial complex but uses a small local business as its metaphor. Kyle William Bishop states that *Return* "presents a scathing criticism of the American military complex" (*American Zombie*, 185). Business, at all levels, also comes under scathing critique for its own nihilistic values, embracing only profit and self-protection.

Frank and Freddy, for example, decide not to tell Burt about the accident that unleashes the trioxin, as "it might make us look stupid." With this, the cover-up begins; but it is not a competent one. At every step of the way the individuals move to protect themselves and, perhaps more importantly, the company. And yet with every step they make the problem worse. Frank's first solution is to spray Lysol to cover up the smell. When they discover the living half-dog, reanimated by the trioxin, they panic and try to kill it by hitting it with a broom. None of these solutions work, obviously.

Freddy calls Frank a "stupid asshole" for leaking the trioxin. "Watch your tongue, boy, if you like this job," is the response. "Like this job?" asks Freddy, the implication being there are greater problems than Freddy insulting his corporate superior, and that there are fates worse than being fired. Not so for Frank, whose first impulse is to protect the company (and himself): "You don't want to call the cops. You know what the cops would do to this company?" he asks Freddy. Freddy's response: "Who cares about the company?" It is clear Frank does. He will not call the police or the number on the side of the containers, which will connect him to the army. His solution is to call the owner of the company.

What is especially remarkable is that when the army is finally contacted, they understand the delay. Colonel Glover's (Jonathan Terry) response, heard as one side of a telephone call, is deadpan to the point of being blasé: "Why didn't you call this number immediately? I see. It's understandable." The military *expects* a cover-up and the protection of the individuals involved as a priority. The military and business are complicit in the larger cover-up which is to follow.

Burt's response to the trioxin leak when he arrives is not concern over the leak and its possible side effects but how it affects him personally as head of the company: "I'm going to be sued by the Darrow Chemical Company. I'm going to be investigated by the government. I might become very famous, Frank. I might even lose my business. I might even go to jail, goddamn it!" If we take these as an ascending order of possible negative consequences, being sued is bad, being investigated by the government is worse, losing one's business is terrible, and the worst thing that can happen is the head of the company going to jail. It is Burt, in fact, who, after this litany, proposes a cover-up: "On the other hand, if we destroy all this evidence around here and keep our mouths shut...." To which an enthusiastic Frank responds, "That's it! Let's do that, Burt!"

Burt, as a business owner, then turns to his friend Ernie, who owns the mortuary and funeral home next door. Burt, Frank and Freddy enter the mortuary and approach Ernie about using the crematorium to dispose of the evidence of the leak. Though Ernie is concerned about having people in the embalming room, telling Burt, "It's illegal!" once Burt explains the plan, Ernie asks, "What's in it for me?" While he pays lip service to obeying the law, especially when it comes to health concerns, Ernie ultimately is out for his own self-interest.

Burt asks, "What do you want?" To this Ernie replies, "Way I see it, this is a pretty big favor." Burt promises Ernie to do whatever he asks later. Ernie then agrees to burn the bodies: "All right, let's take care of your problem. Yesirree, you're going to owe me a big one." In other words, Ernie engages in illicit behavior because it will help a fellow local businessman and put him in a position to profit from Burt. None of them anticipate the aftereffects of the cremation, as none of them are thinking about any possible long-term repercussions. The body is burned, but the smoke and ash coming out of the chimney is shown to form precipitation. An acid rain falls on the cemetery, reanimating the buried corpses.

The military is critiqued in this film, as Bishop suggests; but the military characters are also a synecdoche for the privileged classes in America. The lower class life of the punks (only one of whom has a job), the heavily graffitied and vandalized cemetery, the beat-up car and the kids who have nowhere to go are contrasted with the upper class military family. After the credits, the film transitions from the plastic-wrapped reanimated dead body to a shot of the American flag (suggesting the same opening-credit flag from *Night*). The camera pulls back to reveal a gated and guarded private estate with well-manicured grounds and a private tennis court. Visible behind the house is the ocean, and the sound of waves crashing (perhaps on a private beach?) is clearly audible. The guards spring to attention as a luxury car pulls up and the subtitles tell us it is "4:00 Pacific Daylight Time." We will learn later that this is San Diego. This mansion is a home of privilege. In the next shot, the driver of the car, a uniformed soldier, who we will later learn is Colonel Horace Glover, enters a huge foyer decorated with tapestries and with entranceways into other elaborate and tastefully decorated rooms as classical music plays. He then makes his way into a dining room where his wife, Ethel, wearing a formal dress and pearls, lays out an elaborate table in front of a mural of a Spanish conquistador arriving in the new world. Their home is ornate and full of expensive material possessions. O'Bannon cuts directly from the colonel's dining room to the punk kids in the trashed car literally crossing to the proverbial wrong side of the tracks. These kids are not only on the other side of the country, they are on the *underside* of the country. Their visible poverty contrasts with the conspicuous wealth and privilege of the colonel.

The military is clearly privileged in every sense in this film, the colonel living a life of opulence and wealth. He carries out his work at a distance from any citizens. He is completely disconnected from the everyday lives of the other Americans in the film. His power is substantial. However, authority figures are powerless in the face of the living dead. Two cops arrive to investigate the missing paramedics and are overwhelmed and consumed. Later, a police helicopter and a line of squad cars arrive, and the units on the ground are attacked and the officers also overwhelmed.

As the helicopter flies overhead, the characters hear, "Attention. Attention. This is the police. This area is under police blockade. All persons within this area wishing to surrender should make their way to the perimeter at once." Yet we immediately see the police blockade overwhelmed. The local authorities clearly have no idea how to cope with or contain the situation. The cop Burt calls does not know what is going on, he only knows that he has lost over a dozen men. Then he himself is killed. The zombies request "more cops" over the police radio. In short, the police cannot help in this situation.

Once Burt calls the number on the side of the container, he explains what is happening to Colonel Glover and then is told to wait. The colonel then alerts a superior that the missing "Easter eggs" have been found. The code name for the containers holding trioxin zombies is a pun, both on the round shapes of the containers but also on "Easter" as a holiday of resurrection. We do not hear the response from the superior, but Glover then states, "Well, sir, it would be good news, except that the eggs have hatched." Glover then receives orders on how to deal with a "hatched" egg. We see orders making their way through the chain of command to a man working a missile battery.

At 5:01 A.M., a nuclear missile takes out 20 city blocks and an estimated 4000 people in Louisville. As we witness the smoke and debris from the bomb, we hear the colonel's phone conversation as a voiceover:

> I wouldn't worry about the fires, General. The rain is taking care of that right now. Well, there have been complaints about burning skin, but I shouldn't worry. Minor irritation, General. The rain will wash everything away. That's correct, sir. Everything should be back to normal by morning.

As the last lines are spoken, we are shown the rain falling upon another cemetery, soaking into the earth and down into a casket. The music and images suggest the cycle will begin again and more zombies will be created. The military's solution — to nuke an American city — simply makes the problem worse.

This final solution is the greatest critique of the American military in the film. Not only does the military neither understand the implications nor realize the repercussions of firing a nuclear weapon on an American city with a small zombie outbreak, the unrealistic expectations of the military that everything "will return to normal" without any other efforts on the military's behalf have already been demonstrated to be wrong. This phone conversation displays not only the military's arrogance, hubris and ignorance, but also demonstrates the danger the military solution creates: it does not solve the problem but makes it worse. In a sense, *Return* "out–Herods Herod" and offers an even bleaker ending than *Night* by not only killing the protagonist(s) but by nuking all of Louisville, Kentucky, and showing the inability of the living to stop the trioxin zombies in any meaningful way. Every way the zombies are stopped only results in the creation of more zombies.

Metacinema and the Critique of Romero

At its heart, *Return* is also a critique of Romero's original film and an example of metacinema: a film about film. The events of *Return* occur in a world where *Night* exists and the characters have seen it. Thus, they are already aware of the tropes of zombie cinema. The characters (and O'Bannon's script) remind us of them so that *Return* can immediately begin to deconstruct and change them:

> FRANK: Let me ask you a question, kid. Did you see that movie *Night of the Living Dead*?
> FREDDY: Oh, yeah, yeah, yeah. That's the one where the corpses start eating the people, right? Sure. What about it?
> FRANK: Did you know that movie was based on a true case?
> FREDDY: Aw, c'mon, you're shitting me, right?
> FRANK: I ain't never been more serious in my life.
> FREDDY: That's not possible. I mean, they showed zombies taking over the world.
> FRANK: They changed it all around. What really happened was, back in 1969 in Pittsburgh at the VA hospital, there was a chemical spill. All that stuff kind of leaked down into the morgue and made all the dead bodies kind of jump around as though they was alive.
> FREDDY: What chemical?
> FRANK: 245 Trioxin it's called.

Trioxin, we are told was developed for the army to spray on marijuana. The army wanted to destroy pot as part of the "war on drugs." When the chemical was spilled, corpses reanimated. This story both revises *Night*'s Venus probe radiation cause for the outbreak, and also posits that the Venus probe was merely a cover story for the true origins of the zombie problem: a military accident that caused the dead to reanimate. Frank tells Freddy (and us) that Romero (unnamed) was told that if he told the truth he would be sued, so he "changed it all around."

The mistakes, however, were compounded, as no sooner had the outbreak been contained and the army had shipped out the contaminated dead bodies (ostensibly to a military base where they would be studied), a "typical army fuck up" landed the bodies at the Uneeda Medical Supply warehouse. The barrels have been stored at Uneeda ever since. This backstory not only critiques the military, but rewrites the history of *Night* as a docudrama based on a true story, with many aspects changed to avoid lawsuits and prosecution. *Night* is thus both true and not true: dead bodies were reanimated and attacked the living, but the details have all been changed.

As a result, the characters look to *Night* for answers on how to deal with their zombie crisis. O'Bannon seems to be suggesting that we look not to Hollywood for solutions (which would also be in keeping with his punk aesthetic — using cinema to critique cinema), as even when movies tell the truth they transform, embellish and sometimes simply lie. Burt knows "the movie" as well: "In that movie they destroyed the brain to kill them — is that what they did?" So Burt, Frank and Freddy tried to stop the reanimated cadaver in the freezer by destroying its brain. Frank, upon seeing the still-moving body of the zombie impaled through the head with a fire ax and subsequently beheaded, cries out, "It worked in the movie!" Burt responds, "Well, it ain't working now, Frank!" prompting Freddy's incredulous response, "You mean the movie *lied*?!"

Return is subversive and self-aware. By 1985, Romero's films had established "zombie rules," which *Return* became among the first to intentionally and self-consciously play against. For Romero, kill the brain and you kill the ghoul. *Return* refutes this by showing zombies with head injuries and even no head still animated. *Return*'s zombies are fast, can talk, and violate most of the tropes Romero created. The movie did indeed lie.

Return is also full of moments of reference to *Night*, both as playful allusion but also in order to again show how "the movie lied." The siege imagery of *Night* is repeated at the funeral home when they begin boarding up the windows to prevent the dead from coming in. Iconic images from *Night* are recreated but also undermined. We hear the pounding of hammers and see them cover every window. "How many fucking windows you got in this place?" Spider (Miguel Nunez) asks Ernie, which provokes laughter. The characters race around the home as they (and we) hear glass breaking, representing another zombie incursion. Whereas Ben is able to secure much of the farmhouse by himself, a group of people must work quickly to secure the funeral home.

The location, of course, is also ironic. Ernie and the punks work to secure a mortuary and funeral home against the living dead. They desire to keep the dead *out* of a funeral home. While Ben, Barbara and company defend the family home against hordes of intruders, Ernie, Spider and company defend a mortuary. The funeral home is not actually a home, but the characters of *Return* seek shelter there. There is also irony to be found in the placing of Frank and Freddy in the chapel. After they die and begin to become living dead, the two men are sealed in the chapel by the living, who no longer trust them. The place where the living go to say goodbye to the dead and pray for their repose becomes a place where the dead are sealed off from the living for their protection. Tina stays behind and agrees to be sealed into the chapel because she is not ready to let go of Freddy. A metaphor is literalized by Tina remaining behind, unable to leave those who have already passed on. In the end, this decision is shown to be a mistake, as Freddy then attacks her, seeking to eat her brain.

Ernie (a middle-aged white man) and Spider (a young black man) argue about how to protect themselves from the living dead. Spider wants to leave; Ernie wants to hide.

ERNIE: The crawlspace in the ceiling. We could go up, barricade ourselves in. The only way up is through the hatch, and we could nail that shut.
SPIDER: You must be out of your fucking mind. I'm not barricading myself in no damn roof.

This is a reference to and reversal of *Night*, where Harry wants to hide in the cellar and Ben refuses. The lines themselves echo Ben and Harry's argument in *Night* in which Ben asserts he will not trap himself down in the cellar.

As this example demonstrates, *Return* is very much a self-aware mirror image of *Night* in which the "rules" are revealed to be lies. *Night* sees some characters want to go down in the basement; *Return* sees characters want to go up to the attic. *Night* sees the siege of a farmhouse; *Return* sees the siege of a funeral home. *Night* offers ways to kill the living dead; *Return* reveals that none of them work, and some even make the situation worse. *Night* ends with a local posse stopping the zombies; *Return* ends with the military dropping a nuclear missile on Louisville, only exacerbating the problem. In a very real sense, *Return*'s sociophobic is that *Night* lied: there are no solutions to the problems, the authority figures do not know what they are doing, and any attempt to rescue survivors or fight the monsters will result in epic failure. There are some problems, caused by government, the military and human incompetence, that simply have no easy solutions. While *Return* seems like it will be a film both celebrating and critiquing its youthful punk characters, ultimately it embraces and affirms their nihilistic worldview, even as it shows it to be mere posing on their parts. The best example of this is, of course, trioxin itself.

"There Was Some Chemical That Soaked into the Soil..."

When the majority of characters are gathered together in the funeral home after the attacks of the zombies, Burt tells the punks, "There was a chemical. There was some chemical that soaked into the soil of the graveyard and made the corpses come back to life." He does not tell them that he was one of the ones who put the chemical into the soil, or at least was directly responsible for its release into the graveyard. His language construction is passive: the leaking and soaking was something the chemical did. No one actually did the releasing, in his linguistic construction. It was an act of nature, or an unpreventable occurrence.

This single line exposes one of the dominant sociophobics in *Return*, and why a Venus probe is replaced by a chemical leak. By 1985, American newspapers had, for over a decade, been reporting on chemical leaks — or, more accurately, the discovery of chemical leaks in residential areas. In almost every case, a corporation or industry had engaged in some sort of chemical dump, or purposeful or accidental leak. The dump or leak would be followed by a cover-up of some sort. Once discovered, the government would be required to fix the problem, instead of the original polluter. Usually there were also consequences for local residents, but any legal actions taken generally remained tied up in the courts for years.

The best known example of this situation was Love Canal, a neighborhood in Niagara Falls, New York, in the late 1970s. The neighborhood had been built over a chemical dump containing more than twenty thousand tons of dioxins, the common name for polychlorinated dibenzodioxins — environmental pollutants and causers of cancer and birth defects — put there by Hooker Chemicals. The dioxins had soaked into the soil and water table and caused local residents numerous health problems (see Blum 9–27).

Several other toxic waste sites were discovered over the next decade. Wade Dump in Pennsylvania had PCBs, cyanide, and acid leaking into the groundwater and catching fire when cleanup finally began in 1981. Valley of the Drums was another toxic waste site — this one near Louisville, Kentucky, where cleanup began in 1983, two years before *Return*. Many of these cleanups came about as a direct result of the Comprehensive Environmental Response, Compensation, and Liability Act of 1980 (CERCLA), which also created the so-called "Superfund," which congress developed in order to pay for the cleaning and detoxification of sites contaminated by toxic waste. The Environmental Protection Agency was charged with locating polluters and compelling them to clean up such sites, or, failing to locate a culpable corporation, to arrange for the cleanup. As Valley of the Drums was located in the same city where *Return* is set, it is not too much of a leap of the imagination to see that the dominant sociophobic in *Return* is the chemical spill. Trioxin is a clear reference to dioxins, the toxic chemical of Love Canal and several subsequent toxic waste cleanup sites.

Return is thus a return to the origins of the living dead, positing a truth behind *Night* that *Night* did not tell the truth about. Radiation from a Venus probe did not reanimate the dead — a chemical spill did. When the chemical is re-released into the atmosphere, nearby dead tissue again reanimates. The consequences of doing so are dire, and not just for the individuals who do so but for the entire surrounding area. While the film posits that business and industry are to be feared, as is the military, it is as much for their incompetence at dealing with the very crisis they create as any malevolence on their parts. *Return* seems to say that we should never look for malice when human stupidity, ineptitude, ineffectiveness and shortsightedness can explain the horrible things that happen. *Return* reflects upon the Reagan era with a humorous nihilism that demonstrates an apocalypse more in tune with *Dr. Strangelove* than *Dawn* or *Day*. Everybody dies, and that is, in the end, pretty funny in a black humor kind of way.

Returning Again and Again and Again...

In 1988, *Return of the Living Dead Part II* opened, spawning a series of sequels to an unofficial sequel/remake (of sorts). *Return II* is in many ways a repeat of the first (with several of the same actors). A trioxin zombie falls off a military truck in a new suburban development, causing the dead to rise and attack a group of young people. Two grave robbers, played by Thom Matthews and James Karen from the first film, undergo the same experience as their characters in the first movie — dying and reanimating. In the end, we learn that while decapitation, dismemberment, and being crushed do not stop the living dead, for some reason high voltage electricity does. Unlike the first film, the sequel ends with the possibility of stopping the outbreak. The film also loses its punk edge, with a twelve-year-old kid as hero, aided by his teenaged sister and her boyfriend.

In *Return of the Living Dead 3* (1993), some of the more pertinent themes of the series (and *Day*) appear. The U.S. government experiments with trioxin in order to create trioxin zombies to serve as soldiers that cannot be killed. Introduced in this film is yet another new way to stop the trioxin zombies: freeze the brain and the zombie is at least put into suspended animation. The son of one of the military men overseeing the zombie project brings his girlfriend to the military laboratory. When she accidentally is killed, he reanimates her. She goes punk, with serious piercings, and becomes the soldier the military wants. The idea of the zombie soldier who keeps fighting even though dead comes from *Day*, and will later be seen in *Zombie Strippers*.

In *Return Part II* and *Return 3*, coming at the end of the Reagan-Bush era and the beginning of the Clinton administration, two motifs from the original begin to dominate. First, the focus on young protagonists transform these movies into teen films. Whereas the punks are significant in the original, they are part of a larger story and are all at least college age. In the second and third films, the protagonists are high schoolers. The *Return* sequels are effectively reduced to teen horror, and thus focus on a young sociophobic rather than the concerns of society at large. Second, the films continue their focus on the military; but even though the army's experiments with zombies are central to the third film, it lacks the critique of the military from the first.

The fourth sequel, *Return of the Living Dead 4: Necropolis*, was virtually unrelated to the original three and released twelve years later, in 2005. By now, the film has completely immersed itself in youth culture. A group of high school kids break into a military base in order to rescue a friend who has been zombified. In doing so, they accidentally release a number of zombies, who begin attacking others. Whereas the trioxin zombies of the original are almost unstoppable, the dead can now once again be killed by a shot to the head. The humorous nihilism of the original is gone, replaced with a standard group of stereotypical teenagers fighting the monsters. By the end the zombies are stopped, except for an "or are they?" stinger via a news anchor reporting the zombie outbreak assuring viewers it is over (if it happened at all) and then being attacked on-camera by a zombie, who bites his head.

Produced simultaneously as *Necropolis*, *Return of the Living Dead: Rave to the Grave* (2005) dropped the numbers: and as the title suggests, rave culture has replaced punk culture in this one. Punk in 2005 is retro and mainstream, whereas society was concerned with raves and what happens at them. Although raves had been occurring since the seventies in the United States, it was only in the late nineties and first decade of the twenty-first century that society began to express concern over what occurs at them, not least because of several well-publicized deaths at raves and the popular perception that raves were drug-centric. Ravers, who differ greatly from punks in appearance, music and outlook, embrace a culture of hedonistic partying.

Contemporary nihilism is more of a self centered hedonism and epicurianism — pleasure in the moment. It is not a rejection on philosophical grounds of the mainstream culture but an embracing of its pleasurable aspects while rejecting the previous generation's values. The "Rave to the Grave" is a huge party that zombies interrupt; but the living dead are eventually defeated. The series has come far since the original *Return*, which was a very self-aware horror film that understood its own sociophobics. *Rave to the Grave* exposes a pair of oppositional sociophobics: it relies on an adult fear of raves and what happens at them (drug-taking, rapes, and other problems caused by out-of-control young people), while at the same time focusing on a youth fear that the party will end. The authority figures (parents, teachers, police, the military) will attempt to stop young people from having fun. That is a far cry from concern over nuclear weapons and toxic waste dumps.

III
Day

8

"From now on, everyone is under martial law!": *Day of the Dead* (1985)

The third film in Romero's original trilogy is perhaps the least loved and admired by his fans, but it is nonetheless an excellent and well-made movie. It was a quintessential eighties film (as will be detailed below), not least because of how it was first encountered by most people. *Day*'s opening was not strong, and fans preferred *Return of the Living Dead*, released around the same time, for cutting-edge zombie cinema. As a result, VHS was *Day*'s "primary format of display," not cinema (Felsher, n.p.), which means that *Day* was also the first film in Romero's trilogy to receive multiple viewings at home. By 1985, VHS was the dominant format for home film viewing, having beaten out Beta and Laserdisc. *Day*, as the Romero film that was primarily encountered on VHS, the exemplary eighties format, was thus also the embodiment of eighties zombies. In the past two-and-a-half decades, its reputation has grown as a much better film than first reviewed.

Day echoes and expands the key sociophobic of both *Night* and *Dawn*: that other humans are more dangerous in the end than the living dead. The dead have won in *Day*, but in the face of overwhelming defeat, the humans still prefer to kill each other rather than the zombies. For all practical purposes, the film posits eleven humans left alive in the United States, possibly the world, and they are all armed with guns and willing to kill each other. As Michael Felsher observes, "These folks are in serious danger of losing their only hope for survival by refusing to let go of what once was" (n.p.). The survivors hold on to outdated social structures and beliefs. They follow a command structure that lost everyone outside the bunker. The very real possibility of the end of the human race confronts the characters, and they embrace that possibility rather than work together. It is, altogether, a bleak, pessimistic view of humanity filmed at the height of the Reagan administration.

In this chapter I consider *Day* as very much an archetypal eighties film, influenced by and embracing not only the home video revolution described above, but also the Reagan era's nostalgia for the fifties, the apocalyptic nuclear film such as *The Day After* (itself also a film about the end of the human race and the world as we know it), and eighties films about Vietnam and Vietnam vets. Then I examine the opening sequence in order to tease out *Day*'s themes and sociophobics. Lastly, I consider two major themes of the work: functioning after one's purpose has gone, and science in the service of the military, both major issues during the eighties. Like all films, *Day* reflects the milieu in which it was created, but it also builds upon Romero's earlier work as well. The chapter concludes with a brief observation on the place of *Day* in the canon.

"Mo(u)rning in America" (and in the Movie Theater)

Glenn Kay reminds us that the cinematic context of *Day* was the Hollywood of Reagan's "Morning in America"—nostalgia for the fifties, concern over communism and a celebration of American spirit (132). The dominant films when *Day* came out were such opuses as *Rocky IV, Cocoon*, and *Back to the Future*—bright visions of the future and wish-fulfillment (in fact, on its opening weekend *Day* opened third behind the latter two) (133). Unlike in the earlier films, in which America is celebrated, nostalgia for the past was embraced, and the main characters overcome adversity through sheer strength of will, *Day* was a bleak, pessimistic, progressive zombie movie for the Reagan era.

A contemporary film that *Day* slightly resembled was the made-for-television movie *The Day After* (1983). *The Day After* concerned a nuclear attack on the United States by the Soviet Union and its aftereffects. While not a typical apocalyptic survivalist film, it did use many of the tropes of the disaster movie to demonstrate a possible scenario if nuclear missiles were deployed against a small city in Kansas. While the two are similar in neither imagery nor plot, what both *Day*s did have in common was imagining what the United States might look like after an apocalyptic event wiped out most of the population. *Day of the Dead*, much like *Day After*, does not present heroic survivors gathering together and fighting back against those who attacked the United States and attempting to rebuild society. Both films present survivors simply trying to survive one more day in deplorable conditions, with substandard and ruined equipment. Both films were pessimistic and believed that the military command structure and the government were part of the problem, not part of the solution.

Day of the Dead showed a small group of military survivors living in a bunker. While many critics saw the film as dividing between the scientists and the soldiers, we might note that no one in the bunker is technically a civilian. The scientists are all government employed scientists who were brought to the bunker to research the walking dead and find a cure. While the group subdivides into military and scientists, all of them are former agents of the United States government, so to speak. Just as *Back to the Future* displayed a nostalgia for the fifties and demonstrated how that decade both informed and was undermined by the eighties, *Day of the Dead* also displays a pessimistic, perverse nostalgia for the bomb shelter mentality of the fifties. The characters live in a bomb shelter underground with limited supplies. *Day* is very much the dark cousin of the eighties film celebrating the fifties, echoing Reagan's rhetoric.

If *Night* is an analogy for the Vietnam War as it was experienced at home, *Day* is an analogy for Vietnam veterans, who came to prominence during the Reagan era, often as part of a counter-narrative. *Day* shows broken and angry former soldiers reliving a war long lost. *Day* therefore also fits right in with eighties films about the Vietnam War experience, such as *Apocalypse Now* (1979), *Platoon* (1986) or *Hamburger Hill* (1987), and films about Vietnam veterans, such as *The Deer Hunter* (1978), *First Blood* (1982), and *Rambo: First Blood Part II* (1985). All of these films engage post traumatic stress disorder as experienced by Vietnam vets, as well as the sense of betrayal and loss when, upon returning from combat, they found a nation at best indifferent to them and their needs, and at worst genuinely hostile toward the "baby killers." The overarching narrative of the *First Blood* series, as well as the other Vietnam films of the period, is that the people and government of the United States abandoned soldiers who had been drafted into the military, sent to fight a war not their own, and returned to resentment and a lack of sympathy. It is thus up to Vietnam veterans to care for (and, in the case of *Rambo*, rescue) themselves and other veterans. The eighties was the decade of the angry soldier, fearful and betrayed by his nation. *Day* reflects this mode as well. *Day* also parodies the militarism of eighties films such as *Red Dawn* and *Rambo*. John, Sarah and McDermott climb to safety and freedom through a missile silo!

Tony Williams also reports that the original plan for *Day* was to include a wealthy upper class that "lives in affluent luxury parodying the escapist world for popular Reaganite television series such as *Dallas, Dynasty, The Colbys* and *Falcon Crest*" (130). While not included in the final script, the idea would finally manifest itself in *Land of the Dead* (see chapter 10). It also indicates a desire on Romero's part to link the militaristic culture of the eighties to its economic excesses. *Night* is a critique of the late sixties, *Dawn* is a critique of the late seventies, and *Day* is very much a critique of the mid-eighties.

"The Fact Is ... We Are the Only Ones Left"

To understand the evolution in Romero's narrative, one need only look at the opening sequences of each film in the original trilogy. In *Night*, a brother and sister argue in the cemetery where they have come to visit their father's grave. Normalcy falls apart with the arrival of the Cemetery Zombie. There is no normalcy in *Dawn*. From the opening moment the ongoing crisis dominates. Fran wakes up in a chaotic newsroom. By the beginning of *Day*, however, the crisis is over, replaced, in a sense, with a new crisis. The war is over; the zombies won. The characters have a new normalcy, with new routines and a dwindling population of twelve human beings left alive. *Day* features social disintegration, as society as we know it is gone. We are shown something that barely even qualifies as a microcosm: a few survivors hiding in a bunker.

On the one hand, Romero seems to indicate that we can learn to live with anything, and we certainly did in the eighties. The doctrine of MAD (Mutually Assured Destruction) was one of the guiding principles of the Cold War. The aforementioned *The Day After* emphasized to television audiences in the United States in 1983 the idea that the United States and the Soviet Union, even in a limited exchange of missiles, would end life as we know it. With the threat of global extinction and the very real possibility of global thermonuclear war constantly overhead, most people went on with life as usual, not giving too much thought to the danger and peril America found itself in as a result of these policies.

The opening sequence of *Day* begins with Sarah (Lori Cardille) alone in a concrete bunker devoid of everything. The only other object in the space is a calendar open to October, displaying a picture of a field picked relatively clean, except for a few pumpkins.[1] All thirty-one days are crossed off, which means both the end of the month but also that the current day is the first of November, or All Saints Day, the day after Halloween and the day before *El Dia de los Muertos*. It is a time of year when the dead supposedly walk the Earth, but also when we remember the deceased family members as well as the saints. We remember and honor the dead. The image on the calendar concerns endings, harvest, a dying and no longer fertile Earth. No green exists, and the people in the barren field stand at a distance from the camera. It is the first of many images of isolation and distance in the film.

Sarah reaches up to change the calendar, and dozens of hands come through the wall. She turns away from the wall in fear and despair. She awakens in a helicopter, indicating what we just saw was her highly symbolic bad dream. The first thing she sees upon waking is Miguel (Antoné DiLeo), holding and kissing his saints medallions, further linking the opening to All Saint's

Day. Yet, the suggestion that we are in a holy period is an ironic one. Instead, Romero shows us a world without saints and without anything holy. Miguel (and Sarah) reach for something beyond themselves, for a belief in truly good human beings who point the way to God. No such people exist in Romero's world. In fact, almost no people of any kind exist in Romero's world.

As the helicopter lands, Romero relies on a series of long shots to establish how alone, distant and isolated the living are from their former lives and any other humans that might be alive. The helicopter, viewed from a distance, is small and inconsequential in the new landscape. Miguel begins using a bullhorn once the helicopter lands to call out to any possible survivors in the beachfront community. Again, Sarah and Miguel remain in the distance, centered in a long shot. "Hello? Is anyone there?" Miguel repeatedly calls. The city is shown initially to be abandoned, money blowing in the wind in front of a bank, as does a newspaper that reads "The Dead Walk." The next thing we see is a shambling dead man, the lower half of his face missing, bloody and rotten as the title credit is superimposed. He is seen in medium shot, in direct contradiction to the long shot of the living. This world belongs to the dead, who visually dominate it. The living are small, distant, and in most cases only a memory. Romero follows this shot with a series of close-ups of the dead responding to the living human voice. The response to that voice is a rising chorus of moans and groans from the emerging dead.

The helicopter returns to base, and Romero's camera work continues to demonstrate the isolation and solitary existence which the living now experience. Only two living soldiers are seen at the base initially: one tending to marijuana plants and one sitting in a canvas lean-to flipping through what appears to be a pornographic magazine. They are isolated visually, but also in their activities; these men do not work together, nor are they actively guarding the perimeter. They are indulging in distractions that dull the senses. The choice of activities also symbolizes the decay of military discipline and the self-indulgence of the remaining humans. These shots also create a sense of the hypocrisy of the military, which will allow the soldiers to indulge in these lapses of discipline and readiness while simultaneously expecting the scientists to deliver or die.

This sense of isolation and loneliness will be continually reinforced throughout the film. After returning to the bunker, Sarah goes to meet with Rhodes in a cavernous meeting hall/dining room. A dozen folding tables with a half dozen chairs at each are set up. Rhodes, Dr. Ted Fisher (John Amplas) and Private Steel (G. Howard Klar) sit at one table, Rickles (Ralph Marrero) sits two tables over. Sarah joins the three men to argue over Miguel and then begins to exit. Romero shows that the five of them are small in this sprawling space. As Sarah exits, she and Rhodes exchange words by yelling across the room, but the sense we have is of a small number of people in a huge space, utterly isolated from one another even when in the same room.

Later, in the same space, Romero will gather most of the living: five out of six soldiers; three scientists; and the pilot John, and communications specialist McDermott, who keep themselves separate from both groups. As the scientists and soldiers literally face off across two tables, John and McDermott sit at their own table, at a distance behind the scientists (with whom they nominally ally), with their guns on prominent display. The opening has thus far established that they cannot find anyone living within radio contact distance, and yet the eleven surviving humans cannot meet face to face without weapons or criticizing each other for every aspect of their behavior and personalities. Rhodes tells Sarah to sit down "or so help me God I'll have you shot," and then orders Steel to kill her. Steel initially treats the order as a joke, and Rhodes then points his gun at him and orders him again to shoot Sarah if she does not sit. Steel is hesitant to shoot her, but the scene demonstrates the lengths to which Rhodes will go to maintain the power structure. They may be the only eleven people left alive in the world, and Sarah the only woman among them, but Rhodes is willing to kill her to prove that he is in command.

Logan informs the other characters that the dead now outnumber the living 400,000 to one by his estimate. But again, we have only seen eleven living humans. Sarah assumes there must be other bunkers with other people in them:

> Look ... there have to be survivors in Washington. They have more sophisticated underground shelters than this one. There must be people in those shelters who know about us, who know where we are. With no radio contact, there's a small chance they might come looking for us....

This hope is never conclusively proven, however. Instead, the number of people within this bunker will slowly decrease until only three escape to an island somewhere in the Caribbean.

After the meeting, Sarah visits John and McDermott, apparently for the first time ever. McDermott must show her the way to their living quarters and then shows her around. Her delight at the novelty is apparent on her face, which indicates that she has never been here before. Even in a population of only eleven, these characters are isolated. The collapse of the world seems to bring about a collapse of personal relationships in *Day* (a sentiment that will be central to the remake of *Dawn*; see chapter 7). The only romantic relationship in the film is between Miguel and Sarah, and it is not a positive one. He treats her poorly, sensing her as a threat to his masculinity. He insults her and slaps her and is finally kicked out of their quarters by her for taunting her. The soldiers alternately bully and ignore one another. The only lasting relationships in the film are John and McDermott's friendship, which endures throughout the movie, and the relationship between Logan and Bub (which might be seen best as a master/pet relationship).[2]

In a few opening images and exchanges, Romero establishes the utter isolation and loneliness of his eleven surviving characters. A few of the characters express yearning for something more, something good and connected to God, but that is not possible. Others seek to find and establish society as it was, which is also not possible. The sociophobic here is one of dark wish fulfillment. What if one really was one of the last people left in the world? What if all of society collapsed and only a handful remained. While other films, such as the *Mad Max* series, also imagine an apocalyptic world in which we are free to fight for what we want, Romero sees the apocalypse that shuts down society as not freeing at all. Instead, we hold onto what was, and that is what dooms us. One must dig one's self out of the wreckage of society and not rebuild, but escape.

Functioning After the Purpose Is Gone

With Dr. Logan and his experiments, the audience is finally given some insight into the physiology and biological mechanics of the living dead. The soldiers call Logan "Frankenstein" as a derogatory nickname, but he is actually the reverse of Dr. Frankenstein. Whereas Mary Shelley's creation constructs a new being out of pieces of the dead, Logan deconstructs the dead and reduces them down to component pieces in order to see if they can be controlled. Like his nickname-sake, however, Logan loses control of his creations and is eventually killed — not by them but by the military.

One of Logan's main discoveries is that the zombies continue to try to eat long after the digestive system is removed. The brain is all that is needed for a zombie to continue its existence:

> You don't need any blood flow. You don't need any internal organs. I've severed all the vital organs in this one. There's nothing left of the corpse but brains and limbs, but still it functions. Look, Sarah! [*He dangles his fingers above the zombie's mouth and it tries to bite them.*] See! It wants me. It wants food. It has no stomach. It can take no nourishment from what it ingests. It's working on instinct!

Robin Wood reads this discovery as an enhancement of the satire in *Dawn*: "Above all, they consume *for the sake of consuming* (a revelation of *Day*, it was not apparent in the earlier films)" [emphasis in original] (289). The dead do not need human flesh to survive, they are instinctively driven to consume. America literally becomes a nation of consumers who consume even when they do not need to in this film. Yet there is another way to read this discovery relating specifically to *Day*: the body continues to function after the purpose is gone.

The dead continue their attacking, destructive behavior, even though it serves no practical purpose any more. They are instinctively driven to attack and eat the living, but they gain nothing by it. Romero uses this as a metaphor for what the characters of *Day* themselves are doing, and for America in the eighties. The dead try to eat long after the purpose and function of doing so are gone, just like the people in the base. Long after the purpose and functions are gone, they continue to do the activities they were assigned before the fall of society. They also hold onto outdated social and political structures. Rhodes, after threatening to shoot Sarah, states, "This ain't a goddam field trip, people. THIS IS A FUCKING WAR! I'm not down in this cave for my health, I'm down here on orders!" Fisher reminds him, "Your orders are to facilitate the job of this scientific team. This is a civilian team, Captain, and we don't have to be subjected to your tyranny." Rhodes rejects that structure. He asserts his own authority. But the people who gave the orders that sent Rhodes down into the cave are long dead. The military command structure is gone. The United States as an entity or body politic is gone. The purpose of the military, of the command structure, of everything Rhodes stands for, is gone. He insists on functioning after the purpose is gone.

Even the cave itself in which they stay functions after the purpose is gone. It is a storage facility and a missile base, but the nation it was created to defend no longer exists. The records that are stored there are no longer relevant or useful. John remarks to Sarah:

> We don't believe in what you're doing here, Sarah. Hey, you know what they keep down here in this cave? Man, they got the books and the records of the top 500 companies. They got the Defense Department budget down here. And they got the negatives for all your favorite movies. They got microfilm with tax return and newspaper stories. They got immigration records, census reports, and they got the accounts of all the wars and plane crashes and volcano eruptions and earthquakes and fires and floods and all the other disasters that interrupted the flow of things in the good ole U.S. of A. Now what does it matter, Sarah darling? All this filing and record keeping? We ever gonna give a shit? We even gonna get a chance to see it all? This is a great, big, fourteen mile *tombstone* with an epitaph on it that nobody gonna bother to read. Now, here you come. Here you come with a whole new set of charts and graphs and records. What you gonna do? Bury them down here with all the other relics of what ... once ... was? Let me tell you what else. Yeah, I'm gonna tell you what else. You ain't never gonna figure it out, just like they never figured out why the stars are where they're at. It ain't mankind's job to figure that stuff out. So what you're doing is a waste of time, Sarah. And time is all we got left, you know.

SARAH: What I'm doing ... is all there's left to do.
JOHN: Shame on you. There's plenty to do. Plenty to do, so long as there's you and me and maybe some other people.

Sarah defends her continuing the activities and duties she was assigned, as it is "all there's left to do," and because it gives her meaning and purpose. The soldiers hold on to the command structure and stay at the base helping the scientists because those were their orders. That gives their lives meaning and purpose, even though they don't understand it. "I'm not sure just what the hell it is you're doing in there. Just what it is that my men are risking their asses for," Rhodes grumbles, but he continues to allow it and support it, as those were his orders. John and McDermott do their jobs because it helps the others, but they do not find any meaning or purpose in it. They want to escape the base and go to an island. It is (as I noted earlier as Michael Felsher concludes, "These folks are in serious danger of losing their only hope for survival by refusing to let go of what once was" (n.p.). The only way the survivors of *Day* can continue to survive is to relinquish the old world and the old ways, which are now controlled by the dead anyway, and find new purpose and function.

Romero seems to suggest that America in 1985, by looking back in nostalgia to Cold War fifties-era attitudes, is continuing to do things the same way long after the purpose has ended. The zombies are a metaphor for an America stuck in the past and looking backwards for old solutions to new problems. Logan summarizes the zombies' situation:

> They are us. They are the extension of us. They are the same animal, just functioning less perfectly. They can be fooled, you see? They can be tricked into being good little girls and boys, the same way we were tricked into it: the promise of some reward to come.

This passage contains many recurring ideas and motifs from Romero's work. The idea that "they" are "us" is a key one. Though, beginning in *Night*, the living dead are never identified as the same as human — termed "them" or "those things," or, in this film, "those creatures"— the simple fact of the matter, as Logan states, is that "they" are the same animal that "we" are. Our enemy is ourselves, but also our enemies are very much the same animals as we. The idea that society has trained us to be "good little girls and boys" means that we often are incapable of dealing with crises.

Logan and Sarah compete in terms of their research and attempts to find solutions. Sarah wants to find a "cure." Logan wants to learn to control the zombies. Even the scientists, who ostensibly are on the same side, cannot work together. They criticize each other's approaches. Sarah tells Rhodes that Logan cannot deliver his promised control method in a few weeks: "I don't think there's any way how long it will take. It could be months, it could be years before we know what it is we're dealing with." Logan argues that Sarah's approach will not work at all:

> Sarah's research is more esoteric. She's looking for a way to reverse the process, a way to eradicate the problem with the walking dead. That could take a long time. A very, very long time. She may never find what she is looking for. We have a limited supply of chemical agents, and our lab equipment is hopelessly inadequate for our needs.

Even the most educated individuals, perhaps the only ones who might solve the problem, each other cannot even agree on a solution or even what the problem is. They publicly disrespect and attempt to undermine one another's work with the rest of the group. Even though many critics and viewers see this film as offering a stark choice between science and the military, between the scientists and the soldiers, neither group is unified or working together, as will be discussed later.

The film teaches us, however, that neither approach works. We might be able to train a single zombie, like Bub, but the vast majority will still be killing machines that endanger us. We might be able to try to stop the progress of the disease through a single individual, as Sarah does with Miguel, but it is not through a cure. She cuts off his bitten arm and cauterizes the wound. These actions do not save him. Instead, he is driven to sacrifice himself in order to destroy a corrupt society in the bunker. By letting in the dead, he dies, but in doing so he solves the problem that Logan and Sarah could not.

The problem is, quite simply, that there is no solution; the problem itself is unsolvable. Zombies cannot be trained or cured. We cannot control them. We cannot heal them. We cannot function safely in the same space with them. Similarly, we cannot trust most other human beings, especially ones who hold on to outdated ideas and power structures. We cannot work together at cross purposes in any society modeled or based on the old one. Therefore, the only legitimate solution is John and McDermott's: escape altogether. Leave society and its remnants behind and go to an island where there are no people, and the only materials from the old world are the few things you bring with you to survive.

Science in the Service of the Military

Continuing to function long after the purpose is over, the six soldiers who form the military unit of *Day* are a harsh critique of the military during the Reagan period, but also of the militaristic stance of the American government. In *Day*, although the system has collapsed and everyone is armed, including the scientists, Captain Rhodes asserts his own command and his authority over everything, including life and death, for the eleven remaining living humans:

> But you all better work hard, you better start showing me some results, and you'd better not piss me off. From now on, everyone is under martial law. Nothing goes on around here without my knowing about it! And anybody that fucks with my command ... they get court-martialed ... they get executed. Are we clear?

On the one hand, we might read these lines as a critique of the coercive power of institutions, especially the military. Hantke sees *Day of the Dead*'s employment of "a military base as a site for chronicling the breakdown of social institutions, using the military hierarchy and command structure, with science as its corollary, as the central metaphor for institutional authority" to indicate a fundamental distrust of all official authorities, whether military, governmental or scientific (703). As with *Night* and *Dawn*, the target is the "establishment."

Yet there is something more contained in the lines than the mere threat of death. It is the insistence of Rhodes on his own importance and centrality to the survival of all. He is one of eleven, yet because of his military role before the fall, he now insists that he must know everything and that no one may "fuck with [his] command," presumably referring to whatever he decides is "fucking with." He imposes martial law, but that martial law is a form of tyranny.

The irony, of course, is that both soldiers and scientists were sent to the bunker by the United States government to find a way to stop the crises. As noted above, the soldiers' duty was to protect and facilitate the scientists' work; but once society collapsed, the military took over, and now the scientists study and work at their command. The previous commander was Major Cooper (a reference, perhaps, to *Night*), but his death promotes Captain Rhodes. Rhodes is not necessarily the best one to lead the group, but because of his rank he assumes command. Rhodes imposes martial law, of which he is the sole authority.

None of the soldiers are admirable people. They are racist, sexist, sadistic, violence-prone bullies who take pleasure in the suffering of others. Romero's "bad guys are all thoroughly horrible, prone ... to racist comments just to emphasize their rottenness" (Flint 89). The military in this film is shortsighted, interested solely in preserving its own power and authority. The soldiers do not do anything of actual use or value, other than wrangle the occasional zombie for experimentation. We see no guard duty, no protecting the base or the civilians, and nothing resembling aid to the scientists. They neither protect nor serve.

The soldiers in this film grow pot, read pornography, threaten to rape Sarah, bully and intimidate the civilians, and hang out in the cave that serves as a mess hall. When Sarah, John and McDermott fly one hundred miles each way up the coast, the only soldier to go with them is Miguel, who is Sarah's lover and the least soldier-like of the soldiers. Even he, however, is cruel, selfish and violent toward Sarah. These soldiers have no discipline, no real skills, and are dangerously incompetent, and yet they take authority and control the base. Rhodes proclaims martial law, which is literally the imposition of military rule over the entire population. The population, however, is over half military and only eleven people. From what Sarah and McDermott say, Cooper was already imposing military law over the entire contingent, but Rhodes imposes himself as sole authority and calls it martial law.

In a sense, the second meaning of "day of the dead" is this privileging of the military in American society. Steffen Hantke argues for the conflation of the military with war and hence with death in the popular imagination (702). Military locations, he argues, are "a place of death — imminent, inevitable, violent, inexorably physical and omnipresent: bloody death, grim death, death without metaphysical or transcendent comfort" (702). This description aptly matches the bunker in *Day*. While the military can serve as a great protector of the nation, its primary purpose is to cause death and destruction in doing so. Thus the military (a death-causing organization) has been placed and/or places itself over the scientist's efforts to stop the dead and save the living.

Not merely content to critique the militarism of Reagan's America, *Day* also criticizes the appropriation of science in the service of the military and the scientists' acquiescence to have their work used by the military. For example, with "Star Wars," the popular name for the Strategic Defense Initiative (SDI), a plan to use ground and space-based technology to stop potential missile attacks by the Soviet Union, lasers, particle beams, interceptors, and other tropes from science fiction were posited as ways to defend the United States. It was a source of great public debate. Launched in 1983 by President Reagan, and formally set up within its own agency in the Department of Defense in 1984, SDI was the embodiment of both Reagan's idea of "Peace through Strength" and the blending of scientific advancement with military applications.[3] Conversely, at the same time, the Union of Concerned Scientists regularly gave updates on the doomsday clock, a metaphor for how close the world was to nuclear destruction. In the mid-eighties some scientists publicly opposed the government's militaristic policies, while others directly worked to militarize science and sell their work to the military.

Science is demonstrated to be not much better than the military in terms of civility, preserving society or even being ethical. Logan is "Frankenstein," experimenting on corpses. Possessing no ethics, he is finally revealed to be more than a little unhinged, as he sees himself as a mother to the zombies he is training. Tony Williams sees Logan as representing the "scientific establishment who ignored their responsibility to society and eagerly worked with totalitarian regimes" (135). As noted in the introduction, the pleasure of zombie apocalypse cinema is wish fulfillment: all laws are suspended, and you may indulge urges to shoot, steal, destroy, and pillage without fear of repercussion. Similarly, Logan is free to perform experiments without the ethical controls most societies would impose. His work with the dead is suggestive of World War II experiments by totalitarian regimes in which prisoners of war were experimented upon by scientists (the Japanese in China, Nazi experiments on concentration camp prisoners, etc.). Logan comes from the same line as Josef Mengele, the Nazi medical doctor, and Shirō Ishii, the leader of Japan's Unit 731, the biological warfare unit of the Japanese Imperial Army who was possibly responsible for over ten thousand deaths. Closer to home, Logan also calls to mind the Tuskegee Syphilis Study, in which hundreds of African Americans were deliberately infected with syphilis and others were deliberately not treated in order to observe the progress of the disease. This study was carried out by public health professionals in the United States from 1932 to 1972. The American government, in the form of the U.S. Public Health Service, deliberately infected American citizens with a deadly disease. In 1981, *Bad Blood*, James H. Jones' history of the Tuskegee experiment, was published, calling public attention to the experiment.[4]

Logan dissects, vivisects, and literally deconstructs bodies without fear or restraint. He even uses the corpses of dead soldiers as rewards for his experiments. The living soldiers would be mortified and greatly angered if they knew, and when they finally do discover this fact, they kill Logan. But this behavior is the logical outgrowth of his work for the military. If all flesh is simply regarded as material for experimentation, then no one's flesh is sacrosanct or off limits. The ends justify the means. Peter Dendle perceives it as "the abstruse inquisitiveness of the scientific community fares no better than the brutish territoriality and aggression of the military one" (46–7). Both the scientists and the soldiers fail to solve the problem or even preserve what the few survivors have.

Logan's experiments in control and in developing Bub as a zombie person, however, set a pair of linked tropes that will be repeated many times after *Day*. The first is the idea of zombies retaining memory and/or relearning at the hands of scientists. The second is the idea of zombies being domesticated, with an eye toward using them as soldiers or servants. With Bub, Romero begins a series of characters representing semi-intelligent, domesticated living dead, including Big Daddy in *Land of the Dead* and the families in *Survival of the Dead*. Outside of Romero's own work, many films have appropriated the ideas of zombie soldiers and zombie servants, from *Return of the Living Dead 3* to *Fido*, and from *Resident Evil* to *Zombie Strippers*.

The idea of reanimating dead soldiers to keep them fighting becomes a trope frequently employed in the twenty-first century, especially after 9/11. The government seeks to ensure that even in death our soldiers can continue to fight and kill the enemy. Frequently in such films, however, the *Day* model of the government, and the military being unable to do anything successfully, indicates that the experiments on dead soldiers will result in chaos and more death. From *Fido* to *Zombie Strippers*, the dangers of zombies, even domesticated, are not to be underestimated.

In the end, this observation is actually a conservative one. The enemy cannot be domesticated or lived with, so the enemy must be destroyed. There are no other options; there is no win/win scenario. The enemy must not only be subjugated but destroyed. This rhetoric will heighten in Romero's post–9/11 films (see chapter 10), but even in *Day* the enemy can only be killed, not trained. Given Romero's trope that humans are always more dangerous than zombies, however, this means that the only way to survive the day of the dead is not merely to eliminate the zombies but also to eliminate any human who stands in the way of survival, which is precisely what happens.

Miguel, bitten by a zombie and dying, despite Sarah amputating the limb, opens the gate and then opens the lift, which allows the thousands of zombies surrounding the fence to enter the base. They kill him, tear him apart and devour him. Two soldiers already died in the accident that resulted in Miguel's bite, but the other soldiers are then killed and eaten by the horde. Rhodes is shot at by Bub, who is enraged by the death of Logan. As Rhodes flees, he opens a door to a room filled with zombies, who grab him and tear him apart as he screams, "Choke on 'em!" Only John, McDermott and Sarah escape to a desert island with no zombies — and, as far as we are shown, no humans either.

The film displays a community in conflict, which is often read as the scientists and the soldiers. I would argue, however, that the society Romero depicts is not two groups but eleven individuals divided into three smaller groups: soldiers, scientists and technicians (John and McDermott — who are neither scientists nor military, but men hired to fly a helicopter and work a radio). John and McDermott remain separate from both groups, as they just do their jobs and try to live. They remain separated from both groups physically in every scene, sitting at a distant table in the mess hall and living in trailers far away from both the soldiers' and the scientists' quarters. They live for a reason. They represent the vast majority of Americans who simply do their jobs, try to survive and do not align themselves with any institutional authority. They carry their own guns, and they do not engage in any of the battles between scientists and soldiers. Their solution from the beginning is to opt out, to go away, to find a separate space where they are not in a society at all.

John and McDermott, as the individuals not in any group, are actually more organized and unified, and they work together in a way that none of the others can or do. The scientists do not work together, except to confront Rhodes, and even then will turn on one another in order to secure more material and support for their individual research. As noted above, Sarah and Logan disrespect and undermine each other's work. Likewise, the soldiers are bullies who abuse Miguel, and Rhodes threatens to shoot Steel if Steel does not shoot Sarah. Neither of the groups really function as groups that work cooperatively as a single organized entity. Instead, both are Darwinian, almost animalistic packs whose members struggle for dominance within the group, as well as against those outside the group.

No one in *Day* is a truly good person. Michael Felshen describes *Day* as "a more intimate and claustrophobic tale with a bunch of radically unsympathetic characters who do little to inspire our affection and also have the tendency to de-evolve rapidly from unpleasant to downright psychotic in many cases" [n.p.]. In *Night* and *Dawn* there were characters to empathize with and root for; not so *Day*. Even Sarah, John and McDermott are not genuinely heroic. Logan, who is ostensibly on their side, is a deeply disturbed, amoral psychopath. None of the soldiers are worth saving. John and McDermott are emotionally disconnected from the group. They move to protect Sarah when Steel and Rhodes threaten to kill her in order to kill Miguel, but their instinct is not to save others but flee. McDermott, when helping Sarah, says sarcastically to John, "Well, what do you know? We are heroes after all. What a relief." But his lines are intended ironically, both by McDermott and Romero.

Sarah is a strong woman in a period where feminism and the women's movement was under attack from within the culture. Miguel tells Sarah she is stronger than everyone, but he also concludes, "So fucking what?" The fact that she is not falling apart emotionally and mentally when everyone else is will not save her should the zombies get into the bunker. At the same time he discounts her abilities and her strength, she is the only one he dares criticize or even attack physically. In a time when strength is praised, to have a character claim that strength does not matter when a crisis occurs is a powerful if veiled critique of the Reagan era, but also an even more powerful critique of powerful women. So what if they are strong, women do not count as much as men. Rod Gudino reads *Day* as a battle of "the progressive, active woman versus the repressive, fascist soldier" (17). Yet we also might read it as a retrogressive apocalyptic fantasy in which even the progressive woman is wrong, no matter how strong she is. Again, the only possible solution is to opt out.

Day remains a typical eighties film, an atypical horror film and a classic George Romero film. Like all his other dead films, it is self-referential. McDermott, in complaining to the soldiers about the situation outside the bunker, screams, "All the shopping malls are closed!" In context it makes a good deal of sense, but it is impossible to hear the line and not think of *Dawn*. In some ways, *Day* is not only a continuation of *Dawn* but a remake of it in its own right. A small group, trapped and surviving in a place not designed to be lived in, eventually falls apart; and as the zombies invade an ostensibly safe space, some die and some live. The film ends with a helicopter escape; and two of the survivors are a white woman and a black man. *Day* is simply repetition with variation. Romero calls attention to this when Logan locks the new zombie in a dark room to "think about what he's done"; here the soundtrack plays a modified version of "The Gonk," the song from *Dawn*. But what *Dawn* played for laughs and satire, *Day* plays as absurd tragedy.

Notes

1. Later we will learn that this calendar hangs in the bunker room she shares with Miguel, and it is not as Spartan as in her dream. A bed, some other furniture and even other décor fill the space.
2. They even share a credit screen — both Howard Sherman and Richard Liberty's names appear at the same time during the opening of the film.
3. See Frances FitzGerald's *Way Out There in the Blue: Reagan, Star Wars and the End of the Cold War*.
4. I in no way posit that Romero read or was influenced by Jones' book. I simply cite it here as part of the zeitgeist of the eighties, in which AIDS was also on the rise; in 1985 Reagan had yet to mention it publicly. Many felt that the government was ignoring AIDS and that previous examples of the American government experimenting on its own people were very much part of the public discourse of the time. See Jones' revised edition of *Bad Blood*, published in 1993, for a comparison of the Tuskegee experiment and public perception of the government's handling of the AIDS crisis.

9
"Somebody will come. They have to": *Day of the Dead* (2008)

As Leadville, Colorado, descends into chaos, overrun with its former citizenry now turned into zombies, one of the people trapped at the town's radio station asserts, "Somebody will come. They have to." Of course, no one comes. It is a telling moment in a problematic film. The faith in small-town America that "somebody" will solve the problem, someone will come and rescue the citizens if something goes horribly wrong, has repeatedly been proven misplaced. The boy in the film believes in the idea of rescue by "them"—the government, the military, the American people. Someone will come.

As witnessed in the aftermath of Hurricane Katrina in 2005, no one is coming. Barack Obama often quoted Pulitzer Prize–winning author Alice Walker: "We are the ones we have been waiting for." By the end of the Bush presidency, many Americans distrusted the government's ability to handle crises. Obama's use of Walker's quotation serves as an example of the idea that "rescue" begins with one's self.

Following in the wake of the 2004 remake of *Dawn*, *Day of the Dead* was remade in 2008, clearly under the influence of the *Dawn* remake and other recent zombie films. Yet, in the *Day* remake the monsters are not Romero zombies. Technically, they are not even zombies. Much closer to the infected of *28 Days Later* (2002), the "zombies" of *Day* are human beings infected with a government-developed virus designed to make enemy soldiers calm. Instead, like the infected of *28 Days Later*, side effects of the virus include extreme aggression and rapid transformation into a decaying, infected monster. The tagline on posters and the DVD box for the new *Day* is "Faster, Stronger, Deadlier," as if the infected of this film are in competition with earlier zombie films.

Not a remake in the *Dawn* sense, *Day* is a reimagining of the original. Certain elements, characters (though often in name only) and individual situations echo the earlier version. The plot, context and given circumstances, however, are all radically different from the original. Whereas the original film presented the latter days of the zombie apocalypse, with a small remnant of humanity consisting of scientists and soldiers hiding on a military base somewhere in Florida, the new film is set at the beginning of the outbreak in a Colorado mountain town and deals with the attempt of the military to control viral outbreak.

Some elements, situations and scenes from the original are duplicated in new contexts. Salazar (Nick Cannon) and Sarah (Mena Suvari) debate whether or not to kill Bud (Stark Sands) after he has been bitten, even though she has poured bleach all over the wound—just as in the original Sarah claims that her cauterizing Miguel's wound should prevent him from becoming a zombie. "Bud" is clearly meant to resemble Bub, who also fires a gun and is a semi-intelligent zombie who appears to have bonded with some of the living (although Bub's friendship with Logan in the original is not at all the same to Bud's sexual desire/crush on Sarah in the remake). Lastly, the heroes finally find themselves in an abandoned silo complex, trapped with a crowd of zombies and looking for a way to escape.

The sociophobics offered in the *Day* remake arise from concern over government conspiracies and cover-ups, while also being afraid that the United States is headed in the wrong direction. First, I will examine the cultural forces and cinematic antecedents of the *Day* remake, including relevant films that also riffed on the original *Day*. Next, I look at how popular conspiracy theories are reflected in Day, specifically the "9/11 Truther" movement, and the fears and concerns over the Federal Emergency Management Agency (FEMA) in the wake of Hurricane Katrina. I conclude by considering the *Day* remake as a nostalgic tribute to the eighties milieu of the original. Just as the second President Bush was seen as embodying a return to Reagan's America, so too does the *Day* remake echo a return to the Reagan era.

Hollywood from Vietnam to Resident Evil

If, as noted in the previous chapter, the original *Day* was shaped just as much by movies about the Vietnam War and the Vietnam veterans as it was the political and cultural context of Reagan's America, the remake was as profoundly shaped by the zombie film renaissance and by 9/11 as it was by Hurricane Katrina and the culture of the Bush administration. The influence of previous horror films and other subgenres within this movie are rather obvious. In addition to the direct influence of the remake of *Dawn* and *28 Days Later, Day* also contains element of the slasher flick, the apocalyptic conspiracy movie (such as *The Andromeda Strain, The Stand,* or even Romero's own *The Crazies,* itself remade in 2010), and the military film.

Behind the overarching narrative of *Day*—an accidental release of a government-created supervirus—lies the tropes of the apocalyptic conspiracy film: a disease is inadvertently released in a small municipality; the local population begins to die or go crazy; the protagonists, in the course of investigating the situation, learn that the government was behind the outbreak; and steps are then taken to stop the virus. The heroes in this case are members of the military who are willing to expose and resist the parts of the government that endanger the citizens. In that sense it differs radically from the original *Day*. That film was a liberal critique of the military, and the science and scientists complicit with the military right. This *Day* is a reactionary critique of government: Washington is out to secretly destroy the small town and its people. Only brave soldiers willing to stand up to Washington and "the Government" can solve the town's problems. I will return to this idea later.

Just as the original *Day* was shaped by military films of the eighties, the remake of *Day* can also be read in the wake of zombie films rooted in corporate and government conspiracies. In the years between the release of the remake of *Dawn of the Dead* and the remake of *Day of the Dead*, two films rooted in the original *Day* were released that also shaped the remake of *Day*; these were *Day of the Dead 2: Contagium* and the *Resident Evil* films, especially *Resident Evil: Extinction*.

In 2005 *Day of the Dead 2: Contagium* was released as a direct-to-video prequel to *Day*. Actually, although the filmmakers billed it as a "prequel" to *Day*, the film had nothing to do with the original. Taurus Entertainment owned the rights to Romero's *Day of the Dead* and decided to make a movie using the original Romero film's name. *Contagium* is set in a mental hospital for young patients that was originally a military hospital in 1968. During the Cold War, the Russians engineered a "bio virus" that raised the dead and was subsequently captured by the Americans when a pilot defected. When the young patients find a thermos containing a sample of the virus, they open it, releasing the virus into the hospital population, slowly transforming the residents into zombies.

The film is arguably the lowest quality work in this volume.[1] It contains plot holes you could drive a truck through. The acting is uniformly uneven, much of it not very good at all. The production values are low. The ideas in the film are recycled from other, better films, and it piggybacks on current trends in zombie cinema: zombies caused by a virus; fast zombies; rapid infection through a small, local population.

As noted in the introduction, even bad films reflect the sociocultural concerns of the period from which they emerge. One can read into *Contagium* a concern that both the legacy of the Cold War and the current activities of the military can and will hurt the current generation of Americans. Disconnected and mentally ill young people are drawn into a world in which they can die and reanimate from things that happened before they were even born. The film may not be well executed, but the ideas behind it very much reflect the sociophobics of 2005.

Two years later, in 2007, *Resident Evil: Extinction*, third in the *Resident Evil* series (which had its own "Dawn" in *Resident Evil: Apocalypse*), was released.[2] The film had a bigger budget and far higher production values than *Contagium*, but it also shared key plot and thematic elements with that earlier movie. The villain, Dr. Issacs (Iain Glenn), is a far more evil version of Dr. Logan from *Day*, performing experiments not only on the living dead, but also on his current and former colleagues. Like *Day*, the central location of *Extinction* is a military base, mostly underground, accessed by chopper, surrounded by a mob of thousands of howling zombies, and home to a small group of scientists attempting to domesticate the dead.

The film features a "Bub" moment in which a group of three white-jacketed scientists attempt to domesticate a balding, rotting male zombie. He is given a cellphone, which he picks up and recognizes, echoing Bub's use of the razor. He is then given a children's toy that tests observational and motor skills by requiring shaped objects be inserted into a box with matching shaped holes. As he begins to place the pegs in the holes, the scientists congratulate themselves. Unfortunately, he grows frustrated when one peg does not fit, breaks his chains and attacks the scientists, who are then locked in the lab with him by Dr. Isaacs, leaving them unable to escape slaughter by the now furious zombie.

One of the key similarities between *Day* (where the power structure does not support such experiments and drives Rhodes to kill Logan) and *Resident Evil* (where they are supported and even encouraged by the power structure, even when a failure) is that science is questionable at best and more often dangerous and ethically unsound. Another key similarity is the prominence of women — in the form of Alice (Milla Jovovich), Claire (Ali Larter), the leader of the band of survivalists, and Betty (Ashanti), all three of whom play major roles in the fight against the living dead and the Umbrella Corporation.

Whereas *Day* focused on the former part of the Military/Industrial complex, the *Resident Evil* films have focused on the latter. Corporations, in this case the ubiquitous and evil Umbrella Corporation, are the source of all that is wrong in the world. Umbrella has unleashed a virus that has devastated the world. And the corporation, from its secret labs all over the world, still attempts to dominate the post-apocalyptic landscape. Those who run the corporation, such as Dr. Isaacs, are soulless and happy to sacrifice others in the quest for power, money and dominance.

The opening sequence sets the tone for the entire films. Echoing previous *Resident Evils*, Alice wakes up naked in a shower. She dresses and begins to attempt an escape. She is able to get past monster dogs, guards, various technological traps and devices, only to be stabbed and die. The moment is a surprising one, as Alice has been the main character of the series. Two lackeys then carry her body up and out of the complex and toss it into a refuse pile that contains hundreds of identical Alice corpses. The viewer then realizes that we have seen a clone being put through a test.

This moment works on several levels and also introduces several themes of the film. The piling up of corpses is emblematic of the movie's concern for the decreasing number of living left in the world. It also echoes something seen in 2005's *Land of the Dead* (discussed in the next chapter), in which corpses are also thrown onto a trash pile. Dr. Isaacs and the Umbrella Corporation do not value human life. People are only good for their research value or as consumers, and when one is done with them they can simply be thrown out as refuse. The image is also one that reflects the video game origins of the film, in which one must learn as one plays, watching the protagonist of the game get killed multiple times in order to find out how to beat the current level and move on to the next. The game player and the Umbrella Corporation are equated: both require a large number of deaths in order to advance. Video game aesthetics and ethics dominate the *Resident Evil* series.

A Brand New Day: *The New World Order*

The remake of *Day*, like *Contagium* has little to do with the original and shares more in common with *28 Days Later* or the *Resident Evil* series.[3] The zombies themselves are not Romero zombies, nor is the unfolding of the story done in a traditional Romero style. Nina (AnnaLynne McCord) takes her father (Michael McCoy) to the hospital with the flu. The film takes us inside his body to see the transformation as the virus infects him. As his cells are transformed, the camera pulls out of his body and shows the external macro-transformation matching the micro-transformations taking place within at the cellular level. And, as that transformation is instantaneous, so, too, is the macro one. After talking with his family about the Asian flu, he stops in mid-sentence. He seems distracted. Then his eyes literally glaze over and his skin breaks out into decaying patches, looking like he has been dead for a week. This entire sequence maintains the videogame aesthetic of *Resident Evil*.

He instantly attacks his own family, displaying a speed and aggression not seen in any Romero film or remake. Simultaneously, all other infected patients in the hospital begin to change. The speed of the zombies in their attacks is matched by the speed of transformation. With Romero zombies, the alteration from living, normal human to living dead is a slow one: witness Karen in the original *Night*, Roger in the original *Dawn*, and even Frank in the remake of *Dawn*, all of whom die slowly and then, after a pause, slowly reanimate. In this *Day*, the turn from human to "infected" is much more similar to the transformation of Frank (Brendan Gleeson) in *28 Days Later*, who gets a drop of infected blood in his eye and six seconds later attacks his daughter and friends.

This *Day* is actually a much smaller and localized zombie apocalypse; it takes some of the ideas from the original and transfers them to a much smaller film — in every sense of the word. The original is concerned with a small group of people in a world dominated by the dead; the world of the remake is not dominated by the dead, but the small-town world of Colorado quickly becomes overwhelmed, and the movie focuses on a small group of people in that town. This film is a post–9/11 zombie movie, one influenced by the experience of the attacks of September 11. Unlike the original, this film begins at the beginning of the crisis, not the middle or the end. The original film posits a conflict between scientists and the military, whereas the remake posits a union of government scientists and an uninformed fascistic military pitted against a small group of civilians and soldiers.

The remake transforms several of the characters of the original in order to reflect this small-town apocalypse. Captain Rhodes (Ving Rhames) is no longer the king of the kingdom but a minor tyrant of the roadblock. His death occurs much earlier than his dramatic forebear, and he is neither the threat nor the power of the original. He is first shown overseeing a roadblock. Mr. Leitner (Robert Rais) complains that his son is very sick and needs to get to a "real hospital." Captain Rhodes (his name patch clearly visible before he even speaks) tells him that his orders are "to keep this road sealed for the next twenty-four hours."

Sarah is no longer one of the scientists. She is now "Corporal Cross," a soldier and communications specialist who is part of the unit detached to contain Leadville, which also, coincidentally, happens to be her hometown. As a result, Rhodes asks her to convince Leitner to obey orders. Thus, Sarah and Rhodes' relationship dynamic is no longer as adversarial as in the original. While the original Sarah was a scientist under Rhodes' command, this Sarah is a soldier with Rhodes as her immediate superior. Bub the Zombie is now Private "Bud Crain," whose death will transform him into a Bub-like sympathetic and intelligent zombie.

Doctor Logan's (Matt Rippy) character has undergone the most radical transformation. He is no longer a crazy, mad old scientist whom the audience actually embraces. He is, in fact, a covert government scientist involved in a secret American biological and chemical weapons program, and has more in common with *Resident Evil*'s Dr. Isaacs than the original's Logan. While initially appearing to be a helpful scientist, he is actually one of the chief villains of the piece. Like Sarah, his relationship with Rhodes is fundamentally different than in the original. This Logan does not have an antagonistic relationship with the military. He gives orders to Rhodes, which Rhodes obeys without question. In this *Day*, the reversal in power is made clear between the characters of Rhodes and Logan: the government scientists control the military, and the military must obey and answer to the scientists.

The chief aspect in which this film differs from the original is its concern with the origin of the zombie outbreak. In the original *Day*, Sarah and Logan and the other scientists are carrying out a series of experiments in order to understand how the virus animates the dead and what can be done to cure it. They are no longer concerned with its origins; in fact, the origin of the zombie plague is irrelevant. The new *Day*, rooted in post–9/11 paranoia and the 9/11 truth movement, offers a wholly different sociophobic.

In the wake of the terror attacks of September Eleventh, a small but vocal group began insisting that 9/11 was an inside job. Controlled explosions, missiles striking the pentagon, and supposed government cover-ups are all elements of the belief that somehow the Bush administration and/or Israel were behind the attacks.[4] One of the chief claims of those who believe 9/11 was an inside job is that the last part of the conspiracy is the cover-up carried out by the government — what Michael Barkun terms "suppressed knowledge": "claims that are allegedly known to be valid by authoritative institutions but are suppressed because the institutions fear the consequences of public knowledge or have some evil or selfish motive for hiding the truth" (27). This idea is at the center of the remake of *Day*—that a small cabal within the government is responsible for a major national crisis, but hides the evidence of that responsibility and covers it up. When Sarah convinces Mr. and Mrs. Leitner to return to the hospital in town, she asks Rhodes, "Sir, did I just tell them the truth?" He does not answer that question, but instead tells her, "Corporal, your orders are to keep this shithole town ... excuse me, *your* shithole town sealed off. Now do it." He cynically appeals to her self-interest (as her family and friends are still there), but Sarah is already aware that the information she gives to the people of the town seems more like a cover story than the truth.

Day is here following a model that is not found in horror but in the political conspiracy film. The example *par excellance* is *The Andromeda Strain*, in which the crime is not the introduction of an alien bacteria into a local population but the cover-up which follows (a theme Romero himself tackles in *The Crazies*). In *The Andromeda Strain* the local population is threatened by a virus from a satellite that has fallen to Earth, but the government tells locals a cover-up story. The government uses local media and authority figures to disseminate the story that will replace Barkun's "suppressed knowledge."

In *Day*, Paul the DJ (Ian McNeice), a character with no equivalent in the original, becomes the first civilian to openly question the cover story of a military exercise that coincidentally is occurring at the same time as an outbreak of a particularly bad strain of the flu: "Still, they keep saying this is just an exercise. Now Uncle Sam wouldn't be trying to lie to us, would he?" At this point, the camera pulls back to reveal an armed soldier standing behind him in the broadcast booth. As a song begins to play, Paul asks him, "As a cog in the military industrial complex, are you capable of independent thought?" The soldier replies, "Sir, my orders are to relay the information to you so you can pass it along to the public." The film introduces the distrust of the government, and the distrust of the military as an organization with a vested interest in suppressing knowledge. The national media cannot be trusted either; it is only the local media (the distrustful individual DJ, who is himself capable of independent thought) that will tell people the truth. In a sense, this *Day* is a much more radically conservative film than the original. It is conservative in its filmmaking, but it is also politically conservative. Only an independent media, small-town Americans, and soldiers with a sense of honor and history can protect the people from their own government and military. Salazar reveals that the orders to blockade the town and shut off all communication to and from outside comes from Washington. In his words, "There is some serious shit going down."

As Barkun notes, in the wake of 9/11 many voices on the fringe, and some much closer to the mainstream, argued for advanced knowledge of the attacks by the United States and British governments, or that the governments themselves were actually the destroyers, using controlled demolitions to bring down the towers from within. They maintain that others had advanced warnings of the attacks or were told not to travel on that day, or that Israel was somehow involved (163). The government and/or those involved in the conspiracy "used its power to keep the rest of the population in ignorance" and "utilize[d] its power to keep the truth from being known" (Barkun 27).

Unlike in the post–9/11 *Dawn* remake, in which the cause of the zombie outbreak is never known, *Day* posits a very different reality. The cause is *knowable*; it is, however, not known because of a cover-up by those involved. The scientists working on a virus to use against America's enemies have allowed that virus to escape, mutate, and affect American citizens. The military is then sent in with a cover story, and orders to contain the affected population and discourage investigation of said cover story.

In the case of *Day*, we have an obvious reference to *Andromeda Strain* in the name "Project Wildfire," which was the massive underground complex in that film dedicated to unraveling the mysteries of the alien virus. In this Project Wildfire, overseen by Logan, "a few select scientists studying certain biochemical agents" are actually at work on a biological weapon — activities which the United States claims not to be involved in. Sarah, Salazar and the others discover a videotape left by the last scientist at the project, who describes a bioengineered virus: "It was designed to paralyze enemy troops by shutting down their neural systems for six to seven hours. We didn't think it would mutate." Lack of planning on the part of the scientists, however, resulted in the virus both mutating and escaping, subsequently infecting the local population. Never reluctant to turn a crisis into an opportunity, the government moves to watch the local infected as guinea pigs.

Logan tells them, "This would have allowed us to capture people without killing them. It was intended to save lives." Salazar responds: "Heck of a job, Doc." This exchange carries with it two significant connotations. The first is that the government always claims that the conspiracy and subsequent cover-up were for our own good. Anything done to the American people is justified because it will in the long run help or protect the American people. Second, the exchange carries with it a reference to the Bush administration's handling of Katrina: "Heck of a job, Brownie." "Brownie" refers to Bush's Federal Emergency Management Agency head Michael Brown. FEMA features in many conspiracy theories, as it has the authority to relocate people and use national crises as a justification for instituting martial law.

Concern about FEMA or any other government institution is rooted in the idea that the government does not have the best interests of its citizens at heart; but rather a small ruling cabal uses the government and its institutions (such as the military) to use the American people for its own nefarious purposes. Leonard G. Horowitz, a dentist and conservative conspiracy theorist, saw the 2001 anthrax attacks in the wake of 9/11 as "a military-industrial conspiracy involving chief biological weapons 'preparedness' firms and the CIA," which demonstrates that "America ... [is] under attack from within our own national security system" (qtd. in Barkun 162). Any time the government is moved to aid the civilian population, especially through the use of the military, National Guard or especially FEMA, it is viewed as "particularly sinister" (Barkun 169).[5] Barkun observes concerns among conspiracy theorists as far back as the Reagan administration (after having come to prominence during the Carter administration) that FEMA was planning on establishing "concentration camps" for American citizens (74). When one observes how the government responds to natural disasters by controlling movement in and out of the area, and establishing facilities for those affected, the conspiracy theorists' ideas seem more plausible.

Contrasted with those who have the suppressed knowledge is the ignorance of the citizens. Trevor (Michael Welch), Mr. and Mrs. Leitner, and Paul are trapped in the radio station, which is surrounded by the fast-moving, dangerous zombies. Trevor says, "Somebody will come. They have to." He begins to broadcast. He does not want to do anything to save himself because he still has faith in the government, but the film has shown that the government cannot be trusted, nor will it help its own citizens. More likely than not, according to the conspiracy theorists, the government is actively out to hurt and control its own citizens, and one is foolish to think that someone will come. Even if someone does come, they are not coming to help but to cover-up; and in this case, someone already did come: the military arrived to aid in the cover up, not help the town. The only people who will be saved are those who disbelieve the government lies, recognize the suppressed knowledge, and work to save themselves rather than waiting for the government to come save them.

I Love the Eighties

At the climax of the film, Sarah, Salazar, Nina, Trevor and Bud go looking for the missile silo in the old Nike missile base where Project Wildfire was housed. They are surrounded by hordes of the original zombies, but the military and missile equipment in the base provide weapons with which to fight the zombies. At one point Sarah, the soldier who loves America but will not obey unlawful orders, tells the others, "Find the missile silo — that's our escape route!" This line carries with it a certain weight that indicates a nostalgia for the 1980s.

As noted above, there is a reactionary root to the remake of *Day*. "Washington" is the source of the problems in America, and the good people of the small towns and so-called Red States must both pay the price and resist the government. The irony, of course, is that in both the eighties and the first decade of the twenty-first century, some of the most stringent anti-government voices were coming from the highest levels of government. President Reagan often spoke out against the very government of which he was the executive head. President George W. Bush less frequently invoked his father George H.W. Bush than he did Reagan, to whom he was perceived as being the political heir.

Day imagines a world in which Humvees and guns are good and an intrusive government is bad. Egghead government scientists create problems for the American people that the military, at its higher levels, both perpetuate and cover up. Common soldiers, working with regular citizens, can confront the evils of Washington and return power to the local levels, thus returning America to her former glory. It is no coincidence that the escape route away from government-created Zombies is through the silo of a Nike missile. The Nike missiles were part of the American defense program of the 1950s (although it was begun during World War II) that was subsequently decommissioned in the sixties. Reagan would invoke their spirit as part of his own missile defense plans. Also, Reagan frequently exploited nostalgia for the fifties as part of his political rhetoric, in the same manner that Bush exploited nostalgia for the eighties. It is only by climbing out of a missile silo—remembering when America was strong and its technology was used in defense of the nation, not against its own citizens—that the rugged individualists that are our protagonists can escape the zombie and survive this day of the dead.

Just as *Dawn* and *Land* were prophetic about Hurricane Katrina and the government's response to it, the remake of *Day* was prophetic about the rise of the Tea Party movement in the wake of the election of Obama. Individual conservative citizens who distrust the government speak out against the government and claim awareness of suppressed knowledge (Obama's birth certificate, a secret plan to make America socialist, etc.). The Tea Party movement echoes the concerns of *Day*. Both are conservative reactions against a perceived active, intrusive government. Both see the power of the individual citizen, working in small groups, as a means to change the nation. Interestingly, both left and right see the power of the citizens as a transformative force. Obama proclaimed, "We are the ones we have been waiting for," since no one is coming. The right fears someone is coming, and that their motives are against the best interests of the American people; therefore "we" must confront and take back the government.

Like the *Dawn* remake, the *Day* remake reflects the realities of a post–9/11 America and therefore is much more reactionary. Although nostalgic for the eighties, the new *Day* reflects a new sociophobic, one just as afraid of its government as the original. Whereas Romero's film reflected a progressive's concern for conservative government, the remake reflects a reactionary's concern for progressive government.

Notes

1. With the possible exception of *Children of the Living Dead*, although the *Day* remake is not particularly good either and was released direct to video (the only Romero remake to have suffered this fate).

2. The others are *Resident Evil* (2002), *Resident Evil: Apocalypse* (2004) and *Resident Evil: Afterlife* (2010), all based on the same video game series called "Biohazard" in Japan, its country of origin. The films, however, and their sociophobics, remain resolutely American, despite conforming to the narratives, characters and situations of the games.

3. The *Day* remake and *Contagium* have more in common than this aspect. They were both produced by the same company (Taurus Entertainment), and the director of *Contagium* was one of the producers of the remake. So both films are coming out of the same milieu.

4. For an excellent assessment of the dominant elements of 9/11 conspiracy theories, along with the evidence that refutes them, see Dunbar and Reagan's *Debunking 9/11 Myths: Why Conspiracy Theories Can't Stand Up to the Facts*, which began as a series of articles in *Popular Mechanics*.

5. Remarkably, Barkun observed this primarily of FEMA in 2003, before the Hurricane Katrina debacle made FEMA's name synonymous with government incompetence.

IV
Back for the Dead

10

"Isn't that what we're doing? Pretending to be alive?": *Land, Diary, Surviving* and the World of the Dead

As noted in the introduction, since 9/11 there has been an incredible increase in an already crowded zombie world. This increase is pan-media: film, graphic novel, video games, novels, television, and online content. This increase is also international — from North America, Europe, Asia, Australia and New Zealand. The zombie is king right now: romance novels, zom-rom-com movies, the interjection of zombies into classical literature (*Pride and Prejudice and Zombies*), zombie calendars, zombie crawls, zombie walks, zombie action figures, cartoon zombies, etc. We now live in a dead world. Well, a living dead world.

Also since 9/11, Romero has returned to the genre he pioneered with three new films as of this writing, and a projected two more to come. A whole new generation is growing up with the release of new zombie films: *Land of the Dead, Diary of the Dead* and *Survival of the Dead*. These three movies are original Romeo works, not remakes in the traditional sense; although I will argue they are remakes in the sense of placing new characters into the same circumstances as the original films. This final chapter is concerned with these three films as "remakes" of the world of *Night*.

For *Land, Diary* and *Survival*, Romero's post–9/11 zombie films, I will first consider each as a "remake" of the larger "living dead" narrative of Romero's original films. *Land* completes the series of *Night, Dawn* and *Day*. *Diary*, however, is a "reboot" (to use current film terminology) — a return to the origins and the start of the rising of the dead. It is a "remake" of *Night* in that it is the story of a small group of people attempting to survive the beginning of the outbreak. Yet simultaneously, *Diary* is an erasure of *Dawn*, in the sense that its elements and tropes are all the opposite of *Dawn*. Lastly, *Survival*, as an indirect sequel to *Diary*, directly incorporates elements of *Dawn* and *Day*. Thus, I will also consider the intertextuality of the last two films with the arc of the first four, positing that the former is a continual "remake" of the latter.

Second, I shall consider the sociocultural concerns behind each film and the expressed sociophobics: what does the horror tell us about the fears and concerns of society at the time Romero made them? *Land* is very much a film about Bush's America in the post–9/11 period. *Diary* concerns citizen media and the mediation of disaster. *Survival*, however, engages a much more complex dynamic of conflict and the place of soldiers in society. There is no direct shift, as there was between the original *Dawn* and the remake, but the films still reflect the societal concerns of the periods that produced them. And although there is only four years difference between *Land* and *Survival* (as opposed to the seventeen years between *Night* and *Day*), all three of the latter films also reflect specific concerns from the period and use the zombies in very different ways.

"I Always Wanted to See How the Other Half Lives": Land of the Dead

Romero's original vision for *Day* eventually found its realization in *Land*, albeit under the further shaping influence of September 11. Paul R. Gagne, writing in 1987, reports on the world Romero had envisioned for *Day*:

> The lower class civilian "masses" live above ground in a seedy and fenced-in "stalag" ... where violence, depraved sex, drugs, and disease have run wild. While some of the stalag's denizens are allowed underground to perform various menial tasks, the majority constitute what the script describes as a "cesspool of human dregs" [148].

Above these "human dregs" (socially speaking) are the scientists, and above them, the military (although these two groups live safely in an underground bunker). The post-zombie world is literally separated by social class. This vision for *Day* was realized in *Land*; and as a result, *Land* is Romero's most explicit, overtly political film, even more so than *Dawn*.

Mario DeGiglio-Bellemare sees zombies in Romero's films as "represent[ing] social change" (DeGiglio-Bellemare). In *Land*, the zombies become a literal force for social change with a pair of revolutions, one by the dead and one by the working class survivors, causing not only an overthrow of the ruling class of Pittsburgh but transforming the relationship between the living and the dead. *Land of the Dead* is a not-so-subtle, direct critique of the Bush administration and the war in Iraq.

In *Land*, poor soldiers must go out on the front lines to secure supplies and luxury goods. In the opening sequence, Romero shows a virtual army of individuals, armed to the teeth and with a specially designed war machine, "Dead Reckoning," that initially seems to be gearing up to fight the dead. Instead, they are actually on a supply run, risking their lives to get food and luxury goods, such as Champagne and cigars. The wealthy elite live in "Fiddler's Green," carrying on life as if nothing has changed. They do not sacrifice; they do not contribute to society. Others must do the dirty work, and still others must live poor and undernourished on the streets so that the ruling class may live in luxury. The affluence and ease of Fiddler's Green is built upon the poverty and work of others. Whereas *Night* was about the homeland during Vietnam, *Land* is about the homeland during Iraq.

Mulligan (Bruce McFee), a street preacher and former associate of Riley's, preaches a form of socialism as Riley returns. He wants to overthrow Kaufman's regime and replace it with a fair and equitable society where resources are shared equally. Riley declines to join in his proposed revolution, but after Fiddler's Green is overrun by the living dead (themselves another underclass), Mulligan is offered the opportunity to remake society the way he has preached it.

Cholo (John Leguizamo) is a minority soldier who believes, mistakenly, that hard work and ingratiating himself to the regime will buy him a place in the elite's world. His service, however, gets no reward and grants him no access to the inner circle. Kaufman (Dennis Hopper) tells him, "There is a very long waiting list.... This is an extremely desirable location. Space is very limited." "You mean restricted, don't you?" comes Cholo's reply. Especially telling, Cholo has just poured Champagne into a highball glass for Kaufman. As he delivers the above line to Cholo, Kaufman takes the glass and re-pours the Champagne into a flute glass, as if to reinforce the idea that Cholo has no place in Fiddler's Green because he lacks class, grace and knowledge of the polite manners of good society. Cholo will not fit in well at Fiddler's Green because he does not know the proper behavior of high society, like which glass to use. Though the world has gone to hell, and as Kaufman himself notes, "In a world where the dead are returning to life, the word 'trouble' loses much of its meaning," class difference and things like knowing the proper glass for alcohol are still held onto in order to separate the elite from the working class. No amount of money in the world will buy class. No amount of service to the ruling class will allow one to join that class. Cholo comes to realize that he has been used to do the dirty work of the regime, but that those in power, not him, will reap the rewards. He will not be "approved" for residency in Fiddler's Green.

Cholo serves as Romero's model for the working class soldiers who must serve multiple terms of duty in war zones while those who never served in the military or at least never served active duty during wartime (so called "chicken-hawks"); and who play at military leader (Cheney, Wolfowitz, Rumsfeld, Bush), make speeches about sacrifice and the need for service while never actually contributing themselves. In Fiddler's Green, Cholo is called upon to investigate strange noises. He finds that an older male resident has hung himself from the living room lamp, surrounded by comfort and the trappings of his upper class life.[1] His wife does not want Cholo to hurt the corpse of her husband. As the now reanimated husband bites the son who tries to cut him down and save him, the wife cries out, "What's happening?" Despite living through the reanimation of the dead, her existence is so sheltered that she does not recognize a situation that is an everyday reality for the vast majority of the people on the streets. Fiddler's Green represents a class of people protected from reality.

Compared with this sheltered and clean existence is the dirty and hardscrabble life of those inside the city but outside Fiddler's Green. They live on the streets, struggling for food and medicine. Children are entertained by puppets inside an empty television frame, while more adult entertainment for the masses takes the form of bread and circuses — distractions from an ugly existence.[2] In the underground arena in the city one can "Have your photo taken with a zombie" (cameos from *Shuan of the Dead*'s Simon Pegg and Edgar Wright), watch topless dancers, drink cheap hooch, or seek other, more disturbing fare. Chihuahua (Phil Fondacaro), also affectionately known as "the Little Fat Man," is in league with Kaufman to provide "entertainment" for the masses: drinking, shooting zombies with paint guns, betting on zombie fights, prostitution, etc. Kaufman gets a share of all monies generated from these activities. Slack (Asia Argento) tells Riley (Simon Baker) and Charlie (Robert Joy), "If you can drink it, shoot it up, fuck it, gamble on it, it belongs to him" (referring to Kaufman). Romero critiques the upper class for providing the lower class with opiates of the masses (in some cases, literally). Kaufman has the lower classes working against their own best interests to enrich himself and to maintain the privilege and extravagance of Fiddler's Green. The disparity between the elite and the working class forms the heart of Romero's critique of Bush's America, which is the actual "land of the dead."

When bitten by a zombie, Cholo asks Foxy (Tony Nappo) not to shoot him, saying, "I always wanted to see how the other half lives." The line is ironic, as he will find out how the zombies "live," but Romero is employing a canny metaphor. "How the other half lives" has come to refer to how those of a different social class exist, but its origin is as the title of a work of muckraking journalism published in 1890 by Jacob Riis called *How the Other Half Lives: Studies Among the Tenements of New York*.[3] Riis' purpose was to expose the upper class to the dangerous and squalid living conditions of the working poor in New York's slums. In other words, the title refers to the need of the upper class to learn how the lower class lives. Cholo employs this idea ironically. Though he is working class, with aspirations of joining the ruling elite of Fiddler's Green, now that he is going to die he will learn about the class lower than his: the dead.

The other underclass of the film is the living dead, whose land this has become. As established by the opening sequence, the dead now outnumber the living by a substantial amount. Yet the living destroy and torment the dead, sometimes as a means of survival, but as often as not as a source of amusement or to relieve boredom. As much as the living underclass, the dead begin to resent being preyed upon, taken advantage of, and used and (literally) thrown away. Cholo is shown taking the dead to a garbage dump. Jay McRoy, speaking of Japanese body horror, states, "Larger, socio-national reconsiderations emerge from more immediate, intimate and visceral portrayals of the human body as porous, leaky and violable" (122). The ruined human body is symbolic of the body politic, and both are rotting garbage. The difference is Kaufman's corrupt regime lives in opulence at the expense of others, while the bodies of the poor are treated as refuse. Whereas *Night* ended with the dead being burned, by *Land* the dead no longer even merit mass cremation. They are now simply tossed in a landfill. If McRoy is right, then Romero demonstrates that in Bush's America the working poor are exploited and then thrown away after they have served the needs of the upper classes.

The zombies are drawn to the lights of Fiddler's Green. As they gather at the river, the building serves as a beacon in the dark night. This gathering is the literalization of a metaphor — the disenfranchised dead seek revenge against those who exploit them. The zombies clearly existed in the suburban setting for a long time. The "sky flowers" distract them while the living pillage the town and then slaughter the zombies unnecessarily. The fireworks prevent the zombies from attacking the humans, but the humans kill for fun, leaving Big Daddy (Eugene Clark) to lead a zombie revolution.

What is especially unique is the development of tool use by the living dead. Big Daddy encourages Butcher (Boyd Banks) to use his cleaver to chop a hole in a wooden fence. Number 9 (Jennifer Baxter) carries a bat, which Big Daddy replaces with an assault rifle during the attack on the city. Though terrified of the zombies, the soldier she then shoots is even more terrified that the zombies have learned to use guns. The use of the weapons by zombies indicates that this is not simply a case of the living dead attacking the living as usual, but that this is an armed insurrection of the dead. Gillian Beer reminds us, "Ghost stories are to do with the insurrection, not the resurrection of the dead" (260). What she says of ghosts is easily applicable to zombies:

they are the insurrecting dead. In a very real way, the film creates a moral hierarchy that links Riley and his small band with Big Daddy and his group of zombies, and both are above Kaufman and his regime.

Romero wanted to create a world that reflected the "post–September 11 fear-driven administration of U.S. President George W. Bush" (Blumberg and Hershberger 211). Various lines and images from the first term of Bush's administration fill the movie. Kaufman says in response to Cholo's attempted blackmail, "We don't negotiate with terrorists," a line repeatedly spoken by Bush. Jamie Russell states that *Land* shows "a society whose leaders are willing to profit from a dangerous situation" (190), a criticism frequently leveled against Bush, particularly in regard to the war in Iraq, which was seen as a war for oil that would enrich Bush and Cheney's friends and associates in the petroleum business.

Interestingly, an analogy can be drawn between Kaufman now paying Riley to find and kill Cholo, who is attacking Kaufman, though Kaufman formerly employed Cholo, and Bush now fighting Osama bin Laden and the Taliban, whom the American military trained and supported two decades before 9/11 in their fight against the Russians. Kaufman wants Cholo "captured or killed," just like bin Laden. Cholo even tells Foxy that if Kaufman doesn't give him the money, "We're gonna go Jihad on his ass." In both cases a former ally became a deadly adversary who becomes the most wanted man for "going Jihad" against his former sponsor.

Furthermore, Dennis Hopper based the character of Kaufman on then Secretary of Defense Donald Rumsfeld (Blumberg and Hershberger 211). Hopper, though bearded, is made to resemble Rumsfeld somewhat in appearance and echoes his vocal cadences. Kaufman is clearly selfish, arrogant, and perhaps even evil. His name is also a local criticism for Romero. Kaufman's is a local department store in Pittsburgh. To set a film in post-apocalyptic Pittsburgh and name the chief villain "Kaufman" is a not-very-subtle dig at one of the wealthiest families in Allegheny County. Romero thus takes swipes at the economic and political elites on the local and national level.

Glenn Kay cannily notes that, like Romero's earlier work, *Land* concerns a small group of survivors, but like in *Day*, it is a small group within a larger group that is the focus and that is presented as heroic in the face of the larger group (251). Riley, Charlie and Slack are clearly superior to those who virtually enslave them to preserve the comforts of the moneyed class. However, so is Big Daddy. What all four characters have in common is concern for their community as a whole. Whereas Kaufman and his ilk seek good only for himself and those like him, Riley and Big Daddy seek to aid all within their respective communities.

One might go so far as to argue that Big Daddy is the new Ben. Glenn

Kay sees Big Daddy as being part of a long chain of African American heroes in Romero's work: Ben, Peter, and John from the previous films (250–1). If we accept this observation, the implication is that our sympathies lie as much with Big Daddy and his zombie community as with Riley and his friends. Kaufman and Cholo and the residents of Fiddler's Green might be the true villains, while the zombies are victims in this new world — a dead underclass to match the living underclass of Pittsburgh.

Jamie Russell sees Big Daddy as "a zombified Black Panther, a civil rights revolutionary who leads this living dead underclass on a riot against the establishment" (189). He does not lead a revolution based on race or ethnicity, but on one's life status. Big Daddy fights for zombie rights. Big Daddy tries to save the other zombies when the humans begin to shoot up the town. His anguish is palpable when he sees "his people" being killed by the living. He also recognizes that the fireworks distract the zombies and allow the living to hurt the dead. When a fellow zombie is decapitated in a hail of bullets, Big Daddy looks sad at the still-living head and then performs a "mercy-kill" by stomping on the head so the decapitated zombie is put out of his misery.

While sympathetic zombies are not new in Romero's work (Bub of *Day* being simply the best example, though far from the only one), Blumberg and Hershberger object to the zombies in *Land*, finding both the evolution idea objectionable and the zombies themselves "domesticated" (213). The zombies are, however, hardly "domesticated." These are not the pets or soldiers of *Day* and *Return of the Living Dead 3*. They are, in some ways, distinctly unsympathetic. They are ugly, decaying and their very appearance is hostile. Whereas the dead in the original *Night* had blank stares, the dead of *Land* have malevolent grimaces. Number 9, Butcher and even Big Daddy just plain look angry and mean. Their anger, however, is presented as ultimately being justified, as Romero focuses repeatedly on the brutality of the humans toward the zombies.

If what we are seeing is a zombie revolution, perhaps even zombie Marxism, then the development of class consciousness beyond Big Daddy (the zombie Marx?) is captured as a single moment by Romero. The zombies have broken into the city and ravaged the lower classes first. They make their way to Fiddler's Green, however, and begin to kill and eat the rich. A group of wealthy individuals, all well dressed and clean, stands around outside, not knowing what to do. Like the woman who does not recognize that her husband has become a zombie, they can do nothing for themselves. They do not know how to fight, they do not even know to run away. A man in a suit and tie yells "Hello" into an emergency phone. Without the working class to handle the tasks of zombie-fighting and defense, the upper class is lost and useless, incapable of even protecting themselves. "We're fucked," the man in the tie concludes.

Riley orders the crew of Dead Reckoning to shoot off fireworks to distract the dead in order to protect the inhabitants of the city. The zombies stop advancing and look to the sky. "Oh, thank God," sighs the same man. Romero then slowly focuses in on a single zombie, who suddenly stops looking at the sky and focuses on the people again. It is clear from his expression that he is no longer distracted by the ongoing fireworks, but plans to continue the battle against the living. Like a chain reaction, one after another the zombies stop being distracted and begin advancing toward the crowd. The man in the tie has no more lines; we see in his face that he realizes the zombie revolution will not be stopped and he will most likely die soon. The dead class will no longer be distracted by insubstantial displays; they seek only to destroy the hated living, specifically those who live in Fiddler's Green. Many of the working poor living are free to escape unmolested.

Kaufman himself is killed in an appropriate fashion during the zombie revolution. Big Daddy pours gas all over Kaufman's car, in keeping with his life job as a service station attendant. Cholo then appears, now a zombie, and begins to wrestle with Kaufman. Big Daddy then rolls a burning gas can down the ramp and under Kaufman's car, which explodes, killing both Kaufman and Cholo. Kaufman is killed because of his own choices, but also more directly by petroleum, fire, and two angry dead men.

The zombies kill and devour most of the upper class, and Riley orders Charlie to fire the missiles from Dead Reckoning, since "they're dead already." Both zombies and the living upper class are destroyed in the explosions. Emerging from their hiding places, the surviving humans are all working class, organized by Mulligan, who will rebuild the city "into what we always wanted it to be." Riley and his group plan to leave for Canada, but before they go they see Big Daddy and the remaining zombies walking on a bridge, leaving the city. Riley tells the others not to shoot: "They're just looking for a place to go. Just like us." As I noted in the introduction, Linnie Blake recognizes that zombies and humans have much in common — most notably, both are trying to survive, both can replicate, and both "must destroy the enemy in order to do so" (93). In *Land*, Romero shows zombies and humans trying to survive and fighting one another. And yet Romero also shows zombies and humans choosing to stop the mutual destruction and go their separate ways. The lesson is that the dead want to be left in peace to live their lives, same as the living. The upper class exploited both the dead and the working class, and a revolution has now transformed the social milieu so that there can be a rough peace, or at least non-exploitative co-existence, between living and dead.

The value system that Kaufman's regime represents also comes under critique in the film. A direct line can be drawn from *Land* to *Dawn* in this sense. Whereas *Dawn* critiqued consumer culture, *Land* critiques the valuing of luxury and opulence, even in crisis situations. Kaufman represents Stephen's worst instincts of materialism and self-centered acquisition come to life. A much larger question is why both Kaufman and Cholo value money so much. When Kaufman is fleeing he takes two bags full of money with him. "Whose money?" asks a board member. Likewise, Cholo holds the city hostage with Dead Reckoning for five million dollars. But the money is worthless. Guns, food and water are worth far more than a currency that is no longer legal tender. The fact that money is still so valued by both men tells us something significant about this world.

The final images of the film underscore Romero's critique of the United States in 2005. David Pagano observes, "In *Land*, the immigration to Canada underneath ironically placed fireworks is an obvious nod toward many citizens' despair over George W. Bush America" (80). The fireworks are not merely ironic, they are narratively and thematically brilliant. The fireworks, a symbol of patriotism, distract the zombies from the very real and present dangers in their midst. The zombies themselves are all working class, both metaphorically and in terms of actual work garb: gas station attendant, butcher, security guard, etc. These working-class individuals are distracted by patriotic displays, but such distractions will hurt them, their interests and even their survival in the long run. It is only by learning to ignore such self-serving calls for patriotism that citizens can recognize the true agenda of the ruling class.

Ultimately, *Land* demonstrates that post-zombie apocalypse social structures are just as corrupt and exploitive as our own. *Land* also proved to be prophetic. Glenn Kay rightly reminds us that *Land* was released in June of 2005, and that two months later, on 29 August, Hurricane Katrina made landfall on the Louisiana coast: "An American city was abandoned, reduced to a state of chaos and decay, in many ways mirroring the desolate and ugly city streets of *Land of the Dead*" (251). The elite of New Orleans either evacuated the city or remained safe behind patrolled walls and fences. For weeks and months afterwards, the underclass suffered privation and could not even secure the basic necessities of life. For better or worse, Bush and his administration seemed indifferent to the plight of the suffering poor in New Orleans.

Pagano sees *Land* as an "indictment of oligarchic, self-assured, imperialistic authority. The film's central irony is always that, however bad the zombie plague may be, it is only the logical extension of whatever corruption, ignorance, fear or greed that already exists among the living in America today" (75). In that sense, *Land* is the most overtly political Romero film in terms of its specific criticism of American society. The zombies not only represent the worst of us, we have now managed to exceed and transcend them in being destructive and horrific by remaining in a society more decayed than they are.

And yet, in *Land*, though Romero's sympathies are clearly with the lower classes (both the living and the dead ones), and though we are clearly intended to revel in Kaufman's demise, the situation is more complex, as represented by the hero. Russell argues, "Even though he hates Kaufman's world of bourgeois comfort, Riley's uninterested in the revolution that's fomenting on the streets beneath Fiddler's Green and simply wants to get out while he still can" (186). In a sense, Riley, as the protagonist and the character to which we are most clearly supposed to relate, serves as a representative disconnect from the revolution. He participates in the acquisition of extravagance for the ruling class, and therefore enables the system. He is uninterested in joining any social uprising or resistance movement, or even take the smallest steps toward establishing equality and social justice in the city. His primary solution is to separate himself from society and go alone to the North. The revolution happens, and he is neither part of it nor resists it. The social transformation that the city clearly needs happens without any effort by the protagonist. Rather than try to change the system, as Mulligan does, our protagonists prefer to opt out of society altogether. Fran and Peter get back in the helicopter at the end of *Dawn* because they have no choice — they have nowhere else to go. Riley, Charlie and Slack can stay and work to rebuild an equitable society but choose to leave instead.

Like in *Day*, the small group of main survivors can no longer live in society. Both the corrupt living and the decaying dead are equally dangerous and useless. The only logical option is to leave and find "a place to go" where one is untroubled by other people, living or dead. It is a particularly bleak view, but one that perhaps sums up the sociophobic content of the film. Society is corrupt to the point of being unredeemable. Opting out may be the best option. The zombies are not the worst thing out there, but they are still a terrifying threat. Cholo is called a terrorist by Kaufman, but the zombies of *Land* are also terrorists. They look like us, but they are out to change and overthrow our society. From their perspective, however, they are freedom fighters, seeking to stop an exploitive power devoid of spiritual values. What is truly terrifying about *Land* is the fact that not only are the zombies more morally correct than the living, but the living represent the status quo in America, and the zombies who want to change that are not wrong to want to do so. Romero has made a film sympathetic to anti–American, anti-imperialism sentiments within the United States, but also without. The zombies are not scary, society is. And that is far scarier.

"We Don't Stop to Help; We Stop to Look": Diary of the Dead *and Erasing the* Dawn

George Romero refers to *Diary* as "a return to the roots for me."[4] His previous three zombie films all dealt with later stages of the disaster, whereas

Night dealt with its beginnings. *Diary* also begins at the beginning — with the first night of the zombie outbreak. *Diary* is furthermore a mixture of two genres: the zombie film and the first-person camera pseudodocumentary, which has become a staple in horror cinema.

Beginning with *Cannibal Holocaust* (1980), in which an anthropologist finds the lost footage of four documentary filmmakers who entered the Amazon rainforest and fell victim to gang-rape, torture, murder and the titular cannibalism, all caught on camera, several horror films have followed the model of "found footage" revealing the horrific experiences of the filmmakers.[5] *The Last Broadcast* (1998) features the two creators and hosts of a cable access show entering the Pine Barrens of New Jersey to film a special on the Jersey Devil. They are ostensibly killed by a member of their crew, but the film itself is a documentary into what might have actually happened, with an ending that is not as effective as the rest of the movie. Because of the success of its internet marketing, *The Blair Witch Project* (1999) remains the genre example *par excellance* in the popular imagination. Three student filmmakers vanish in the Maryland woods in 1994 while making a documentary about a local witch legend, and their footage, supposedly located a year later, reveals the group's slow psychological devolution and leaves more questions unanswered than answered. More recently, *REC* (2007), its American remake *Quarantine* (2008), and *Cloverfield* (2008) all purport to be found footage. The former two concern a reporter spending a night with a group of firemen who are called to a building which is subsequently placed under quarantine, and the latter with the going-away party of a young man being interrupted by some sort of monster attacking New York City. In both cases the film purports to be literally unedited footage, as it is found in the camera. Most recently, the film *Paranormal Activity* is purported to be "found footage" of a San Diego couple documenting the haunting of their house and the slow possession of the woman. As of this writing, *Paranormal Activity 2* is slated to be released in October 2010.

Already tropes are beginning to emerge in the form: the protagonist (or one of the protagonists) is somehow involved in filming horrific events as they happen in real time, (perhaps obsessively). Heather in *The Blair Witch Project*, Hud in *Cloverfield*, the reporter in *REC/Quarantine* (both named Angela Vidal), and Micah in *Paranormal Activity* all insist on keeping the camera going no matter what, as does Jason Creed in *Diary of the Dead*. Each film is a first-person camera project in which "found" footage has been edited together, including glitches, jumps, awkward cuts, giving the sense of non-professionals attempting to capture events as they happen and as they get caught up in them. Each film also features the obligatory turn-the-camera-on-the-obsessive-filmmaker moment.

What is unique about *Diary* is that while it is constructed mostly as a first-person camera narrative, it is not "found footage" per se. *Diary* is actually Michelle's edit of Jason's documentary, which she has now named *The Death of Death*. There is a narrator behind the footage who has edited not only Jason's footage but has also added other footage found on the web. It is this extra level of narration and media control which shifts Romero's film away from the earlier first-person pseudo-documentaries and "found footage" films and allows it to comment in a much larger fashion on the mediatized nature of our existence in the twenty-first century. It is metacinema "about this emerging social media and citizen journalism," as Romero told Stuart F. Andrews ("At home" 33).

Diary is also a recap of *Night*. Like the original film, it starts at night. It is set at the beginning of the falling apart of society. It features a small group attempting to survive the rise of the dead but who are slowly getting smaller due to infighting and accidents. *Night* takes place over 12 hours, give or take. *Diary* is a longer narrative, taking place just slightly over 48 hours: *Diary* begins at seven o'clock in the evening on the 24th of October, runs through the entire day of the 25th, and ends at dawn on the 26th. There is a visual reference to *Night* in the barn scene. We see the zombies arriving, marching up to surround the building and start pounding on the walls. Those inside look out through the boards to see the dead slowly moving toward the building. There is also an audio reference to *Night*: When a zombie is loose in the warehouse, right before Stranger tells them to turn off the television, the television soundtrack is one of the broadcasts from *Night*, telling people what to do.

At heart, though, *Diary of the Dead* is an erasure of *Dawn of the Dead*. The former seems to have the same elements as the latter, echoing *Dawn*'s collapse of society, with the officials in charge of public safety becoming self-saving looters. Yet *Diary* also "erases" *Dawn* in terms of narrative, theme and character. The action (and characters) of *Dawn* move from Philadelphia to western Pennsylvania, with a brief stop in central Pennsylvania; *Diary* begins in rural western Pennsylvania and moves to the suburbs of Philadelphia, with a brief stop in central Pennsylvania.[6] *Dawn* features a gang that is a threat to the survivors and takes their possessions; *Diary* features a gang that is helpful and organized, and a military squad that is the threat to the survivors and takes their possessions. *Dawn* begins with the collapse of the media — a television station in Philadelphia going off the air; *Diary* shows that the entire world remains available through the internet — the characters are about to watch uploads from throughout the United States and even other nations, such as Japan. *Dawn* shows the end of the media and the flow of information. In *Dairy*, Jason and his friends continue to document and continue to upload. *Dawn* shuts down the media and isolates the survivors. *Diary* keeps the media going, and in doing so reminds the survivors of how isolated they truly are. The overall effect is the same.

Dawn ends with the surviving protagonists leaving their place of hiding; *Diary* ends with the surviving protagonists going into hiding. The final images of *Diary* reverse the final images of *Dawn*. *Dawn* shows Peter and Francine escaping the mall and rising up into the air, leaving a claustrophobic, secure space for open space and potential freedom. Diary ends with its three surviving characters leaving the open air and closing themselves into the panic room — they gather what few luxuries they can and leave the open space for claustrophobic space and potential security.

There are key differences between the films — most notably, *Dawn* is presented seemingly unmediated as a straightforward narrative film; whereas *Diary* is presented as mediated. It was filmed by Jason (Joshua Close) and edited by Debra (Michelle Morgan), and acknowledges its own subjective, constructed nature from the very beginning. In one of the film's most telling moments, Romero employs the trope of the camera turned on the filmmaker: the filmmaker becomes the subject/object. Most famous recently, perhaps, is the iconic image from *The Blair Witch Project* when Heather (Heather Donahue) turns the camera on herself and apologizes to the families of her fellow filmmaking students for getting them killed, although all of *Blair Witch* was filmmaker as subject/object as well. The same idea holds true for *Paranormal Activity*. In that film the camera is on filmmakers as often as it is on the phenomena.

What *Diary* does new is camera-to-camera shots: Jason and Debra filming each other. This moment in the film, as Romero cuts back and forth between Debra's shot of Jason filming her and Jason's shot of Debra filming him, reflects the echo chamber of modern media. Reporting the story can become the story, and more and more often partisan media begin showing clips from other media in order to raise questions. The twenty-four-hour news cycle is as much about the media as it is about the actual news. Behind *Diary* is the fear of the media and the fear of mediation of our lives.

Romero says, "We're captivated and obsessed by alternative media. The film is mostly about ignoring what's happening around you, no matter how tragic or extraordinary it is in favor of shooting it, making a document of it" (qtd. in Andrews, "When There's No" 26). *Diary* critiques its young protagonists for being completely disconnected from the world around them and even each other in any meaningful way. Nothing is real unless it comes through a computer, television or phone, and that mediation also has the effect of making it unreal. Throughout the film we are shown screens and the images on screens: the thief in the girls' dorm is stealing a television; hanging behind Tony (Shawn Roberts) in the RV is a small flatscreen; in the warehouse controlled by the looters are shelves of televisions, cameras and other equipment. In an empty room Jason and Eliot (Joe Dinicol) find a computer with an internet link which thrills them, as they can "finally upload [their] footage." Carina Chocano observes in the *Los Angeles Times* of the characters that "it's their thoroughly mediated lives that make them incapable of actually experiencing anything first hand" (E4). This charge is frequently leveled against Jason in the film.

Chocano's observation is also about a generational difference. Younger than the characters in *Night, Dawn,* and *Day,* the characters in *Diary* do not respond as their older counterparts do. As Chocano notes, their instinct in response to the zombie uprising is "running home to mom and dad" (E4). And as they do, they bring with them cellphones, cameras, computers, and the other electronic communication ephemera of their lives. At the hospital, Jason "can't leave without his camera. The camera is the whole thing." Romero's film seems to be an older filmmaker growing more concerned about the mediation of the lives of the young. In fairness, however, it is not just the college-and-under set whose lives are fully mediated. Romero's critique is that our entire society is mediated and media saturated — to the point where the media is given deference and might even be perceived as the most important and influential sector within our society.

The opening sequence is of a local news crew reporting on a murder/suicide. As a cop gives details of the man killing his wife and child, an ambulance pulls up in front of the building, sirens blaring. Immediately, the cameraman runs into frame, toward the ambulance, and says, "Hey guys? Channel 10 news. Listen, you're kinda blocking our shot. Can I get you to pull forward a little?" The ambulance driver complies. The media trumps even first responders in Romero's vision.

The report is further interrupted, to the reporter's annoyance, by the bodies beginning to move. A voiceover reports that the footage was downloaded off the web, followed by the reporter being attacked and killed by one of the reanimated corpses. The cameraman catches her as she falls, in the first human moment of the film. The voiceover continues over footage, all supposedly "from the web," some of which was actually real: Romero includes footage from New Orleans after Hurricane Katrina, showing looting.

What follows are fake credits and a voiceover introducing a fake film incorporating real footage. Debra states, "We made a film. The one I'm going to show you. Actually, Jason was the one who wanted to make it. Like that cameraman from channel 10, he wanted to upload it so that people, you, could be told the truth." Thus *Diary* is metacinema: a film about citizen filmmaking. The film within the film is entitled "The Death of Death" and subtitled "A film by Jason Creed." It was filmed on cameras, edited on a computer and purports to be a cautionary tale. We are thus watching the story after it occurred. Debra has edited the footage together, and combined it with things she found on the web to create a narrative of what happened in the first forty-eight hours of the dead coming back to life.

At the end of the film, as Debra closes herself in the panic room with Tony and Professor Andrew Maxwell (Scott Wentworth), we realize she has created the film with the cameras and the computer in the panic room. The end of the events is the beginning of the mediation of the events, and that is what we have seen — not the events as they happened but as Debra has chosen to construct them. The editing sometimes reminds us of what has been left on the cutting room floor (a metaphor at this point, as the editing is done digitally in the computer). Anything on the screen is incomplete, as Romero repeatedly reminds us by framing the shot so that heads are out of frame, or part of the conversation is off-camera. The camera creates an illusion of completeness, but it is only an illusion.

Even documentary is a constructed medium, structuring its narrative to frame a particular point of view or interpretation. There is no such thing as unmediated media, and documentary (as well as news) is just as much constructed as fictional narrative, a point made by Romero in the post-credit opening of the film, which he also uses to critique the more recent zombie movies as well. On October 24, 7:00 P.M., in the rural countryside outside of Pittsburgh, a woman runs through the woods, chased by a mummy. Suddenly, an off-camera director yells "cut," and the camera pans to reveal a student film crew. Jason, the director, tells his actors, "How many times have I told you, dead things don't move fast! You're a corpse, for Christ's sake. If you run that fast your ankles are going to snap off!" Not only does this statement demonstrate the construction of the threat in the film (a slow-moving dead thing under control of the storyteller), it is Romero offering a criticism of such fast-zombie films as the remake of *Dawn* and *28 Days Later*. The "reality" of *Diary* demonstrates that Jason (and Romero) are correct: later, after Ridley (Philip Riccio) reanimates and begins shambling after Amy (Tracy Thurman), Jason calls out, "See, I told you dead things don't move fast."

Over the radio comes a report that the dead are reanimating and attacking others. The students begin to panic and want to leave. Two drive to Philadelphia, the others agree to head back to the University of Pittsburgh. As they go, Jason films virtually every second of their journey, asking the others to identify themselves oncamera, even though these are his friends and fellow students. They pick up Debra in a dorm mostly abandoned by the other students. After Mary (Tatiana Maslany) shoots herself, the others take her to a hospital, where they begin to recognize the depth of the crisis. It is also where Romero more fully develops his themes.

In the hospital, Debra picks up a camera she has found, points it at Jason and says, "Tell us your name," as he did to the other characters previously. Romero then shows us Jason through her camera. He is lit from behind. We cannot see his face clearly. The most distinctive thing about him is the camera on his shoulder. Unlike Debra, whose face is clearly visible, Jason only truly exists behind the lens. He is a cipher at best in front of it. He even has trouble saying his name: "Uh ... Gimme a break. Jay. Jason. Jason Creed." Jason does not exist without a camera. When it is off, he ceases to be.

Frequently in the film, Jason's face is not visible. It is hidden behind a camera. When Debra makes her final plea to him to try to survive with the group, we cannot see his face. It is behind a viewfinder and obscured by the shadow of his camera. To the very end, he is nothing without the camera and a void behind it. There is no there, there.

Conversely, anything that is not caught by the camera is not real. Jason hears a conflict down the hall and then sees Debra, who has blood on her. She talks about how she was attacked in the other room. Jason does not film the attack (nor, for that matter, does Romero), causing Debra to remark, "If it didn't happen on camera, it's like it didn't happen, right?" She tells him what happened in the other room. It is one of the only unmediated moments in the entire film. Someone simply narrates what happened to them. The other time this occurs again is in the last section, when Ridley gives a disjointed narrative about what happened to Francine and his family.

Later, in Stranger's headquarters, Eliot and Jason upload everything to the web. We see them edit the film we just saw, including an explanation as to why they have security footage from the warehouse. They self-justify why they are doing it: "72,000 hits in 8 minutes." Despite the world-ending crisis occurring around them, they want to ensure their website or YouTube channel maintains a high profile and receives numerous hits. On the positive side, people can learn how to survive by watching Jason and his friends and what they have learned (by contrast, a Japanese girl is shown to have uploaded a video recording the situation in Tokyo, and states that only destroying the head works), but they do not upload for that purpose. Jason and Eliot want their crisis video to go viral. Although any opportunity for a film career is rapidly vanishing, the students value how much flow their site receives from the web as a form of self-validation. This is not citizen media as public service; it is citizen media as self-aggrandizement.

Another telling moment occurs when Professor Maxwell shoots one of the living dead attacking the students in the hospital. The moment, although seen through a camera lens, is a bit too close and a bit too real for Jason. Maxwell tells him, "You're stuttering, Mr. Creed. Don't try to speak. Just shoot. Shoot your picture. Shoot for as long as your hard drive holds out, as long as you have power." He then hands Tony the gun, saying, "Take this. It's too easy to use." In the following scene, after Gordo (Chris Violette) is bitten, Debra films Tracy holding him, but then sees Jason filming her film them. She hands the camera to Maxwell, repeating the line, "Take this. It is too easy to use."

This idea — that a camera is as destructive in its own way as a gun — forms a major recurrent motif in *Diary*. Debra refers to the filmmakers as "the shooters." The colonel in the National Guard (who later becomes "Sarge" in *Survival*) points his M-16 at Jason, who is pointing a camera at him. Both are weapons that can be used destructively or threateningly in order to get one's way. The conflation of gun and camera is complete at the climax of the film. Bitten by a zombie, Jason says, "Shoot me," an ambiguous request by this point in the film; and in the very next shot Debra picks up his camera. We see his face unhindered by camera or shadow for the first time when Debra then shoots him in the head with her pistol. This is followed by a "confessional" of his thesis statement for this new film project. Shooting Jason with a gun is what prompts Debra to finish shooting his movie. The camera and the gun are one in the same. The violent, intrusive nature of filming: "shooting."

The two dominant comments on filmmaking in *Diary*, therefore, are that it is an act of violence upon its object but also a distancing practice that removes sympathy, empathy and the ability to connect with the people on the other side of the lens. As Debra exits the hospital, Romero cuts to archival footage of a crowd of people, most of whom are viewing something off-screen through cameras as a voiceover gives the statistic that there are over two hundred million video cameras worldwide. Romero then uses what seems to be actual footage from a bombing in Israel, a riot from somewhere in Africa, a fire, and a series of images of people hurt or injured. "We don't stop to help," Debra intones in a voiceover, "We stop to look." Olsen's conclusion: "rather than bring people closer together," new media "actually served to isolate us from one another" (E3). If the characters of *Night* understand the zombie apocalypse through media, the characters of *Diary* have only a mediated zombie apocalypse.

Along the way to Philadelphia the students have three different encounters. The RV suffers mechanical problems, and they stop at a farm to fix it. Samuel (R.D. Reid), the deaf-mute Amish man in whose barn they hide, writes on an erasable slate. His communication consists of pre-modern mediation: he writes on a slate to communicate and be understood. And yet his mediation makes him much closer to the students than the internet, the cameras, and their cell phones. Samuel uses dynamite to stop the living dead and gives the students refuge so that they might complete their repairs. In the end, he is attacked by a zombie, bitten, and kills both himself and his assailant by slamming a scythe through both of their heads. While it is a comically graphic moment in the film, it also demonstrates the power and effectiveness of simplicity. Romero did not choose to make Samuel Amish by accident. The Amish (Pennsylvania Dutch) reject contemporary technology and live lives of simplicity. They adopt plain dress, eschew modernity, value rural life and separate themselves from the non–Amish society that surrounds them. Samuel and his people are the exact opposite of the students. His life is the opposite of theirs. He is helpful, humble, and lives a simple, unmediated life. It is ironic that he dies attempting to save them as they repair their RV, but his death displays his power and the power of his lifestyle. Jason points a camera but does not care very much about the people he films. Samuel gives his life to save others.

The second encounter is with Stranger (Martin Roach) and his group. Like Ben, Peter and Big Daddy, Stranger is African American. He has organized a group who has gathered up all the supplies in the area. While many have left the area because of the living dead, Stranger and his group see the rising of the dead as an opportunity for social change. Stranger tells Debra and the other students that he and his men will not leave, "Cuz we got the power. For the first time in our lives, we got the power. Cuz everybody else left. All the folks without suntans." Tony responds, "They'll be back. The army. The National Guard. I mean somebody's got to put all this shit back together." This attitude is the same one we have seen expressed in film after film (indeed, it was the title of the previous chapter). Stranger tells Tony, "Kid, I'm in the National Guard." The National Guard abandoned rural Pennsylvania, so the rural Pennsylvanians abandoned the National Guard. Stranger unifies the people he knows from his life, and they reorganize the community.

Debra objects, arguing, "It's called looting." Stranger responds, "No ma'am. It's called doing what you have to do." Stranger protects his family, his community, and the people who have banded together during the crisis. He is not out to lord over others or make himself the center of power. When Debra demands gasoline, weapons and food, Stranger at first resists, but then agrees to "give her what she wants." He sees himself in her, and, recognizing a kindred spirit interested in protecting the group, not enriching herself, he gives freely. Romero suggests that real communities work to protect and help each other. Stranger is the polar opposite of *Land*'s Kaufman.

Stranger's other polar opposite is the Colonel, who will become known as "Sarge" in *Survival*. After receiving supplies from the second encounter, the students have their third encounter, this time with the National Guard, whom Tony had previously believed would come and help and protect the people. Instead, the soldiers point guns at the students and steal all their supplies. The collapse of society transforms those who have taken an oath to protect it into predators that prey on those weaker than themselves. Samuel and Stranger each help the students, the actual authority figures from society do not. Romero is practically in Biblical territory here, demonstrating that those who are outside society, who are different or even potentially dangerous (as the very name "Stranger" suggests) are of more help during a crisis than the institutions designed to protect us. *Diary* was Romero's first film after Katrina, and reflects that reality.

While arguing with Debra, who questions Jason's priorities, Jason questions the point in surviving, but paradoxically wishes to record the events for those who do survive: "Survival? Who the fuck wants to survive in a world like this? All that's left is to record what is happening for whoever remains when it's over." Jason is completely unaware of the irony in not wanting to be a survivor, but needing survivors for his audience. While possibly framing his filming and uploading as an altruistic act, Jason fails to recognize that he is completely separate from both those he films and those who watch his films, and that he values the fact that his work might be viewed by those who survive more highly than his own survival. The danger is that Jason values media over his own life, but the media he creates is simply not that valuable. As one character notes, "In the end, it's all just noise." *Diary* is a critique of not just the media, but of a society that values viral videos over genuine information, and of a generation that lives a life so mediated it is incapable of genuine empathy.

"We Were Just Looking for a Place Where There Was No Them": Survival of the Dead

I hope that if this book has demonstrated anything thus far it has shown that shifts from original to remake indicate a shift in concerns or causes of fear. Shifts in titles also mean things. Romero uses the suffix "of the dead" in order to indicate a shift in situation and a shift in focus. *Night* concerns a single night's events. *Dawn*, as discussed in chapter 6, reflects the rise of the dominance of the dead over the living. *Day* depicts the final collapse of civilization and the rule of the dead over the lands formerly controlled by the living. *Land* represents the totality of the control of the dead but also the emergence of a détente between the lower class dead and the lower class living against the wealthy elite who profit off of both. *Diary* indicates the recording of the events, demonstrating its focus on first-person media.

"Survival" in the title *Survival of the Dead* can refer to at least two things: the dead themselves surviving death and living again, and "how to" survive the dead (dead in this case being both subject and object). The empathy for the living dead in this film is not as open as it was in *Land*. Whereas Big Daddy and his flock are clearly sympathetic figures in that movie, the dead here are dangerous. Like *Diary*, *Survival* resists the tropes of twenty-first century zombie trends. Nick Muntean and Matthew Thomas Payne argue that contemporary zombies are "enraged" monsters who are "overtly coded as disease carries" (246–7). *Survival* rejects this model in favor of a more complex understanding. Muldoon may want to domesticate the living dead, but so does Romero. His zombies are not "coded as disease carriers."[7] They are not the fighting-for-their-freedom zombies of *Land*, either. They are closer to rabid pets. They can be chained up and taught to repeat basic tasks, but when given the opportunity, individually or collectively, they will attack, bite, and kill anyone they can.

Some have criticized *Survival* for being lacking in horror. In the world after *28 Days Later* and the *Dawn* remake, the slow-moving, easily killed zombies of Romero's films "pose more of a nuisance than a threat," which cuts down on the fear factor (Ordoña, "Humans" D6). As *Los Angeles Times* film critic Michael Ordoña concludes, "When there's social commentary present, a spoonful of gut-wrenching terror might help the medicine go down" ("Humans" D6). Perhaps that might be a third, subconscious way to read the title "Survival of the Dead": the series continues, but it is merely surviving right now, not succeeding as horror.

Yet as the title of this section suggests, there is also a nostalgia that is rooted in present fears: "We were just looking for a place where there was no them" might refer specifically to the zombies, but we also might take it to refer to the problems caused by the living dead — the conflict and stress and need to loot and kill merely to survive. It might also refer to other people in general. We are looking for a place where life can return to "normal" without the interference of others, living or dead. Sarge's statement is one of nostalgia — a desire to return to the way things used to be before the dead rose. We can read into this a post–9/11 American desire for a return to normalcy — in the airport, in our concerns, in how our national political processes occur. We, as a nation in the midst of an unending war on terror and the worst economic downturn since the Great Depression, are now simply trying to survive. While not the explicit horror of aggressive, running zombies, the slow, shuffling zombies from whom there is no escape and who are a constant threat of slow death represent the very real fears of 2009 America. We will not die quickly in the onrush of a horde of fast, maniacal undead, but in the slow crush of attempting to live in a world in which the dead dominate and in which all our nostalgic wishes for life back then will never come true. It is a slow, quiet horror, but a horror nonetheless.

In a voiceover which begins the film, Sarge (Alan van Sprang) states, "Last time anyone counted, 53 million people were dying every year, 150,000 every day, 107 every minute. And that was in normal times." We are given statistics, and then Romero introduces the idea of "normal times," implying that we are no longer in "normal times." "Now every one of those dead people gets up and kills another person, and every one of those gets up and kills," Sarge warns. We are aware of what normal was, but we know it no longer is. Yet "now" we also are aware of how things are, and a world in which the dead rise and try to kill the living is the new normal. The reality of a post–9/11 world now includes scrutiny and aggressive security at airports, the PATRIOT act, and a color-coded terror scale, and we accept these things as the new normal. Sarge and his soldiers accept their world as the new normal.

The voiceover switches to a live shot of Sarge and his men having to deal with one of their own reanimating, as chaos reigns about them. "We've added more than our fair share to the body count," Sarge tiredly intones. He's sitting in camouflage fatigues, lighting up a cigarette as we hear a helicopter pass overhead. Bodies are carried past him. "We should have been afraid of them, but we weren't. They were easy enough to kill, except when they were buddies." The opening shots reflect the socioreality of an America still fighting a war on terror and two geographical wars (Iraq and Afghanistan), the latter of which is the longest military conflict in American history.

In the immediate aftermath of the 9/11 attacks, President Bush announced a "Global War on Terror" that commenced with an American attack on Taliban-controlled Afghanistan in October 2001 under the name "Operation Enduring Freedom." As of this writing, that war continues, making it the longest war in United States history, surpassing the Vietnam War on 7 June, 2010 (Bradley). The Second Gulf War, also known as Operation Iraqi Freedom, began on 20 March, 2003, under President Bush. On 19 August, 2010, President Obama declared the end of major combat operations, despite the continued presence of 50,000 American soldiers in Iraq. The war was initially justified by the supposed presence of weapons of mass destruction, which were never found. Subsequently, the Bush administration offered other reasons for the invasion and occupation. While the actual combat against Saddam Hussein and his army took mere weeks, the occupation and rebuilding of Iraq took over seven years (to date).

These two wars together have resulted in hundreds of thousands of soldiers serving multiple tours of duty in one or both combat zones. It is a simple fact that the "war on terror" affects military more than civilians, and the hot wars in the Middle East, involving multiple tours of duty by service members who are voluntary soldiers, sometimes require them to take multiple tours out of necessity. An entire generation of soldiers have been exposed to combat and are returning to the United States with injuries and post-traumatic stress disorder (PTSD). As with Sarge in this opening sequence, in the current American conflicts one is not always aware of the danger or the presence of the enemy until it is too late. IEDs and suicide bombers have made the wars in Iraq and Afghanistan particularly challenging. The living dead of *Survival* become a metaphor for the dangerous conditions under which the American military now fights in all of our names. The war on terror is also more conceptual than real to most Americans — longer lines at airports and arguments about the role of the government in pursuing the war is the extent of the impact on most American lives — "except when they were buddies." In other words, when the horror is close to you, you feel it. When it is not, you do not.

Sarge has to shoot one of his buddies, then "Lou," then the zombie that just bit Lou. He then complains, "This sucks. I didn't sign up for this shit. We're better off on our own." Like *Dawn*, once society breaks down, the soldiers are no longer responsible to or for anything other than themselves. This group of soldiers was among the villains in *Diary*, but now they are the protagonists, and their actions are treated with more sympathy here. What Sarge is asked to do when the dead start to rise is not what he "signed up for." What is presented as a negative in *Diary* is seen here as a positive. The National Guard in *Diary* were a synecdoche for institutional American society: the government, the military, and the structures that failed the "little people" when crises occurred. Here the soldiers stand for human beings who opt out of that system when it no longer does what it did when they "signed up." In this case the authority figures abandon their duties and responsibilities, yet they take advantage of their official positions of power to escape to an island from which the dead might be eliminated.

Romero has set this film primarily on Plum Island, off the coast of Delaware, serving as a microcosm of American society. Islands as a place of refuge (or at least an idealize place of refuge, is a recurring theme in Romero's work. The cops stealing a boat in the original *Dawn* plan to go to "any island." The escapees from the mall in the remake of *Dawn* head for islands in the Great Lakes. The survivors of *Day* head for a tropical island. Islands have always represented a safe escape from the world of the dead. The irony in *Survival* is that Plum Island is advertised on the net by O'Flynn (Kenneth Welsh) (the soldiers themselves are tricked by "Captain Courageous" to come to the docks, where an ambush waits), but it is not a place of refuge. Not only are the animate dead there, but the always-more-dangerous living humans are in the midst of a feud.

After showing the section of *Diary* in which Sarge and his men rob the students at gunpoint, he remarks in the voiceover, "It's become an 'us vs.

them' world. We were just looking for a place where there was no them." It is clear from the context that he is not actually referring to the zombies, but specifically to other people. At the heart of "Survival" is the idea that human conflict on the small group level is a fundamental danger in this world, the same argument found in *Night*, which is referenced by the hunters out in the woods. The hunters are a posse that has been out shooting zombies. They decapitate zombies and place their still living heads on stakes. They have also beaten a young man and stolen his possessions. The soldiers (who might have done the same thing a few months before) shoot the hunters, who, admittedly, were about to shoot them.

This scene establishes Sarge and his men as slightly more moral than the hunters, but we already know they have become highway robbers, literally. The other thing it establishes is that any time in this film when two groups come upon each other, people die. Romero himself describes the sociophobic at the heart of *Survival*:

> I thought there's nothing particular happening right now that I really want to talk about, so I set out to do a broader thing about war and the fact that people can't bury the hatchet and can't lay down their hatreds. And now all day today on CNN, all it's about is that people can't disagree without being disagreeable and so suddenly I think the film is timely..." [qtd. in Andrews, "At home" 33].

He has also said, "I think all of North America needs to take an anger-management class" (qtd. in Lacher D3). At the heart of the film is the O'Flynn and Muldoon (Richard Fitzpatrick) feud. Even after dying and reanimating, the two old men continue to fight and try to kill each other.

Patrick O'Flynn organizes a posse to kill all the dead on Plum Island. Seamus Muldoon believes a cure can be found. O'Flynn believes that "we're putting the dead to sleep." Whereas Muldoon argues, "We're killing our own kind!" He sees himself as "doing the Lord's will." The historic feud becomes, in a time of the living dead, what Andy Klein calls "a strategic disagreement with religious overtones" (20). *Survival* was inspired by William Wyler's 1958 film *The Big Country*, concerning a ranch war in the old west; but beyond the personal animosity of the two men is their intractable positions. Both hold views in which compromise is impossible; therefore the enemy is not the dead but the living who disagree with one's position.

In contrast to these two men is Sarge, who believes "we're better off on our own." He literally wants to be an army of one. He is the logical extension of Riley from *Land*, who also has no interest in preserving, rebuilding or transforming society. Riley and Sarge are only interested in escaping the troubles of living with other human beings. It is these three positions that Romero places in combat and conversation: two inviolate beliefs about the dead and the man who wants to be left alone. Both come from what they believe is a morally correct stance. Both believe they are doing the right thing. Eventually, Sarge comes to realize that the other two, because of their belief that they are right and the other is wrong, will not leave him alone; so in order to achieve the security and solitary state he wishes, he will have to side with one of them and join the fight.

Sarge claims he will not take a bullet for anyone. He does, however, and the experience only convinces him of the futility of such gestures, as the comrade in arms he attempted to protect dies anyway. Everything O'Flynn and Muldoon do to make a difference is futile, but the same holds true for Sarge. O'Flynn argues, "We're all on the same side—those who are living." Sarge responds, "I'm not on anyone's side." The tension in his character, like in Riley's, is between the instinct to help others and do right, and the instinct to go off by himself and live alone. What is troubling about *Survival* is that nothing one does makes any difference. Try to help the dead, as Muldoon does, and one gets killed. Try to put down the dead, as O'Flynn does, and one gets killed. Try to escape, and one dies. Try to save others, and they die. Even success, as when the dead begin eating the horse at the end, is not really a success. It is merely another example of how human effort is futile and nothing can change the situation for the better.

The conclusion of *Survival* is the same conclusion as *Dawn*, *Day* and *Land*—a very small number of people escape the collapsing society and head out for somewhere far away. In this case, Sarge leads others back onto the ferry. After *Night*, this idea—that the best solution to the collapse of society is to abandon it altogether—dominates Romero's work. Sarge is not on anyone's side, but society (and the zombie crisis) will not allow one to stand idly by. Even in 2010, if you are not with "us" then you are with "them." So the only option left is to go somewhere where there is no "them" at all—not just the living dead, but anyone at all.

Although not as groundbreaking, genre-redefining or seminal as *Night* or *Dawn*, *Land*, *Diary* and *Survival* all continue Romero's trend of staging sociophobics within the film and offering an interpretation of the threats facing society, noting that most of those threats were created by society in the first place. These three more recent films are, as noted in the introduction, in their own way all remakes of *Night*. At heart they use the idea of a small group attempting to survive the living dead and failing because of societal problems: greed and economic inequality; the media as a distancing tool rather than a genuinely informative way of creating empathy for others; and the inability to compromise with those who hold views opposite from one's own. Romero makes these arguments in a world where the overt threat is zombies, but the covert threat does so much more damage.

NOTES

1. This scene was not in the theatrical release of *Land* but was included on the DVD — yet another example of John Bryant's idea of a "fluid text," as described in chapter 6. I saw the film in the theater upon its release in June 2005. When the disc came out a year later, the additional scenes transformed my memories of the film, so the film text is unstable.

2. The (uncredited) puppeteer's voice is George Romero's himself, presenting a violent Punch and Judy show. One might be tempted to read into this moment a bit of self-effacing criticism: Romero is the man behind the entertaining and distracting puppet show that is aimed at children.

3. Although W.W. Norton has published a critical edition of Riis' text, complete with photographs, the original edition (with photos) is also available online at http://www.authentichistory.com/1865–1897/progressive/riis/index.html.

4. This statement is made in "The Roots," a behind-the-scenes documentary on the DVD for *Diary of the Dead*.

5. Interestingly, despite its graphic gore and sexual violence, *Cannibal Holocaust* remains much more controversial because of its depiction of actual cruelty to animals. Seven animals were killed during the filming, six of which are visible onscreen. A large sea turtle is captured, decapitated, cooked and eaten. Monkeys, a snake, a pig, a spider and a coatimundi are all killed onscreen, most often violently with a machete. It is this animal cruelty that caused the film to be banned in Italy and several other countries, not to mention generating legal problems for the director and releasing company.

6. There is a significant problem with the geography of the journey in *Diary*, which is surprising, given Romero's intimate knowledge of Philadelphia. The characters stop in Scranton on the way from Pittsburgh to Pennsylvania. Scranton is not on the way from Pittsburgh to Philadelphia. One would leave the Pennsylvania Turnpike, which connects the two, to get on I-81 and drive 122 miles northeast. To go to Scranton, turn around, and continue to the other side of the state would add at least five hours to the drive.

7. Given that the initial explanation for the rise of the dead in *Night* was "some kind of radiation," it seems Romero has stayed with this idea of zombies rising from an external source and not a virus or disease. The lack of viral infection would also explain why characters that die from causes other than zombie bite(s) still reanimate.

Conclusion

I began this book with the Zombie Jamboree. I now conclude it with another *Night of the Living Dead* event. On 18 September, 2010, the original *Night of the Living Dead* was shown in Hollywood Forever Cemetery in Los Angeles. The event sold out, and thousands of people sat in the graveyard watching the film projected on the side of a mausoleum wall.[1] Forty-two years after its initial release, the film still has power to draw an audience, the majority of whom (including this author) had not yet been born when it was initially released. The crowd is also, however, a sign of the ascendant living dead. Zombies have gone mainstream.

This book itself is an example of the huge zombie culture prevalent in the twenty-first-century United States. As noted in the introduction, zombies are everywhere: film, television (as of this writing, an adaptation of the graphic novel *The Walking Dead* is being produced by AMC), novels, graphic novels, cartoons, toys, etc. In zombie literature we are seeing the blending of genres. Zombie stories used to be a genre unto themselves, but now there is blending, bending and transformation. *Pride and Prejudice and Zombies* combines the actual text of the classic novel with new passages incorporating zombies. *Patient Zero*, Jonathan Maberry's blending of the technothriller and the zombie novel, performs the same type of genre blend that *Shaun of the Dead* does with romantic comedy and zombie film. Zombies are not just a subgenre of horror; they can be, and have been, added to every type and genre of film imaginable: western, action, romantic comedy, mockumentary, pseudodocumentary, epic, war, drama, etc. We have seen these things before (*Dead Heat*, anyone?), but previous blends were individual and isolated. Currently there is a wave of zombie culture.

No longer is *Night* the sole model as well. Other genre blends demonstrate the next generation of zombie cinema also both engages contemporary political concerns and makes obvious the sociophobics behind them. The "mockumentary" *American Zombie* purports to follow regular Americans who also happen to be the living dead as they attempt to continue their existence and fight for equality and what they perceive as their rights. While obviously a zombie film, one can read into the movie a metaphor for gays, illegal immigrants, Muslims, or any other social or ethnic group that American society fears. *Homecoming*, an episode of Showtime's *Masters of Horror* series, in which dead soldiers return to life in order to vote in an election after a politician claims that if the dead soldiers could vote they would do so to continue the war, is very much a direct critique of the Bush administration.

The recent popularity of zombie culture demonstrates that the zombie film as sociophobic metaphor is still dominant and still relevant. In this conclusion, I wish to indicate three films that introduce the overtly and covertly political into their zombie narratives.

Jay Lee's *Zombie Strippers* (2008) is, like *Homecoming*, an overt political satire (admittedly delivered with all the subtlety of a sledgehammer to the forehead, as the title suggests). The opening of the film references ongoing wars in Iraq, Iran, Syria, Canada, and Alaska during George Bush's fourth term. A satire, *Zombie Strippers* uses the extreme to mock (even Alaska is a place Bush might invade, believing it somehow a foreign country). Also, the fact that Bush's fourth term is announced expresses comically the concern of the Left that Bush and Cheney desired to maintain power after their term was over, and that the PATRIOT Act might somehow supersede the twenty-second amendment of the Constitution. As in *Day of the Dead*, the government seeks to reanimate soldiers in this film, expressly to allow dead soldiers to keep fighting after they die. An escaped zombie soldier hides in an illegal underground strip club (the religious right in the film having outlawed any displays of sexuality). In the film, sexual morality is juxtaposed with the morality of war and violence, as the language of sexuality and the language of war become interchangeable. Two of the soldiers look like strippers. The blonde soldier even has her tank top torn off by a zombie so that she fights in her bra. Simultaneously, the strippers use the language of violence and war to talk about their relationships with each other and their patrons: "It's on," "I'll kill you," etc. Similarly, the film not only targets the morality and political posing of conservatives, but also uses the strippers who turn into zombies to comment on American society in general. In the *Los Angeles Times* review of *Zombie Strippers*, Michael Ordoña wrote, "The commentary on social concepts of beauty, particularly in casting sex goddess [Jenna] Jameson as a monster whose appeal to the strip club's clientele increases with her with her desiccation, is meaty" (E10). While Romero also gave us the "smart zombie film" model, *Zombie Strippers* combines low and high in the film: Sartre, Ionesco, Nietzsche are all referenced, and Kat (Jenna Jameson) states that Nietzsche "makes so much more sense" when one is dead. Lastly, the non-zombified strippers seek to become zombies after they see the zombie strippers becoming popular with the club patrons. While one might not think an exploitively titled film such as *Zombie Strippers* would prove to be a rumination on the dangers of conformity, compromise and following fads for popularity's and money's sakes, that is precisely what Lee delivers.

ZMD: Zombies of Mass Destruction (2009) has a title that references WMDs: "weapons of mass destruction," which was the United States' justification for invading and occupying Iraq. Like *Survival of the Dead*, which was produced at roughly the same time, it is also set on an island, with slow-moving zombies. The film evinces many Romero tropes, including the siege aspect and characters gaining information from media. The protagonists, however, are a gay couple and a Muslim-American girl, Frida Abbas (Janette Armand), in this case Iranian (director Kevin Hamedani is also Iranian-American). The zombies are caused by a terrorist bio-attack (perhaps from Muslim terrorists). The film's true villains, however, are the rednecks and fundamentalists who serve as a metaphor for "Red State" America. Her neighbors think Frida is Iraqi, and when the zombies begin to attack, they focus their efforts on capturing and stopping her. Meanwhile, a church group attempts to capture and "stop" the gay couple. The implication here is that while there are real dangers to be found from terrorism and enemies outside, the real threats of mass destruction come from American ignorance and conservatism rather than imaginary enemies.

Lastly, *Zombieland* (2009), arguably the most mainstream of zombie films in 2009, and perhaps even since *Shaun of the Dead*, paradoxically avoids many of Romero's tropes while still embodying the zombie ideal that Romero's work has espoused. None of the main characters die or become zombies, although Bill Murray, playing himself, is accidentally shot by Columbus (Jesse Eisenberg) and dies. Thus, the Romero formula of main characters dying and reanimating (seen in every film) does not occur; the major death in the film is caused not by zombies but by a trigger-happy living human.

The character known only as "406" (her dorm room number, played by Amber Heard) is the only character we see first as a living person, then as a zombie. She is also possibly scarier as a human than she is as a zombie, as she is shallow and self-centered. As a zombie, she is easily outwitted and killed by Columbus.

The real danger in *Zombieland* comes not from zombies (which can be outwitted rather easily, killed by a nun with a piano, outrun with a few minutes of cardio a day, or merely serve as distractions while looking for Twinkies or love) but from, as always, other human beings — namely, the main characters. Columbus, Tallahassee, Wichita, and Little Rock join forces, abandon one another, steal cars and guns from one another and threaten each other with bodily harm far more than any of the walking dead. *Zombieland* embodies the Romeroesque principle that in any disaster the most dangerous things around are other people behaving stupidly and selfishly.

Zombieland shows the end of the United States as we know it, following the model of *Dawn* and *Day*; whereas *Strippers* and *ZMD* follow *Night* in that the outbreak is eventually contained and stopped. Yet, in all zombie films the potential for the end (or, more accurately, "The End") is always there. As Kim Paffenroth reminds us in *Gospel of the Living Dead*, the living dead are a sign of the end times and always indicate the end of the world as we know it, even if the plague is stopped. If that is true, however, Bruce Milne also indicates that eschatology and narratives about the end of the world are "always moral teaching. It is concerned with the way we are to live in light of it" (46). Zombie films, like all end-of-the-world films, tell us how we might avoid disaster, or, if it is unavoidable, what sort of moral quandaries might be faced by survivors. In doing so, they also tell us about what we value and who we are. The best of the new generation of zombie films, like *Dawn* and *Night*, engage sociophobics and prove didactic. They show us who we really are and ask us if that is indeed what we want to be.

As of this writing, Romero, the original zombie prophet, has two more dead films under contract and currently in development. Stuart F. Andrews reports that Romero writes with CNN on in the background, "so if there's any sort of stimulation or any sort of crazy ideas or things that come from the real world, it comes in through Wolf Blitzer" ("At home" 33). Romero continues to find zombie narratives in contemporary cultural contexts and explore current sociophobics. Given his legacy, it is not unreasonable to wonder if *Land*, *Diary* or *Survival* (or the as-yet-unmade films) might someday be remade themselves, as *Night*, *Dawn* and *Day* have been. Considering the continuing popularity of zombies and the cycles of remakes in Hollywood, both new Romero and remade Romero seem to be definite presences in the future American cultural landscape.

It is an odd thing to like and enjoy reanimated corpses, and to seek them out in various media. The continuing popularity of the living dead and the emergence of the zombie into mainstream popular culture spells something larger. There is something in the reanimated dead that now speaks to a mainstream audience — the fears and pleasures of zombies resonate with those of us who have lived through 9/11, a seemingly unending series of wars and conflicts, and a cinema grown stale with serial killers and CGI monsters. Zombies have become the beautiful dead.

A week after *Land of the Dead* was released, Stephen King dedicated his *Entertainment Weekly* column to a celebration of Romero's work:

> George Romero made these movies with no major stars, no consistent studio backing, and amid ongoing battles for just enough budget so the picture could

be made if every dollar spent did the work of two. Yet in spite of the strangled budgets (maybe even because of them), there are strangely beautiful images in *Land of the Dead* [76].[2]

In all of Romero's work, I would argue, there are strangely beautiful images, ones that haunt the viewer. The same is true for many of the remakes of Romero's work. Like all other texts in this zombie renaissance, they speak to us. In some cases our real fears are played out on the screen, domesticated and made safe in the dark of a movie theater, den, or dorm room. In other cases, Aristotelian catharsis allows us to live through the zombie apocalypse, purging ourselves of negative emotions of fear and pity, but also allowing us to vicariously work out our anger, rage and frustrations at the system.

In all cases, the zombie films of George Romero and their remakes express not only the personal fears and hopes of both the artists and the audience, but also the societal fears and concerns of the era in which they were created. The brilliance of the Romero films is that, forty-two years later, sitting in a cemetery in Hollywood, the audience is still frightened by some scenes, amused by others, and, most important of all for the purposes of this book, find meaning and relevance in the films. Vietnam is over, Iraq is ending, Afghanistan is ongoing and an African American president sits in the White House, but the film still speaks to us about our society's fears. And, most likely, forty-two years from now, with new conflicts and concerns, these films will continue to speak and be seen by the audience as raising these fears again and again.

> *"Zombies, man. They creep me out..."*
> — Kaufman (Dennis Hopper), *Land of the Dead*

> *"For the living know that they shall die:*
> *but the dead know not any thing."*
> — Ecclesiastes 9:5

Notes

1. Wonderful though this event was, it was not unique. An organization called Cinespia shows films almost every weekend in Hollywood Forever Cemetery from May through September. Though some of the most memorable experiences have been horror films (watching *The Exorcist* in a cemetery was particularly creepy and thrilling), more often than not the films are from a variety of other genres. I have seen *The Stunt Man*, *The Maltese Falcon*, and even *Ferris Bueller's Day Off* in Hollywood Forever. The cemetery scene that opens *Night*, however, takes on a particular resonance when watched in a cemetery.

2. Ironically, in the same issue of *Entertainment Weekly*, film critic Owen Gleiberman panned the film in a review subtitled "The zombie flick has seen better *Days*, *Nights* and *Dawns*" (47). "I'm compelled to report that in *Land of the Dead* there are virtually no good parts," he informs the reader, and it is "listless and uninspired" (47). I raise this negative review only to note that reactions to *Land* and Romero's subsequent films have been mixed, but I have found they always reward the viewer upon multiple viewings.

Filmography

I. Romero — Remakes and Related Works

Children of the Living Dead. Dir. Tor Ramsey. Screenplay by Karen L. Wolf. Westwood Artists, 2001.
Dawn of the Dead. Dir. George A. Romero. Screenplay by George A. Romero. Laurel Group, 1978.
Dawn of the Dead. Dir. Zach Snyder. Screenplay by James Gunn. Strike Entertainment, 2004.
Day of the Dead. Dir. George A. Romero. Screenplay by George A. Romero. Dead Films, 1985.
Day of the Dead. Dir. Steve Miner. Screenplay by Jeffrey Riddick. Millennium Films, 2008.
Day of the Dead 2: Contagium. Dirs. Ana Clavell and James Dudelson. Screenplay by Ryann Carrass and Ana Clavell. Taurus Entertainment, 2005.
The Dead Will Walk. Dir. Perry Martin. Screenplay by Perry Martin. Anchor Bay Entertainment, 2004.
Diary of the Dead. Dir. George A. Romero. Screenplay by George A. Romero. Artfire Films, 2007.
Document of the Dead. Dir. Roy Frumkes. Screenplay by Roy Frumkes. 1985.
Land of the Dead. Dir. George A. Romero. Screenplay by George A. Romero. Universal, 2005.
Night of the Living Dead. Dir. George A. Romero. Screenplay by John Russo and George A. Romero. Image Ten, 1968.
Night of the Living Dead. Dir. Tom Savini. Screenplay by George A. Romero. 21st Century Film, 1990.
Night of the Living Dead: Origins. Dir. Zebediah DeSoto. Screenplay by Zebediah DeSoto. Simon West, 2011.
Night of the Living Dead: Reanimated. Dir. Mike Schneider. Neoflux Productions, 2009.
Night of the Living Dead: Survivor's Cut. Dir. Dean Lachiusa. Screenplay by George A. Romero and John A. Russo. NLD Film, 2005.
Night of the Living Dead 3D. Dir. Jeff Broadstreet. Screenplay by Robert Valding. Horrorworks, 2006.
Return of the Living Dead. Dir. Dan O'Bannon. Screenplay by Dan O'Bannon and Rudy Ricci, John Russo and Russell Streiner. Hemdale Film, 1985.
Return of the Living Dead Part II. Dir. Ken Wiederhorn. Screenplay by Ken Weiderhorn. Winhall Films, 1988.
Return of the Living Dead 3. Dir. Brian Yunza. Screenplay by John Penney. Bandai Visual Company, 1993.
Return of the Living Dead: Necropolis. Dir. Ellory Elkayem. Screenplay by William Butler and Aaron Strongoni. Denholm Trading, 2005.
Return of the Living Dead: Rave to the Grave. Dir. Ellory Elkayem. Screenplay by William Butler and Aaron Strongoni. Denholm Trading, 2005.
Survival of the Dead. Dir. George A. Romero. Screenplay by George A. Romero. Artfire Films, 2009.

Zombie Jamboree: The 25th Anniversary of Night of the Living Dead. Dir. John Russo. Screenplay by John Russo. Imagine, Inc., 1993.

II. Other Films

Alien. Dir. Ridley Scott. Screenplay by Dan O'Bannon and Ronald Shusette. Brandywine, 1979.
Aliens. Dir. James Cameron. Screenplay by James Cameron, David Giler and Walter Hill. Twentieth Century–Fox, 1986.
American Nightmare. Dir. Adam Simon. Screenplay by Adam Simon. Minerva Pictures, 2000.
American Zombie. Dir. Grace Lee. Screenplay by Grace Lee and Rebecca Sonnenshine. Lee Lee Films, 2008.
The Andromeda Strain. Dir. Robert Wise. Screenplay by Nelson Gidding. Universal Pictures, 1971.
Apocalypse Now. Dir. Francis Ford Coppola. Screenplay by John Milius and Francis Ford Coppola. Zoetrope Films, 1979.
Back to the Future. Dir. Robert Zemeckis. Screenplay by Robert Zemeckis and Bob Gale. Universal Pictures, 1985.
Black Christmas. Dir. Bob Clark. Screenplay by Roy Moore. Warner Brothers, 1974.
Black Christmas. Dir. Glen Morgan. Screenplay by Glen Morgan. Dimension Films, 2006.
The Blair Witch Project. Dirs. Daniel Myrick and Eduardo Sánchez. Screenplay by Daniel Myrick and Eduardo Sánchez. Haxan Films, 1999.
Cannibal Holocaust. Dir. Ruggero Deodato. Screenplay by Gianfranco Clerici. F.D. Cinematografica, 1980.
Children Shouldn't Play with Dead Things. Dir. Bob Clark. Screenplay by Bob Clark and Alan Ormsby. Geneni Films, 1973.
Cloverfield. Dir. Matt Reeves. Screenplay by Drew Goddard. Bad Robot, 2008.
The Collector. Dir. Marcus Dunstan. Screenplay by Marcus Dunstan and Patrick Melton. Liddell Entertainment, 2009.
The Crazies. Dir. George A. Romero. Screenplay by Paul McCullough and George A. Romero. Pittsburgh Films, 1973.
The Crazies. Dir. Breck Eisner. Screenplay by Scott Kosar and Ray Wright. Overture Films, 2010.
The Day After. Dir. Nicholas Meyer. Screenplay by Edward Hume. ABC Circle Films, 1983.
Dead Heat. Dir. Mark Goldblatt. Screenplay by Terry Black. Helpern/Meltzer, 1988.
The Deer Hunter. Dir. Michael Cimino. Screenplay by Deric Washburn. EMI Films, 1978.
Deliverance. Dir. John Boorman. Screenplay by James Dickey. Warner Brothers, 1972.
Fido. Dir. Andrew Currie. Screenplay by Andrew Currie, Robert Chomiak and Dennis Heaton. Lions Gate Films, 2006.
First Blood. Dir. Ted Kocheff. Screenplay by Michael Kozoll (based on the novel by David Morrell). Anabasis N.V., 1982.
Friday the 13th. Dir. Sean S. Cunningham. Screenplay by Victor Miller. Paramount, 1980.
Friday the 13th. Dir. Marcus Nispel. Screenplay by Damien Shannon and Mark Swift. New Line, 2009.
Guess Who's Coming to Dinner. Dir. Stanley Kramer. Screenplay by William Rose. Columbia Pictures, 1967.
Halloween. Dir. John Carpenter. Screenplay by John Carpenter and Debra Hill. Compass Entertainment, 1978.
Halloween. Dir. Rob Zombie. Screenplay by Rob Zombie. Dimension Films, 2007.
Halloween II. Dir. Rick Rosenthal. Screenplay by John Carpenter and Debra Hill. DeLaurentis Productions, 1981.
Hamburger Hill. Dir. John Irvin. Screenplay by James Carabtsos. RKO Pictures, 1987.
The Hills Have Eyes. Dir. Wes Craven. Screenplay by Wes Craven. Blood Relations Co., 1977.

I Am Legend. Dir. Francis Lawrence. Screenplay by Mark Protosevich and Akiva Goldman. Warner Brothers, 2007.
I Spit on Your Grave. Dir. Meir Zarchi. Screenplay by Meir Zarchi. Cinemagic Pictures, 1978.
I Walked with a Zombie. Dir. Jacques Tourneur. Screenplay by Curt Siodmak and Ardel Wray. RKO Radio Pictures, 1943.
The Incredibly Strange Creatures Who Stopped Living and Became Mixed up Zombies. Dir. Ray Dennis Steckler. Screenplay by Gene Pollock and Robert Silliphant. Morgan Steckler Productions, 1964.
The Last Broadcast. Dirs. Stefan Avalos and Lance Weiler. Screenplay by Stefan Avalos and Lance Weiler. FFM Productions, 1998.
Last of the Living. Dir. Logan McMillan. Screenplay by Logan McMillan. Gorilla Pictures, 2008.
M. Dir. Fritz Lang. Screenplay by Fritz Lang and Thea von Harbow. Nerofilm A.G., 1931.
Masters of Horror: Homecoming. Dir. Joe Dante. Screenplay by Sam Hamm. IDT Entertainment, 2005.
Ms. 45. Dir. Abel Ferrara. Written by Nicholas St. John. Navaron Films, 1981.
My Bloody Valentine. Dir. George Mihalka. Screenplay by Stephen A. Miller and John Beaird. Canadian Film Development Corp., 1981.
My Bloody Valentine. Dir. Patrick Lussier. Screenplay by Todd Farmer and Zane Smith. Lionsgate, 2009.
The Omega Man. Dir. Boris Sagal. Screenplay by John William Corrington and Joyce Hooper Corrington. Warner Brothers, 1971.
Platoon. Dir. Oliver Stone. Screenplay by Oliver Stone. Hemdale, 1986.
Poltergeist. Dir. Tobe Hooper. Screenplay by Steven Spielberg, Michael Grais and Mark Victor. MGM, 1982.
Psycho. Dir. Gus van Sant. Screenplay by Joseph Stefano (from the novel by Robert Bloch). Universal Pictures, 1998.
Quarantine. Dir. John Erick Dowdle. Screenplay by John Erick Dowdle and Drew Dowdle. Andale Pictures, 2008.
Rambo: First Blood Part II. Dir. George P. Cosmatos. Screenplay by Sylvester Stallone and James Cameron. Anabasis N.V., 1985.
REC. Dirs. Jaume Balagueró and Paco Plaza. Screenplay by Jaume Balagueró and Luis Berdejo. Filmax, 2007.
Resident Evil. Dir. Paul W.S. Anderson. Screenplay by Paul W.S. Anderson. Constantin Film Produktion, 2002.
Resident Evil: Apocalypse. Dir. Alexander Witt. Screenplay by Paul W.S. Anderson. Constantin Film Produktion, 2004.
Resident Evil: Extinction. Dir. Russell Mulcahy. Screenplay by Paul W.S. Anderson. Resident Evil Productions, 2007.
Scream. Dir. Wes Craven. Screenplay by Kevin Williamson. Dimension Films, 1996.
Shaun of the Dead. Dir. Edgar Wright. Screenplay by Simon Pegg and Edgar Wright. Universal Pictures, 2004.
The Stand. Dir. Mick Garris. Screenplay by Stephen King. Greengrass Productions, 1994.
The Terminator. Dir. James Cameron. Screenplay by James Cameron and Gale Ann Hurd. Hemdale, 1984.
Terminator 2. Dir. James Cameron. Screenplay by James Cameron and William Wisher, Jr. Carolco Pictures, 1991.
The Texas Chainsaw Massacre. Dir. Tobe Hooper. Screenplay by Tobe Hooper and Kim Henkel. Vortex, 1974.
Thriller. Dir. John Landis. Screenplay by John Landis and Michael Jackson. Optimum Productions, 1983.
28 Days Later. Dir. Danny Boyle. Screenplay by Alex Garland. DNA Films, 2002.
Wall Street. Dir. Oliver Stone. Screenplay by Oliver Stone and Stanley Weiser. Twentieth Century–Fox, 1987.

The War of the Worlds. Dir. Byron Haskin. Screenplay by Barré Lyndon. Paramount Pictures, 1953.
War of the Worlds. Dir. Stephen Spielberg. Screenplay by Josh Friedman and David Koepp. Paramount Pictures, 2005.
White Zombie. Dir. Victor Halperin. Screenplay by Garnett Weston. Edward Halperin Productions, 1932.
ZMD: Zombies of Mass Destruction. Dir. Kevin Hamedani. Screenplay by Kevin Hamedani and Ramon Isao. Typecast Pictures, 2009.
Zombie Strippers. Dir. Jay Lee. Screenplay by Jay Lee. Stage Six Films, 2008.
Zombieland. Dir. Ruben Fleischer. Screenplay by Rhett Reese and Paul Wernick. Columbia Pictures, 2009.

Bibliography

Abele, Robert. "A Zombie Plot?" *Los Angeles Times*, 1 October 2009, D1, D6–D7.
Adams, John Joseph, ed. *The Living Dead*. San Francisco: Night Shade Books, 2008.
Alexander, Chris. "Knight of the Living Dead." *Fangoria* 284 (June 2009): 12–17.
Andrews, Stuart. "At Home with the Dead." *Rue Morgue* 101 (June 2010): 32–35.
_____. "When There's No More Room in Hell..." *Rue Morgue* 75 (Jan/Feb 2008): 24–26, 28.
Austen, Jane, and Seth Grahame-Smith. *Pride and Prejudice and Zombies*. Philadelphia: Quirk, 2009.
Barkun, Michael. *A Culture of Conspiracy: Apocalyptic Visions in Contemporary America*. Berkely: University of California Press, 2003.
Beard, Steve. "No Particular Place to Go" *Sight and Sound* 3.4 (1993): 30–31.
Bearman, Joshua. "Zombie Zeitgeist." *L.A. Weekly* (November 3–9, 2008): 112–113.
Beer, Gillian. "Ghosts." *Essays in Criticism* 28 (July 1978): 259–64.
Biguenet, John. "Double Takes: The Role of Allusion in Cinema." In *Play It Again, Sam: Retakes on Remakes*, edited by Andrew Horton and Stuart Y. McDougal, 131–143. Berkeley: University of California Press, 1998.
Bishop, Kyle William. *American Zombie Gothic: The Rise and Fall (and Rise) of the Walking Dead in Popular Culture*. Jefferson, NC: McFarland, 2009.
_____. "The Idle Proletariat: *Dawn of the Dead*, Consumer Ideology and the Loss of Productive Labor." *Journal of Popular Culture* 43, no. 2 (2010): 234–248.
Black, Andy. *The Dead Walk*. Hereford: Noir, 2000.
Blake, Linnie. *The Wounds of Nations: Horror Cinema, Historical Trauma, and National Identity*. Manchester: Manchester University Press, 2008.
Bloch, Robert. "Heritage of Horror." In *The Best of H.P. Lovecraft*. New York: Del Rey, 1982, vii–xxv.
Blum, Elizabeth. *Love Canal Revisited*. Kansas City: University Press of Kansas, 2008.
Blumberg, Arnold T., and Andrew Hershberger. *Zombiemania*. Tolworth: Telos, 2006.
Borrowman, Shane. "Remaking Romero." In *Fear, Cultural Anxiety and Transformation: Horror, Science Fiction and Fantasy Films Remade*, edited by Scott A. Lukas and John Marmysz, 61–82. Lanham, MD: Lexington Books, 2009.
Bosco, Sally. "Theatre Review: Jobsite's *Night of the Living Dead*." *Arts Net, Tampa Bay*, 30 October 2009, http://networkhost2.org/wp/?p=1088 (accessed 15 July 2010).
Bradley, Bill. "America's War in Afghanistan Now Officially Longer Than Vietnam." *Vanity Fair*, 7 June 2010, http://www.vanityfair.com/online/daily/2010/06/americas-war-in-afghanistan-now-officially-longer-than-vietnam.html (accessed 22 May 2010).
Braudy, Leo. "Afterword: Rethinking Remakes." In *Play It Again, Sam: Retakes on Remakes*, edited by Andrew Horton and Stuart Y. McDougal, 327–334. Berkeley: University of California Press, 1998.
Bryant, John. *The Fluid Text: A Theory of Revision and Editing for Book and Screen*. Ann Arbor: University of Michigan Press, 2002.

Chocano, Carina. "The Zombies Are Just Cleaning Up." *Los Angeles Times*, 15 Feb. 2008, E4.
Clear, Marty. "Light Thrills, Big Fun." *St. Petersburg Times*, 23 October 2009, http://www.tampabay.com/features/performingarts/light-thrills-big-fun/1046503, (accessed 16 July 2010).
Clover, Carol J. *Men, Women and Chainsaws: Gender in the Modern Horror Film*. Princeton: Princeton University Press, 1992.
"Corpses Scandal at U.S. Crematorium." *BBC News*, posted 17 February 2002, http://news.bbc.co.uk/2/hi/americas/1825248.stm (accessed 29 September 2008).
DeGiglio-Bellemare, Mario. "Film Review: *Land of the Dead*." *Journal of Religion and Film* 9, no. 2 (October 2005), http://www.unomaha.edu/jrf/Vol9No2/Reviews/LandDead.htm, (accessed 22 September 2008).
Dendle, Peter. *The Zombie Movie Encyclopedia*. Jefferson, NC: McFarland, 2001.
Dillard, R.H.W. "*Night of the Living Dead*: It's Not Like Just a Wind That's Passing Through." In *American Horrors: Essays on the Modern American Horror Film*, edited by Gregory A. Waller, 14–29. Urbana: University of Illinois Press, 1987.
Dunbar, David, and Brad Reagan, eds. *Debunking 9/11 Myths: Why Conspiracy Theories Can't Stand Up to the Facts*. New York: Hearst, 2006.
Felsher, Michael. "*Day of the Dead*: From the Files of Dr. M. Logan, Ph.D." DVD Booklet, *Day of the Dead*. Anchor Bay, 2003.
FitzGerald, Frances. *Way Out There in the Blue: Reagan, Star Wars and the End of the Cold War*. New York: Simon and Shuster, 2001.
Flint, David. *Zombie Holocaust: How the Living Dead Devoured Pop Culture*. London: Plexus, 2009.
Frank, Thomas. *What's the Matter with Kansas?* New York: Metropolitan Books, 2004.
French, Stanley. "The Cemetery as Cultural Institution: The Establishment of Mount Auburn and the 'Rural Cemetery' Movement." In *Death in America*, edited by David E. Stannard, 69–84. Philadelphia: University of Pennsylvania Press, 1975.
Gagne, Paul R. *The Zombies That Ate Pittsburgh: The Films of George A. Romero*. New York: Dodd, Mead, 1987.
Gleiberman, Owen. "Review: *Land of the Dead* and *Undead*." *Entertainment Weekly*, 8 July 2005.
Grant, Barry Keith. "Taking Back the *Night of the Living Dead*: George Romero, Feminism, and the Horror Film." In *The Dread of Difference: Gender and the Horror Film*, edited by Barry Keith Grant, 200–212. Austin: University of Texas Press, 1996.
Greene, Richard, and K. Silem Mohammed, eds. *The Undead and Philosophy*. Chicago: Open Court, 2006.
Gudino, Rod. "The Dead Walk ... Again!" *Rue Morgue* 34 (July/August 2003): 14–21.
Gutiérrez, Peter. "They're Still Coming to Get Us!" *Night of the Living Dead: Reanimated* DVD Insert, Wild Eye Releasing, 2010.
Halberstam, Judith. *Skin Shows: Gothic Horror and the Technology of Monsters*. Durham, NC: Duke University Press, 1995.
Halsell, Grace. *Forcing God's Hand*. Beltsville, MD: Amana Publications, 1999.
Hannon, Thomas J. "Western Pennsylvania Cemeteries in Transition: A Model for Sociological Analysis." In *Cemeteries and Gravemarkers: Voices of American Culture*, edited by Richard E. Meyer, 237–257. Ann Arbor: University of Michigan Research Press, 1989.
Hantke, Steffan. "The Military Horror Film: Speculations on a Hybrid Genre." *The Journal of Popular Culture* 43, no. 4 (2010): 701–719.
Harper, Jim. *Flowers from Hell: The Modern Japanese Horror Film*. London: Noir, 2008.
Harries, Martin. *Forgetting Lot's Wife: On Destructive Spectatorship*. New York: Fordham University Press, 2007.
Heffernan, Kevin. *Ghouls, Gimmicks and Gold: Horror Films and the American Movie Business 1953–1968*. Durham, NC: Duke University Press, 2004.
Hervey, Ben. *Night of the Living Dead*. BFI Film Classics. New York: Palgrave Macmillan, 2008.
Humphries, Reynold. *The American Horror Film: An Introduction*. Edinburgh: Edinburgh University Press, 2002.

Hutcheon, Linda. *A Theory of Adaptation*. New York: Routledge, 2006.
Jackson, Rosemary. *Fantasy: The Literature of Subversion*. New York: Metheun, 1981.
"Jacob Wetterling Crimes Against Children and Sexually Violent Offender Registration Program." *Cornell University Law School United States Code Collection*, http://www4.law.cornell.edu/uscode/html/uscode42/usc_sec_42_00014071----000-.html (accessed 15 August 2009).
Jones, James H. *Bad Blood: The Tuskegee Syphilis Experiment*. New York: Free Press, 1981 (Revised Edition, 1993).
Kahn, Herman. *On Thermonuclear War*. Princeton: Princeton University Press, 1960.
Kay, Glenn. *Zombie Movies: The Ultimate Guide*. Chicago: Chicago Review Press, 2008.
Keene, Brian. *City of the Dead*. New York: Leisure, 2005.
———. *The Rising*. New York: Leisure, 2004.
King, Stephen. *Danse Macabre*. New York: Berkeley, 1981.
———. "Long Live the Dead." *Entertainment Weekly* (8 July 2005): 76.
Kirsch, Jonathan. *A History of the End of the World*. San Francisco: HarperCollins, 2006.
Klein, Andy. "Zombies Keep a-Comin.'" *Brand X* 2, no. 7 (26 May 2010): 20.
Kleinberg, Elliot. "After 8 Years, 350 Victims' Families Share $40 Million from Menorah Gardens Cemetery Scandal." *Palm Beach Post*, 28 April 2009, http://www.palmbeachpost.com/news/content/local_news/epaper/2009/04/28/0428menorah.html (accessed 3 June 2010).
Lacher, Irene. "Dean of '...the Dead.'" *Los Angeles Times*, 20 May 2010, D3.
LaHaye, Tim, and Jerry B. Jenkins. *Left Behind*. Wheaton, IL: Tyndale House Publishers, 1972.
Larkin, William S. "*Res Corporealis*: Persons, Bodies and Zombies." In *The Undead and Philosophy*, edited by Richard Greene and K. Silem Mohammad, 15–26. Chicago: Open Court, 2006.
Leitch, Thomas. "Twice Told Tales: Disavowal and the Rhetoric of the Remake." In *Dead Ringers: The Remake in Theory and Practice*, edited by Jennifer Forrest and Leonard R. Koos, 37–62. Albany: State University of New York Press, 2002.
Lindsey, Hal. *The Late, Great Planet Earth*. Grand Rapids, MI: Zondervan Publishing House, 1970.
Loudermilk, A. "Eating 'Dawn' in the Dark: Zombie Desire and Commodified Identity in George A. Romero's 'Dawn of the Dead.'" *The Journal of Consumer Culture* 3, no. 1 (2003): 83–108.
Lukas, Scott A., and John Marmysz. "Horror, Science Fiction and Fantasy Films Remade." In *Fear, Cultural Anxiety and Transformation: Horror, Science Fiction and Fantasy Films Remade*, edited by Scott A. Lukas and John Marmysz, 1–20. Lanham, MD: Lexington Books, 2009.
Mayberry, Jonathan. *Patient Zero*. New York: Saint Martin's Griffin, 2009.
———. *Zombie CSU: The Forensics of the Living Dead*. New York: Citadel Press, 2008.
McIntosh, Shawn, and Marc Leverette, eds. *Zombie Culture: Autopsies of the Living Dead*. Lanham, MD: Scarecrow, 2008.
McRoy, Jay. *Nightmare Japan: Contemporary Japanese Horror Cinema*. Amsterdam: Rodopi, 2008.
Milne, Bruce. *The End of the World: The Doctrine of Last Things*. East Gorne: Kingsway Publications, 1983.
Mitford, Jessica. *The American Way of Death*. New York: Simon and Schuster, 1963.
Muntean, Nick, and Matthew Thomas Payne. "Attack of the Livid Dead: Recalibrating Terror in the Post-September 11 Zombie Film." In *The War on Terror and American Popular Culture: September 11 and Beyond*, edited by Andrew Schopp and Matthew B. Hill, 239–258. Madison, NJ: Fairleigh Dickinson University Press, 2009.
Newitz, Annalee. *Pretend We're Dead: Capitalist Monsters in American Pop Culture*. Durham, NC: Duke University Press, 2006.
Newman, Kim. *Apocalypse Movies: End of the World Cinema*. New York: St. Martin's Griffin, 1999.
Nunes, Jesse. "Top 20 Zombie Movies of All Time." *Boston.com*, 1 October 2009, http://www.boston.com/ae/movies/gallery/bestzombiemovies/ (accessed 1 October 2009).
Ohm, Lori Allen. *Night of the Living Dead*. Woodstock, IL: Dramatic Publishing, 2003.

Olsen, Mark. "Undead Reckoning." *Los Angeles Times*, 13 February 2008, E3.
Ordoña, Michael. "Humans Bicker, Zombies Rampage." *Los Angeles Times*, 28 May 2010, D6.
_____. "A Waste of Time, Zombies and Plastic Eyeglasses." *Los Angeles Times*, 13 November 2006, E2.
_____. "'Zombie' Sends a Message." *Los Angeles Times*, 18 April 2008, E10.
Oswald, John. "Plunderphonics, or Audio Piracy as a Compositional Prerogative." *Musicworks* 34 (1985), http://www.plunderphonics.com/xhtml/xplunder.html (accessed 27 August 2010).
Paffenroth, Kim. *Gospel of the Living Dead*. Waco: Baylor University Press, 2006.
Pagano, David. "The Space of Apocalypse in Zombie Cinema." In *Zombie Culture: Autopsies of the Living Dead*, edited by Shawn McIntosh and Marc Levertte, 71–86. Lanham, MD: Scarecrow, 2008.
Palmerini, Luca, and Gaetano Mistretta. *Spaghetti Nightmares: Italian Fantasy-Horrors as Seen Through the Eyes of Their Protagonists*, translated by Gilliam M. A. Kirkpatrick. Key Wesy, FL: Fantasma, 1996.
Phillips, Kendall R. *Projected Fears: Horror Films and American Culture*. Westport: Praeger, 2005.
Pinedo, Isabel Cristina. *Recreational Terror: Woman and the Pleasures of Horror Film Viewing*. Albany: State University of New York Press, 1997.
Postman, Neil. *Amusing Ourselves to Death: Public Discourse in the Age of Show Business*. New York: Penguin, 1985.
Prior, Lindsay. "Actuarial Visions of Death: Life, Death and Chance in the Modern World." In *The Changing Face of Death: Historical Accounts of Death and Disposal*, edited by Peter C. Jupp and Glennys Howarth, 177–191. Hampshire: Macmillan Press, 1997.
Ramos, George. "No Peace, Only Grief in Cemetery Scandal." *Los Angeles Times*, 17 August 2002, A7.
Riis, Jacob A, and David Leviatin (ed.). *How the Other Half Lives*. New York: W.W. Norton, 2010.
Roach, Mary. *Stiff: The Curious Lives of Human Cadavers*. New York: W.W. Norton, 2003.
Rodgers, Mark E. *The Dead*. Nashville: Permuted Press, 2009.
Rowe, Dana P., and John Dempsey. *Zombie Prom*. New York: Samuel French, 1996.
Russell, Jamie. *Book of the Dead*. Goldaming: Fab Press, 2005.
Russo, John. *The Complete Night of the Living Dead Filmbook*. New York: Harmony Books, 1985.
Sartre, Jean-Paul. *No Exit and Three Other Plays*. New York: Vintage, 1989.
Scruton, David L. "The Anthropology of an Emotion." In *Sociophobics: The Anthropology of Fear*, edited by David L. Scruton, 7–49. Boulder, CO: Westview Press, 1986.
Shaw, Eva. *Eve of Destruction: Prophecies, Theories and Preparations for the End of the World*. Los Angeles: Lowell House, 1996.
Skal, David J. *The Monster Show, Revised Edition*. New York: Faber and Faber, 2001.
Snellings, April. "*Night of the Living Dead* Re-Envisioned as Animated Epic." *Rue Morgue* 98 (March 2010): 9.
Sontag, Susan. *Against Interpretation*. New York: Farrar, 1961.
_____. "Film and Theatre." In *Film Theory and Criticism*, edited by Gerald Mast, et al. Oxford: Oxford University Press, 1992.
"10 Questions." *Time Magazine*, 7 June 2010, 4.
Thursby, Jacqueline S. *Funeral Festivals in America: Rituals for the Living*. Lexington: University of Kentucky Press, 2006.
Twitchell, James. *Dreadful Pleasures: An Anatomy of Modern Horror*. Oxford: Oxford University Press, 1985.
Verevis, Constantine. *Film Remakes*. New York: Palgrave McMillan, 2005.
Walker, Alice. *We Are the Ones We Have Been Waiting For: Inner Light in a Time of Darkness*. New York: New Press, 2006.

Waller, Gregory A. "Introduction." In *American Horrors: Essays on the Modern American Horror Film*, edited by Gregory A. Waller, 1–13. Urbana: University of Illinois Press, 1987.

———. *The Living and the Undead: From Stoker's* Dracula *to Romero's* Dawn of the Dead. Urbana: University of Illinois Press, 1986.

Williams, Tony. *The Cinema of George Romero: Knight of the Living Dead*. London: Wallflower, 2003.

Wood, Robin. *Hollywood from Vietnam to Reagan ... and Beyond, Revised Edition*. New York: Columbia University Press, 2003.

Zinoman, Jason. "Killer Instincts." *Vanity Fair*, March 2008, 304–312.

Index

Alien 47
Alien vs. Predator 18
Aliens 47
The American Way of Death 22, 37, 45, 86
American Zombie 226
America's Most Wanted 67, 68
The Andromeda Strain 188, 193–195
Apocalypse Now 173
Assault on Precinct 13 29

Back to the Future 173
Barsotti, Scott 115
Benefit of the Living Dead see *Night of the Living Dead: Survivor's Cut*
The Big Country 223
Birth of a Nation 40
Black Christmas 89, 92
Black Like Me 40
Black Panthers 9, 42
The Blair Witch Project 23, 211, 213
The Blob 29
Blue Monkey Theatre Company (Portland, OR) 105
Branch Davidians 69–70, 83
Buffy the Vampire Slayer 95
Bug Theatre Company (Denver, CO) 107–108, 111, 113
Bunicula 95
Bush, George H.W. 7, 57, 196
Bush, George W. 7, 8, 82, 92, 147, 187, 188, 193, 196–197, 202, 203, 204, 206, 209, 221, 227

Cannibal Holocaust 23, 211, 225
Carter, Jimmy 7, 8
Children of the Living Dead 23, 24, 65, 73–77, 114, 197
Children Shouldn't Play with Dead Things 77, 98, 109
Child's Play 48
Child's Play 2 48

Civil Rights Movement 9, 21, 22, 31, 39, 42, 43, 45
Clinton, Bill 7, 8, 92
Cloverfield 100, 153, 211
CNN 59, 229
The Collector 153
Coterie Theatre (Kansas City, MO) 105, 113
The Crazies 188, 193
Cronkite, Walter 43

Dawn of the Dead (1978) 1, 3, 4, 7, 10, 13, 14, 15, 16, 17, 19, 20, 21, 22, 24, 35, 42, 45, 50, 73, 81, 106, 117, 121–135, 137, 138, 144, 147, 149, 153, 156, 167, 171, 174, 177, 181, 185, 186, 187, 188, 192, 194, 197, 201, 202, 208, 210, 212–213, 214, 219, 222, 224, 229
Dawn of the Dead (2004) 2, 3, 7, 8, 11, 16, 17, 19–20, 22, 92, 97, 100, 114, 129, 136–153, 176, 189, 192, 197, 215, 220, 222
The Day After 172, 174
Day of the Dead (1985) 1, 7, 10, 11, 12, 15, 16, 21, 22, 45, 47, 78, 100, 106, 117, 125, 126, 129, 132, 155, 167, 171–186, 187, 190, 193, 201, 202, 206, 207, 210, 214, 219, 224, 227, 229
Day of the Dead (2008) 8, 18, 22, 100, 187–198
Day of the Dead 2: Contagium 18, 24, 189–190, 191, 198
Day of the Triffids 29
Dead Heat 226
Dead Rising 101
Dead Space 101
The Deer Hunter 173
Deliverance 57
Descent 2 18
Diary of the Dead 8, 13, 15, 16, 17, 19, 21, 22, 23, 42, 45, 201, 202, 210–219, 220, 222, 224, 225

Index

Dr. Strangelove 166
Document of the Dead 121, 135
Doom 97

Eastman, Marilyn 1, 32

Fido 184
Final Destination 3 18
First Blood 173
400 Lonely Things 115–117
Freddy vs. Jason 18
Friday the 13th 18, 29, 89, 90, 91

Gangbusters Theatre Company (Los Angeles, CA) 106, 110–112, 113
Ghoulies 48
Ghoulies 2 48
Goonies 48
Gremlins 48
Gremlins 2: The New Batch 48
Guess Who's Coming to Dinner 40

Hair 39
Halloween 18, 89, 92
Halloween II 79
Hamburger Hill 173
Hardman, Karl 1, 30
Hatchet 89
The Haunting 18
The Hills Have Eyes 57
Hinzman, Bill 30, 50, 65
Homecoming (Masters of Horror) 8, 227
House of the Dead 101
House of Wax 18
House on Haunted Hill 18
House on Sorority Row 18
How the Other Half Lives (Riis) 204–205
Hurricane Katrina 147, 187, 188, 198, 209, 214, 219

I Am Legend 100, 147
I Spit on Your Grave 50, 62
I Walked with a Zombie 8, 9, 10, 34
The Incredibly Strange Creatures Who Stopped Living and Became Mixed-Up Zombies 10
Indian Jones and the Temple of Doom 48

Jaws 3D 78
Jobsite Theatre Company (Tampa, FL) 106, 113–114
Johnson, Lyndon B. 7
Jones, Duane 9, 39, 51, 52, 56

Karloff, Boris 49, 84
Keene, Brian 77
Kennedy, Robert 33

King, Martin Luther, Jr. 33, 42
King, Stephen 5–6
Koresh, David 69

Land of the Dead 4, 6, 7, 8, 10, 12, 13, 16, 17, 19, 21, 22, 45, 135, 137, 156, 173, 183, 191, 197, 201, 202–210, 218, 220, 223, 224, 225, 229
The Last Broadcast 23, 211
Last of the Living 147
Left Behind 66, 67, 70, 71, 73, 81
Left for Dead 101
Licina, Scott Vladmir 65
Lindsey, Hal 70, 72
Love Canal 6, 166

M 67–68
Mad Max 177
Mad Movies 99
Malcolm X 9
Maverick Theatre (Fullerton, CA) 104, 105
Mayfair Theatre 107
Megan's Law 68
The Misfits 103, 115, 157–158
The Monster Squad 48
mortuary scandals 79, 87–88
Ms. 45 50
MTV 59
My Bloody Valentine 18, 92

NASCAR 61
Night of the Living Dead (1968) 1, 3, 4, 7, 8, 9–17, 19, 22, 29–46, 47, 57, 60, 61, 67, 73, 74, 78, 79, 80, 81, 85, 88, 90, 94, 95, 98, 103, 106, 116, 121, 122, 124, 125, 127, 128, 129, 131, 132, 149, 154, 157, 161, 162–165, 171, 173, 174, 179, 181, 185, 192, 201, 203, 205, 207, 211, 212, 214, 217, 219, 223, 224, 225, 229
Night of the Living Dead (1990) 1, 2, 7, 14, 22, 35, 47–63, 73, 81, 84, 85, 88, 90, 103, 107, 110, 136
Night of the Living Dead (stage adaptation) 21, 103–115
Night of the Living Dead (in 30 Seconds and Re-enacted by Bunnies) 94–95
Night of the Living Dead: Origins 22, 78, 95, 100–102
Night of the Living Dead: Reanimated 2, 43, 96–100, 101
Night of the Living Dead: Survivor's Cut 95–96, 101
Night of the Living Dead: The Musical 112
Night of the Living Dead: The Opera 107
Night of the Living Dead: Thirtieth Anniver-

sary Edition 2, 7, 24, 63, 64–73, 75, 76, 81, 95, 105
Night of the Living Dead 3D 6, 8, 18, 22, 23, 24, 74, 75, 78–93, 114
A Nightmare on Elm Street 18, 92
9/11 *see* September 11
Nixon, Richard 8, 38
No Exit (Sartre) 132

Obama, Barack 8, 187, 197, 221
O'Bannon, Dan 154, 157, 161, 163
O'Dea, Judith 30
Ohm, Lori Allen 105, 108, 109, 111, 113, 117
The Omega Man 100

Paranormal Activity 211, 213
Paranormal Activity 2 211
Pilato, Joseph 100
Pittsburgh 1, 34, 61, 81, 100, 122, 127, 163, 206, 207, 215, 225
Platoon 173
Polanski, Roman 38
Poltergeist 74
Pride and Prejudice and Zombies 11, 154, 201, 226
Prom Night 92
Psycho (original) 49
Psycho (remake) 20

Quarantine 211

Rambo: First Blood Part II 173
Reagan, Ronald 7, 57, 92, 166, 171, 180, 182, 188, 195, 196–197
REC 153, 211
Red Dawn 173
Ren and Stimpy 97
Resident Evil 97, 184, 189, 190, 191, 193, 197
Resident Evil: Afterlife 197
Resident Evil: Apocalypse 190, 197
Resident Evil: Extinction 189, 190
Return of the Living Dead 3, 5, 6, 11, 17, 22, 45, 65, 109, 123, 154–168, 171, 207
Return of the Living Dead Part II 167
Return of the Living Dead 3 19, 167, 184
Return of the Living Dead 4: Necropolis 167–168
Return of the Living Dead: Rave to the Grave 3, 168
The Revenants 115
Ridley, Judith 30
Rio Bravo 29
Riverfront Playhouse (Aurora, IL) 112
Roadhouse Theatre for Contemporary Art (Erie, PA) 108
Robot Chicken 11, 24
The Rocky Horror Picture Show 107

Romero, George 1, 4, 6, 7, 8, 9, 15, 21, 32, 33, 43, 53, 58, 79, 93, 121, 123, 126, 127, 131, 132, 134, 137, 153, 156, 162–165, 174, 175, 176, 178, 179, 184, 186, 188, 189, 197, 201, 203, 204, 206, 207, 209, 210, 212, 214, 215, 216, 217, 219, 221, 224, 228, 229
Rosemary's Baby 29, 38, 45
Rural Cemetery Movement 34–35, 45
Russo, John 1, 32, 45, 62, 63, 64, 66, 73, 76, 77, 103, 154

Savini, Tom 1, 49, 57, 62, 73, 129, 146
Saw films 18
Schon, Kyra 1, 30
Scott-Heron, Gil 59
Scream 89, 92
September 11 (9/11) 36, 76, 79, 83, 86, 92, 100, 101, 106, 137, 138, 143–144, 145–148, 153, 184, 188, 192, 193, 194, 195, 197, 198, 201, 202, 206, 220, 221
The 700 Club 67, 148
The Shape of Things to Come 29
Shaun of the Dead 4, 114, 204, 226, 228
The Simpsons 11, 24, 97
Sleepaway Camp 90
Snyder, Zach 136, 137, 143, 145, 152
sociophobics 5–6, 21, 23, 30, 48, 65, 66, 83, 99, 106, 111, 127, 138, 143, 165, 177, 197
Sontag, Susan 7
Sorority Row 92
South Park 97
Squonk Opera 106–107, 111, 112, 117
The Stand 188
Star Wars 64, 105
The Strangers 153
Streiner, Russ 1, 30
Survival of the Dead 8, 10, 13, 15, 16, 17, 21, 22, 45, 153, 183–184, 201–202, 217, 218, 219–224, 229
Survivor 141

Tallman, Patricia 49, 53
The Terminator 47
Terminator 2: Judgment Day 47–48
The Texas Chainsaw Massacre 57, 92
13 Ghosts 18
Thriller 47, 109
Todd, Tony 51, 52, 56
"Tonight of the Living Dead" 115–117
28 Days Later 6, 9, 17, 18, 19, 97, 136, 147, 187, 191, 192, 215, 220
28 Weeks Later 17, 18

Urban Legend 89

Vietnam 7, 21, 22, 30, 31, 33, 43, 45, 172, 173, 203, 221, 229

The Walking Dead 226
Wall Street 47
The War of the Worlds 100
Wayne, Keith 30
White Zombie 8, 9, 10, 34
Wood, Robin 33, 41, 177

ZMD: Zombies of Mass Destruction 8, 228, 229

Zombi 128, 129
Zombie Jamboree 1, 23
Zombie Prom 114, 115
Zombie Strippers 8, 167, 184, 227–228, 229
Zombieland 228–229